DATE DUE			

China's
Foreign
Aid

China's Foreign Aid

An Instrument of Peking's Foreign Policy

John Franklin Copper
University of Maryland
Far East Division

Lexington Books
D.C. Heath and Company
Lexington, Massachusetts
Toronto   London

Library of Congress Cataloging in Publication Data

Copper, John Franklin.
China's foreign aid.

Bibliography: p.
Includes index.
1. Economic assistance, Chinese. I. Title.
HC60.C6565   338.91'51   75-39318
ISBN 0-669-00441-3

International Standard Book Number: 0-669-00441-3

Library of Congress Catalog Card Number: 75-39318

To my mother

Contents

List of Tables

Preface

It is now more than a quarter of a century since the Communist regime in China came to power. During this time there have been few works by Western scholars on China's foreign policy or foreign relations. Most works available have been simple descriptions of Peking's activities aborad or appraisals of Mao's external goals based on analyses of Chinese history or Chinese Communist ideology. Almost no studies have been undertaken based on empirical data in an effort to produce meaningful, inductively derived conclusions.

This situation results in part from a lack of concern about China until very recently among political scientists and students of international relations. Most scholars in these fields were trained in European history or in Western political systems. Even now few scholars possess the ability to read Chinese, documents are scarce, and visiting China is difficult. Furthermore, China is a closed nation and Chinese leaders conduct foreign policy decisionmaking in secret, frequently attempting to deceive or confuse foreign observers. Thus an analysis of decision making, which has produced results in analyzing other nations' foreign policies, does not work for China.

In the 1960s China approached and then attained nuclear status. Commensurately, interest in China's foreign policy increased. Many political leaders felt that China had to be recognized as a world power. Some said China was soon to become a superpower. Concern for China's place in the world community was renewed after the Cultural Revolution when Chinese leaders ended a period of self-imposed isolationism and made a serious effort to become a legitimate, recognized member of the world community. At that juncture Peking made a successful bid for China's seat in the United Nations. At the same time it sought détente with the United States. The effect on world affairs was far-reaching.

Mao had for a long time entertained the hope that China would become a world power on a par with the United States and the Soviet Union—a superpower. China's sacrifices and persistent efforts to become a nuclear power reflect this drive. And China's image among other nations did change. Foreign aid is another means that Mao employed to gain the status of a world power. He embarked on a foreign aid program officially in 1953 and, since then, has used foreign economic assistance as an important tool of diplomacy. Moreover, China's economic assistance has increased many times since its aid diplomacy was inaugurated. Now it is competitive with aid given by the United States and the Soviet Union.

Mao found that foreign aid was a useful tool of foreign policy for a variety of reasons. It was a way of competing with the Western "imperialists" without risking nuclear war. Later this applied to the Soviet Union as well. Aid-giving allowed Peking to relate to a number of Asian countries as it had prior to the era of Western imperialism. Also China's economic aid made it possible for Chinese leaders to embarrass the richer countries and maintain an attitude of moral superiority—which in the past was a Chinese custom in dealing with foreigners. Frequently aid-giving served as a convenient means for Mao to manipulate, or further, revolutionary movements or wars of national liberation that China, because of its strong anti-status-quo feelings, but weaker capabilities, found compatible with its own views of the world.

Chinese leaders also discovered that many of the underdeveloped countries were dissatisfied with Western aid, and many were disappointed equally with Soviet efforts in this realm. They were receptive to Chinese aid. China found diplomatic recognition difficult to attain in an arena of world politics dominated by a United States' effort, and later a Soviet effort as well, to keep China isolated. A little aid often paved the way for better relations, including eventually diplomatic recognition.

Now Peking is trying to win a position of leadership with the poor countries. Mao perceives that a wide division exists between the rich and poor nations and sees this gap as a fundamental contradiction in world politics. As a corollary, China is competing with India for leadership of the nonaligned nations. China as well offers its political and economic system as a model for the developing countries. Its economic aid program helps further these aims. In fact, it has gained considerable acclaim and attention among the poorer nations. China is a poor and backward country. However, it is the only poor country in the world that is not receiving aid but rather has an extensive foreign aid program itself.

Thus a thorough study of China's foreign aid program is warranted. Foreign aid has been a tool of Peking's diplomacy for more than twenty years. It is of increasing importance both to China and to the aid-giving countries with whom China competes. And it is important to China's aid recipients. Finally, China's foreign aid program can be seen as a model, since no other underdeveloped nation is in the aid business.

China's foreign aid program is also a barometer of its external interests, commitments, and goals. It reflects views and decisions by Chinese leaders which are not easily accessible or cannot be analyzed directly at all. And, although foreign aid donations do not always accurately reflect foreign policy thinking, they are quantifiable in a way that other aspects of Peking's external intentions are not. In addition, there are two sources of information—China and the recipient country. Thus the views on two sides can be compared, and it can usually be ascertained whether aid was actually given, and why. Even when there is no announcement of aid by either side, trade balances are affected. Or Chinese products might be seen in the recipient country, thereby furnishing evidence of an aid relationship.

In retrospect, China's aid relations with a number of countries provide firm evidence of changes or new directions in Chinese foreign policy. This is true of the Sino-Soviet dispute, China's suspicions of India and New Delhi's growing influence in Asia, Peking's switch of emphasis in Africa from West to East Africa, and Mao's effort to establish a permanent sphere of influence on the African continent. China's foreign aid program in the future most certainly will continue to mirror its strategic concerns, shifts in policy lines, internationalist versus isolationist trends, etc. And all this can be put in quantifiable terms.

The first chapter deals with the roots of China's foreign aid program. Here the question of why China is in the aid business is answered by likening it to the historical tribute mission, its current perspectives on international politics, and the complementary and supplementary aspects of aid-giving in relation to other tools of foreign policy. Chapters 2, 3, 4, and 5 comprise an examination of China's economic aid to four blocs or regions: the Communist bloc, non-Communist Asia, the Middle East, and Africa. Different motives and styles of aid diplomacy are analyzed in each chapter. In addition, these four chapters reflect a chronology of the changing focus of China's aid diplomacy and its expansion over a period of more than two decades. These chapters also elucidate differing perspectives and problems in Peking's throughout each period: the Sino-Soviet dispute; the ups and downs or cyclic patterns in Chinese foreign policy in terms of China's positive attitude toward the external world and its desire to participate in it, and hence the importance given to foreign relations; changing areas of geographical interest.

Chapter 6 contains a summary and conclusions. An attempt is made to assess the successes and failures of China's foreign aid program. Also its unique aspects are discussed. Aid-giving is examined with foreign policy motives and strategies to determine how accurately economic assistance is a measure of foreign policy ends and how reliably it may be used as a means of forecasting future trends in China's foreign policy. Finally, an attempt is made to predict the future course of China's economic aid diplomacy.

It is hoped that this study will be of use to China scholars, especially those studying China's foreign policy. In addition, students of international relations should find that this book offers revealing evidence concerning the importance of China in world affairs. Scholars of foreign aid and economic development also may find this work useful.

**China's
Foreign
Aid**

1

The Roots of China's Foreign Aid Diplomacy

By almost any criterion China is a poor country. Statistics published by the United Nations indicate that China falls into the lower one-third of the world nations in terms of the usual standards used to measure economic development.[1] China's gross national product per capita registers only one-fifteenth of Japan and one-fortieth of the United States. In some senses China is among the very poorest nations. It is one of the few countries where mass malnutrition has been a problem in recent years and where famine conditions have existed over an extended period of time. In 1959 the government had to ask the people to alternate liquid meals with solid meals.[2] And in 1962 the average caloric intake dropped to between 1,300 and 1,600 per day—a level which makes survival questionable.[3]

Despite major efforts made by the regime, economic development is plagued by uncertainty. Economic growth has been erratic. Setbacks in industrial progress have occurred periodically. Agricultural production has barely kept up with population growth and in recent years it has fallen behind, forcing China to import grain from Australia, Canada, and the United States. Since 1952 China's economic growth rate, measured in increases in gross national product, has been less than the world's average.[4] In short, China's leaders face serious problems associated with economic stability and growth; and no simple solutions seem to be in sight.

In spite of this, Chinese leaders appear to be committed to giving foreign aid. Peking has been in the aid business officially since 1953 (unofficially before that), and to date has aided more than fifty-five countries on five continents. (See Table 1-1 for a list of these nations.) If donations of less than a million U.S. dollars and emergency aid are considered, the number of recipients is considerably more. China's economic aid program has increased many times in size and scope since 1953, giving testimony to the view that China is in the aid business permanently. Recent aid promises offer further evidence: In 1970 Chinese aid nearly matched its total official aid to non-Communist countries up to that time and amounted to nearly sixty-five percent of the total Communist bloc aid to underdeveloped countries. Since 1970 China has nearly sustained this level of aid-giving.

Also China gives aid on generous terms. Much of China's foreign assistance is in the form of gifts. The rest is under low interest or noninterest provision loads with long-term repayment conditions. Very little Chinese aid is comprised of loans at standard interest rates, and none has been given at higher than normal

1

Table 1-1
China's Foreign Aid Recipients according to Bloc or Region[a]

Communist	Non-Communist Asia	Middle East	Africa	South America	Non-Communist Europe
North Korea	Cambodia	Egypt	Algeria	Chile	Malta
North Vietnam	Burma	Syria	Ghana	Peru	
Outer Mongolia	Nepal	Yemen	Congo (B)	Guyana	
Hungary	Laos	Southern Yemen	Zambia		
Albania	Indonesia	Sudan	Mauritania		
Cuba	Sri Lanka	Iraq	Kenya		
Rumania	Afghanistan	Tunisia	Central African Republic		
	Pakistan	Morocco	Uganda		
	Maldive Islands		Guinea		
			Tanzania[b]		
			Mali		
			Somalia		
			Ethiopia		
			Equatorial Guinea		
			Sierra Leone		
			Burundi		
			Rwanda		
			Togo		
			Nigeria		
			Dahomey		
			Cameroon		
			Zaire		
			Mauritius		
			Malagasy Republic		
			Niger		
			Upper Volta		
			Chad		
			Mozambique		
			Gabon		
			Angola		

[a]Cambodia and Laos are not considered Communist bloc countries here because China's aid relationship with these two nations started before they were ruled by Communist regimes.
[b]Tanzania is a union of Tanganyika and Zanzibar, both of whom had received aid before the federation was formed in April 1964.

interest rates. Furthermore, Peking has often given aid to nations that are economically better off than China. In fact, most of the nations that China has aided have higher standards of living than China. (See Table 1-2 for a comparison of GNPs of nations that are recipients of Chinese aid.) China has also undertaken major projects that require long-term financing and commitments. The Tan-Zam Railroad Project is a good example, costing China more than $400 million to be repaid over a thirty year period.

This evokes a number of questions: Why is China, an underdeveloped

Table 1-2

Chinese Aid to Nations with Higher and Lower GNPs per Capita (Amounts in U.S. Dollars)

Direction of Aid	Higher per Capita Income	Lower per Capita Income
Communist Bloc	Hungary 1,600 Rumania 930 Albania 600 Cuba 530 Outer Mongolia 460 North Korea 330	North Vietnam 100
Non-Communist Asia	Cambodia 130 Laos 120 Sri Lanka 110	Pakistan 100 Nepal 80 Burma 80 Indonesia 80 Afghanistan 80 Maldive Islands
Middle East	Iraq 320 Syria 290 Tunisia 250 Egypt 210 Morocco 190 Sudan 120 Southern Yemen 120	Yemen 80
Africa	Gabon 410 Zambia 400 Ghana 310 Algeria 300 Congo (B) 300 Mauritius 240 Equatorial Guinea 210 Sierra Leone 190 Angola 190 Cameroon 180 Mozambique 180 Kenya 150 Central African Republic 140 Mauritania 140 Togo 140 Uganda 130 Nigeria 120 Guinea 120	Tanzania 100 Malagasy Republic 100 Dahomey 90 Zaire 90 Ethiopia 80 Somalia 70 Mali 70 Niger 70 Chad 70 Burundi 60 Rwanda 60 Upper Volta 50
South America	Chile 720 Peru 450 Guyana 370	
Europe	Malta 810	

Source: *World Bank Atlas* (Washington, D.C.: International Bank for Reconstruction and Development, 1972) for all of the GNPs except China's. China's GNP according to this source has a wide margin of error. According to other sources it varies from $50 to $200. The latter is a Soviet figure. Here $105 to $i10 is assumed to be an accurate estimate. This estimate confirms generally with U.S., British and Japanese sources.

country itself that faces serious problems regarding its own economic growth, willing to give economic aid to other countries? Can and will Peking continue its foreign aid program? What are the motives of Chinese leaders, causing them to make such sacrifices? Is aid-giving a useful instrument of foreign policy?

Part of the explanation lies in Chinese history. China's traditional style of foreign relations gave emphasis to the tribute mission, whereby foreign countries brought gifts to the Chinese emperor and received more valuable gifts or trade concessions in return. China's current view of world politics is also important. Mao sees powerful economic forces at work as well as a great potential for revolution and change. He sees China's role as that of a leader of the "progressive forces" in the world. This was first manifested in China's allegiance to the Communist bloc and now in its efforts to win leadership of the have-not nations. Chinese leaders have found that economic aid conveniently complements or supplements other instruments of foreign policy. And finally, Mao has found that an aid program gives China the status of a superpower.

The Historical Background

China's style of foreign relations as well as its view of the world developed over many centuries of relative isolation. China had few contacts with other civilized people; and other cultures had only an attenuated influence on China. Historical contacts were primarily with nomadic tribes and other less-developed or less-sophisticated cultures. This resulted in a strong sense of superiority on the part of Chinese toward other nationalities and races. The Chinese people acquired a hierarchical view of the world with China at the pinnacle.[5] This view was furthered by the fact that the Emperor conferred or invested titles for kings and nobles both inside and beyond China's borders. China's rigid class system also reinforced a class view of the world.

Since China was a cultural concept, not a territorial one, it had no clearly defined borders. The Middle Kingdom's outer limits were defined in terms of the intensity of cultural development. The Chinese people considered it their responsibility to spread their superior civilization to the culturally deprived, and thus espoused a patronizing attitude toward other peoples and cultures. Throughout the centuries foreign emissaries visited China to learn from the Chinese or to bargain for protection or trade. In deference to Chinese custom they always brought gifts or payments with them.

The tribute system was a logical outgrowth of China's view of the world and its political and economic relations with non-Chinese. The practice of tribute is old; the foundations are found in Chinese prehistory. It developed and matured through the ages. In recent centuries tribute missions were regularized and became the basis not only of China's foreign relations, but the foundation as well for an Asian "international political system."[6] The tribute system was generally respected by China's neighbors, since the sending of tribute missions usually meant peace. The missions also facilitated trade and brought prosperity and the spread of learning. An interruption of the tribute missions was a sign of decay and war.

Initial contacts with the West reinforced the Chinese tribute system and the hierarchical view of the world which served as its underpinnings. Europeans and Americans traveled great distances to China and brought unusual gifts to the Chinese emperor. With few exceptions they performed the kowtow and other rites expected of them by the Chinese and done by other peoples with whom China had contact. At the same time they asked for trade, and initially at least sought Chinese learning. The tribute system was so much a part of China's system of diplomacy, as well as that of neighboring countries, that even after the Opium War and successive military defeats by the West, China continued to receive tribute missions from other Asian countries.[7]

Although Western imperialism and colonialism destroyed China's tributary relations with neighboring nations and peoples, the nation-state system was not quickly adopted by most Asian countries, particularly China. Asians did not understand the balance-of-power system which characterized European politics. Nor do they now understand or accept the bipolar system which grew out of World War II. And, since China lost its position of dominance and leadership due to the impact of the West, it suffered the most humiliation. Of all the Asian countries, China no doubt has the most affection for the past—despite Mao's future oriented ideology and system of rule. China would like to change the present international system and return to the past glories of China; even Mao reflects this in some of his statements and aims.

For this reason, many parallels can be drawn between China's traditional mode of international relations and its current diplomatic practices and attitudes. The hierarchical view of nations may explain Peking's unequal treatment of ambassadors and other foreign officials residing in China. It also provides some insight into China's antipathy toward much of the world, especially the West, and its self-imposed isolationism.[8] Likewise, the tribute mission, which was an integral part of China's historical diplomacy, can be seen to relate to its current foreign aid diplomacy. More than this, aid can be seen as at least a vague attempt to restore China's historical style of relations with other countries.

With the exceptions of Malaysia and Thailand, all of the nations which were historically tribute bearers have, in the past two decades, received aid from China. When China initiated its foreign aid program, aid was given only to nations on China's borders with whom China once carried on tribute relations. The most important tribute nations of the past were the first to receive aid and in the largest quantities: Korea, Vietnam, and Mongolia. Judging from the date of the first aid donations, it made little difference whether recipients were Communist or not. Cambodia, Burma, and Nepal were granted aid only three years after Peking's first official aid, which went to North Korea.

Although Peking has sent out a large number of aid missions and its diplomatic representation abroad is usually large, the greater portion of aid agreements have been signed in Peking—again resembling the past tribute system. Many heads of state have gone to China, and many have received promises of aid for their politeness. In no case has Mao left China to go on any aid missions; in fact, he has never visited any of the nations that China has aided.

Also resembling tribute missions of the past, important diplomatic business is carried on during aid missions or when grants or loans are made. To the Chinese this is the ideal framework in which cultural exchanges, alliances, border settlements, etc., are discussed. The granting of aid also involves considerable fanfare and ritual, as was true of the tribute missions. Other similarities can be gleaned: Tribute missions represented exchanges of loyalty and friendship and enhanced the prestige of ruling groups on both sides.[9] Similarly today, visits to Peking by heads of state provide a measure of legitimacy and favorable publicity for Mao and his associates, as do return visits by Chinese diplomats to the guest countries.[10] Chinese aid is, by almost any standard, given on quite generous terms. The tribute missions were more beneficial to the tribute bearer than to China. Foreign aid provides an avenue for the export of Chinese products. Almost all of China's aid has been in the form of Chinese products or credits to purchase Chinese goods, rather than in foreign currency. China is short of foreign exchange; but this may not be the only reason for granting aid in the form of goods. Tribute missions that went to China were presented with Chinese products which represented the advanced nature of Chinese culture, civilization, science, and general achievement. Today, China offers aid projects which demonstrate China's technological skills, and favors roads and railroads—perhaps because foreigners once built these in China. Based on this as well as other evidence discussed in subsequent chapters, Chinese aid appears to be motivated more by political than economic concerns, just as the tribute missions of the past gave priority to political over economic goals.

One may reasonably ask why China clings to the past, especially when it appears, at first sight at least, to be so costly and impractical to do so. The answer to this question seems to be that China cannot escape from its past, despite Mao's revolutionary style of rule. Even Mao must be concerned about the legitimacy and prestige of his government. Part of the ritual that accompanies aid announcements is for the benefit of the Chinese people—to convince them that their government is powerful, just, and universal. The respect and laudatory comments of foreign missions afford proof. Otherwise, even though the Chinese people do not know much about the outside world, Peking would hardly be willing to announce publicly its aid donations while there are economic hardships at home.

Foreign aid, like the generosity extended to tribute missions of the past, relates especially closely to the concept of virtuous government. According to the Confucian system of ethics, the ruler has to rule with propriety lest the Mandate of Heaven be withdrawn. Helping less cultured neighbors was traditional proof of the virtue of the rule.[11] Today, the praise and thanks of aid recipients help Mao's image and create an aura of virtue. The need for this relates to the importance of ideology in China as a means of political control. Mao still finds it difficult to adapt Communist ideology to China and fully popularize his ideological tenets. This in turn relates to the problem of bringing 800 to 900 million people under effective political control.[12]

Mao's concern about an image of correct rule similarly relates to China's difficult adjustment to a hostile world and to an alien international system. At the onset of the Western impact, Chinese leaders rationalized their shortcomings by proclaiming a superior moral creed. This was later embodied in Chinese nationalism, and since 1949 in China's strong anti-imperialist, anticolonialist stance. It is now reflected in Peking's bid for leadership of the third world and its lectures to the superpowers and the developed countries about the status of the poorer countries. This point must be expanded upon in the context of China's place in contemporary international politics. Here is another source of explanation of China's foreign aid program.

Mao's View of International Politics and China's Foreign Policy Goals

China's foreign aid program can also be related to specific perspectives of the world espoused by Mao and his colleagues. Mao holds very distinct views concerning the forces at work in world politics and China's role in the future of world affairs. Mao's attitudes, as well as those of other Chinese leaders, are crucial to understanding the purpose and direction of China's foreign aid.

Mao's thoughts on international politics were in large part conditioned by Marxism-Leninism. Like Marx, Mao is an economic determinist who feels that economic forces are largely responsible for political-historical trends and even specific events. He also believes strongly that the forces of imperialism can be dealt with and that the colonial and semicolonial areas (of which China has been the latter) are crucial to the defeat of imperialism. Based on the success of the Chinese revolution, Mao deems that China's role in this struggle is vital.[13]

Mao does not, however, underestimate the power of the imperialist West. He feels that he has to fight fire with fire. He observes that the economic devices of trade and aid and the close relationship between economics, or business, and politics have to be understood and utilized in order to defeat imperialism. Thus business and politics are to Mao inextricably related. Manipulating trade and using economic assistance as a tool of foreign policy are not only legitimate but also are necessary to accomplish Mao's aims and make China a powerful and important nation.

Mao as well realizes that China is poor and backward and that its future development will relate to the economic progress of other countries. At first he perceived China's economic growth to be tied to the Communist bloc. Since politics and economics are tied and the Communist countries are the most progressive ideologically, they could be expected to develop more quickly economically, although the capitalist nations would try to prevent this. The Communist nations therefore would serve as a model for the less developed world. And they should aid the poorer nations in order to ultimately defeat imperialism.

As Sino-Soviet differences sharpened, Mao came to realize that he could not rely on a Communist bloc under Moscow's leadership. He perceived that Moscow had joined the ranks of the rich capitalist West and could no longer be considered reliable. Moscow's aid to the poorer countries was not genuine; China's own experience proved that this was true. Mao then carved up the world mentally into rich and poor nations. He assumed a position of leadership of the poor nations in opposition to Moscow's brand of Communism and New Delhi's so-called neutral or nonaligned nations.[14]

Mao regards the poorer countries as the weak link in a system where international economic and political relations are controlled by the imperialist countries. He also sees them as the most revolutionary. To Mao revolutionary movements are potentially the major force of change in international politics.[15] He perceives that class struggle is being waged on a global scale and this is a vital determinant of world history. By aiding the poorer countries China makes its revolutionary experience universally significant, as was its cultures in the past.

Based on Mao's view of the world, China's foreign policy and the aims of its foreign aid program can be related to changing perspectives in Peking. In the early years of the new Communist regime, Mao and other Chinese decision-makers were concerned about immediate and proximate problems. Later, as these matters were dealt with, or the realization came that favorable solutions could not be had, China's foreign policy outlook broadened. Since Mao sees the world in economic terms, it is natural that foreign-aid donations paralleled the new course in China's external policy. In many cases aid preceded policy changes.

In 1949, when the Chinese Communists came to power, Mao's paramount goals were to consolidate the power he had won and to preserve China's territorial integrity. In short, his overriding concern was security.[16] The major threats to the new regime in subsequent years came first from Korea—the Korean War, then from Vietnam—the Vietnam War. It is no coincidence therefore that Peking's first major expenditures of foreign aid went to North Korea and North Vietnam. Chinese leaders perceived a direct threat to their existence, and it is understandable that Peking was willing to supply economic assistance, as well as military aid and manpower. China has given virtually no meaningful military aid to any other countries, and nowhere else has it committed its army.

Both Korea and Vietnam were coveted spheres of influence. Both were traditional tribute bearers, and both are crucial to China in its feud with the Soviet Union. Thus China was willing to give Korea economic aid even after the conflict there ended and the threat from the imperialist enemy subsided. The same may also be true of Vietnam. This explains why Vietnam is by far the largest recipient of Chinese aid and why North Korea is probably second.

Given China's concern for security, attaining secure borders was a paramount objective of China's policy makers in the early years of the new regime. And aid was seen as a useful tool. Traditionally China's borders were unmarked and changed during periods of strength and weakness. Generally, they didn't follow natural land formations, and thus were difficult to defend. During the 1950s and 1960s border settlements were concluded with a number of countries on China's periphery simultaneous with aid talks; or Peking gave aid to make China appear reasonable and generous.[17] Aid was used in a number of cases to create an environment of friendliness and probably made possible more changes in the border and thus more secure frontiers than would otherwise have been possible. It is hardly a coincidence that China has given aid to all nations on its border (except the Soviet Union and India), and that aid agreements were made simultaneously with all border treaties. At first China's desire for secure borders came in response to the American threat, particularly in Southeast Asia. More recently China has been concerned about the Soviety Union and India. Its amicable border settlements with other countries have been flaunted—with the help of aid—to show that China is reasonable about border questions while the Soviet Union and India are not.

Finally Chinese leaders regarded American bases in Asia as a direct threat to China. The same was true of U.S. military alliances with Asian countries, and particularly the Southeast Asia Treaty Organization. Thus during the 1950s China used economic aid to entice the neutral countries of Asia not to join SEATO or any other alliance with the United States. In some cases, aid promises or deliveries resulted in friendship pacts that stipulated that neither would join any alliance against the other.[18] Thus China increased its security and in some cases established buffer zones on its borders.

In the absence of direct threats to its security, China has employed aid to extend its influence in Asia and elsewhere and deal with what it considers potential threats. In addition to the United States, China has come to regard the Soviet Union and India as major challenges to its spheres of interest in Asia. China's aid to Pakistan, the third largest recipient of China's largess, can be seen in the context of Chinese efforts to preserve a balance of power on the Indian subcontinent.[19] If India becomes the dominant power in South Asia, China's southern border will be less secure. Also, Indian influence might spread to Southeast Asia. A stronger Pakistan offsets India's strength in South Asia and prevents the spread of India's influence outside that region. Most recently the Indian threat has been seen by Chinese decision makers in relation to deteriorating Sino-Soviet relations and an alliance between Moscow and New Delhi assumed to be aimed at China. This goes far in explaining why Peking sees no contradiction in aiding countries that are also recipients of U.S. aid—particularly Pakistan.

The same kind of thinking now applies to China's concern about Soviet expansionism and efforts to encircle and contain China. Continued aid to nations in non-Communist Southeast Asia, aid competition in the new Indochina Communist states, and the focus on East Africa and the southern Middle Eastern countries are thus accountable. Much Chinese aid has been dispersed in non-Communist Asia even though these nations are not revolutionary in Mao's terms. Moreover, they are developing economically faster than China; and China has won diplomatic relations with them already, or diplomatic relations cannot be bought with aid. Fear of Soviet influence also explains Mao's statements to the effect that U.S. troops should remain in certain Asian countries and the fact that Chinese foreign policy aims generally no longer conflict with U.S. goals. Recent aid donations prove this.

A second major objective of China's foreign policy is building trade ties to facilitate China's economic development and to destroy Western "neocolonialism and imperialism."[20] This now applies to Soviet "social imperialism" as well. In the early years of Mao's regime, trade links were built with other Communist countries and nearly all of China's trade was with bloc countries; most important were the Soviet Union and other Asian Communist nations. Aid facilitated China's trade with the Soviet Union; likewise it initiated trade ties with North Korea, North Vietnam, and Outer Mongolia. China sought to be economically independent of the Western capitalist countries that had in the past preyed on China. The success of Mao's revolution was largely a product of Chinese nationalism and China's reaction to foreign imperialism. It was natural that Mao sought to avoid trade ties with the West.

In almost all cases Chinese aid stimulated trade, since China's aid is tied to Chinese products. Economic assistance has thus been effective in introducing Chinese products to the recipient countries. In most cases aid continues to support trade ties, but has been less successful, as we shall see, in establishing permanent trade relations that are maintained without continuing aid. In the case of trade with neutral nations, China's aid has been most important. Because of the period of colonialism, China's traditional trade ties with other Asian nations were cut. And as a result of the United States embargo on China during and after the Korean War, it was difficult for Peking to establish trade contacts with non-Communist countries. Thus Peking sought to win a sphere of influence in Asia and attract Asian neutrals, and later, neutrals in the Middle East and Africa. Aid provided an introduction after which trade and other economic contacts followed.

In the 1950s Mao perceived that China would soon become an industrial nation and that symbiotic trade relations could result with the less developed countries, especially in Asia.[21] Thus he had another reason for seeking trade ties. In the late 1950s Peking could clearly see that its efforts to industrialize and become a manufacturing giant were not materializing. Almost at the same time, however, Sino-Soviet differences became more acute, and Moscow cut off its aid to China and reduced the level of trade. As a result China had to seek other trade ties forthwith. Chinese leaders went to Japan and several Western European nations and found substitutes for Soviet goods. Aid to these nations was not appropriate. At the same time Peking sought to diversify its trade to avoid the difficulty of overreliance on a single trading partner. Aid to the smaller and poorer countries helped initiate trade ties and afforded a greater diversity in China's foreign trade.

In recent years Peking has endeavored to win a position of leadership in the third world and thus has increased its trade with third world countries. Since natural trade bonds between the underdeveloped nations and the developed ones are the strongest, China has found it difficult to establish trade ties. In many cases aid has been helpful. In other cases aid has been beneficial in establishing business contacts which involve critical imports for Peking. Some of these will be discussed later, particularly in the chapter on Chinese aid to African countries.

A third major aim of Chinese foreign policy is winning international recognition. Mao wants to restore China's former place in the world—a position of world leadership.[22] China's status in the community of nations declined during the period of Western imperialism because China was weak. Now China is strong again and will, in Mao's view, play a major role in international politics. On the other hand, neither the imperialist powers nor the Soviet Union wants to grant Mao his due role. Thus Mao employs the tool of economic aid to break out of the isolation imposed by Washington and Moscow. Aid has been used on numerous occasions to buy or set the proper environment for diplomatic relations. The timing of a number of aid promises and deliveries clearly suggests that aid was given for the purpose of winning diplomatic ties. (See Table 1-3.) In fact, the majority of small, underdeveloped nations with whom China has attained diplomatic accords since the late 1950s have also been recipients of Chinese aid. The same is true of votes in the United Nations on seating Peking in place of Taipei. Nearly all of the nations that voted for Mao on the resolution which seated his regime and expelled the Nationalist Chinese had received aid from China, many of them recently. (See Table 1-4.)

Mao has also sought international recognition in a less orthodox way. For years, seeing that he could not win recognition from the world community for his regime, Mao used aid to support wars of national liberation. With usually a small amount of funds, supplies, or weapons China could exert considerable influence abroad. Help to rebel groups was costly for the United States or other "imperialist" powers to counteract. And at the same time it exposed the Soviet Union for its "revisionist" and "counterrevolutionary" tendencies. There was little danger of direct retaliation against China, and Mao could win support from many dissatisfied Third World leaders. This was an easy way to gain at least nominal international recognition for his regime.[23]

Now, China is represented in the United Nations and is recognized by most of the nations of the world. Further, China's relations have improved consider-

Table 1-3

Dates of Diplomatic Relations with China by Aid Recipients and the Dates of Initial Aid

Country	Recognition	Diplomatic Relations	Initial Aid
Rumania	Oct. 3, 1949	Oct. 5, 1949	Nov. 1970
Hungary	Oct. 4, 1949	Oct. 6, 1949	Nov. 1956
Korea (North)	Oct. 5, 1949	Oct. 6, 1949	Nov. 1953
Mongolia	Oct. 6, 1949	Oct. 16, 1949	Aug. 1956
Albania	Nov. 21, 1949	Nov. 23, 1949	Oct. 1954
Burma	Dec. 16, 1949	June 8, 1950	Jan. 1958
Pakistan	Jan. 5, 1950	May 21, 1951	Feb. 1965
Ceylon	Jan. 5, 1950	Feb. 7, 1957	Sept. 1957
Afghanistan	Jan. 12, 1950	Jan. 20, 1955	Mar. 1965
Vietnam (North)	Jan. 15, 1950	Jan. 18, 1950	July, 1955
Indonesia	April 13, 1950	June 9, 1950	Nov. 1956
Nepal	Aug. 1, 1955	Aug. 1, 1955	Oct. 1956
UAR	May 16, 1956	May 30, 1956	Nov. 1956
Syria	July 3, 1956	Aug. 10, 1956	Feb. 1963
Yemen	Aug. 21, 1956	Sept. 24, 1956	Jan. 1958
Cambodia	July 18, 1958	July 23, 1958	June 1956
Sudan	Feb. 4, 1959	June 7, 1959	June 1970
Guinea	Oct. 4, 1959	Oct. 4, 1959	Sept. 1960
Ghana	July 5, 1960	July 5, 1960	Aug. 1961
Cuba	Sept. 2, 1960	Sept. 28, 1960	Nov. 1960
Mali	Oct. 14, 1960	Oct. 27, 1960	Sept. 1961
Somalia	Dec. 14, 1960	Dec. 16, 1960	Aug. 1963
Tanzania	Dec. 9, 1961	Dec. 9, 1961	Feb. 1964
Laos	June 28, 1962	June 28, 1962	Jan. 1962
Algeria	July 3, 1962	July 3, 1962	Nov. 1958
Uganda	Oct. 18, 1962	Oct. 18, 1962	April 1965
Kenya	Dec. 14, 1963	Dec. 14, 1963	May 1964
Congo (B)	Feb. 18, 1964	Feb. 22, 1964	July 1964
Central African Republic	Sept. 27, 1964	Sept. 29, 1964	Sept. 1964
Zambia	Oct. 25, 1964	Oct. 29, 1964	Jan. 1967
Mauritania	July 17, 1965	July 17, 1965	Feb. 1967
Southern Yemen	Jan. 11, 1968	Jan. 11, 1968	1968
Ethiopia	Nov. 20, 1970	Nov. 24, 1970	Oct. 1971
Chile	Dec. 15, 1970	Dec. 15, 1970	June 1971

ably with the United States. However, Peking still seeks influence in the Third World in the form of a leadership role. And Chinese leaders continue to strive to put forward their kind of Communism and expose Soviet revisionism and social imperialism. Thus Mao finds aid useful in winning support for his kind of Communism and as a means to underscore the gap between rich and poor nations.

Clearly one of the prominent elements of Chinese foreign policy in the 1970s is Peking's concern for the poorer countries, and the fact that international trade and economic relations generally favor the rich countries. Mao endeavors to represent the poorer, backward countries. He wants to isolate the richer

Table 1-4
Voting of Recipients of Chinese Aid on the Admission of China to the United Nations

Country	Albania Resolution 1971	Albania Resolution 1970	Important Question Resolution
Afghanistan	Yes	Yes	No
Albania	Yes	Yes	No
Algeria	Yes	Yes	No
Burma	Yes	Yes	No
Cambodia	No	No	Yes
Central African Republic	No	Abstention	Yes
Ceylon	Yes	Yes	No
Chile	Yes	Yes	No
Congo (Brazzaville)	Yes	Yes	No
Cuba	Yes	Yes	No
Ethiopia	Yes	Yes	No
Ghana	Yes	Yes	Yes
Guinea	Yes	Yes	No
Hungary	Yes	Yes	No
Indonesia	Abstention	Didn't vote	Yes
Kenya	Yes	Yes	No
Laos	Yes	Abstention	Abstention
Mali	Yes	Yes	No
Mauritania	Yes	Yes	No
Mongolia	Yes	Yes	No
Morocco	Yes	Yes	Abstention
Nepal	Yes	Yes	No
Pakistan	Yes	Yes	No
Rumania	Yes	Yes	No
Southern Yemen	Yes	Yes	No
Somalia	Yes	Yes	No
Sudan	Yes	Yes	No
Syria	Yes	Yes	Abstention
Tunisia	Yes	Abstention	No
Uganda	Yes	Yes	No
United Arab Republic	Yes	Yes	No
Tanzania	Yes	Yes	No
Yemen	Yes	Yes	No
Zambia	Yes	Yes	No

countries and the superpowers and thus become a major world power without attaining superpower status—which is beyond China's reach for now. Even if this is an exaggeration of Peking's hopes and aims, China does want to force the developed countries to help or allow the less developed countries to grow economically.

In this effort China uses its aid as a model and a basis for propaganda. This explains, in addition to the other reasons already mentioned, why Chinese aid is so generous. Mao wants to make the developed countries appear ungenerous and their aid exploiting. The principles of Chinese aid thus appear to be altruistic

and deriding of the rich nations. (See Appendixes A, B, and C.) Although, as we
will see in subsequent pages, China's aid is not as unselfish as it appears, this is
still a major motive behind China's foreign-aid giving.

Aid and Other Tools of China's Foreign Policy

In addition to relating China's foreign aid program to the historical tribute
system and to Mao's global perspectives, as well as the important tenets of
Chinese foreign policy, aid is also an important tool of foreign policy that supplements, complements, or even substitutes for other policy instrumentalities. This
is especially important to China since Peking lacks or is weak in some of the
means of carrying out foreign policy and has been isolated for so many years.
Finally foreign aid is a policy instrumentality that gives China's diplomacy
needed flexibility.

Initially aid was used to cement relations with other bloc countries. China's
foreign assistance was an extension of Soviet aid and a manifestation of bloc
economic ties.[24] China received aid from the Soviet Union at the same time that
it purveyed economic help to North Korea, North Vietnam, and subsequently
other bloc countries, and even nonbloc nations. Mao perceived an international
brotherhood of Communist nations and made China a part of the so-called
Socialist Union of Nations. Mao and the other Chinese leaders saw no contradiction in giving aid while at the same time receiving it. Aid was a means of conducting business with other Communist countries and a way of strengthening
interbloc relations. Given China's historical method of conducting foreign affairs
with other Asian countries, aid was a natural milieu for conducting diplomatic
relations while at the same time enhancing Peking's contacts with Asian Communist countries. It also strengthened relations with the Soviet Union and
demonstrated that China could play an important role in bloc affairs—that it was
not just another minor member of the Communist world. China's aid to Hungary is a case in point.

Thus China's economic aid served as a tool of its external relations and was
a central factor in its economic ties with the Soviet Union and the Asian Communist countries. It supplemented and complemented all other means of carrying
out foreign policy. China sorely needed Soviet aid. But at the same time Mao
wanted to establish diplomatic, trade and other relations with bloc countries,
especially the Asian members. Aid served these purposes well.

At the onset of China's foreign aid program economic assistance also provided China with a means of assisting a friendly country without making a direct
challenge to the United States. In Korea, China gave aid before getting involved
in the war directly, and subsequently used economic and military assistance to
support the aims of the Communist North. In Vietnam, China did not commit

forces directly to combat situations; aid was generally supplied in lieu of soldiers. In short, China was able to respond in direct ways to outside threats and yet not risk armed confrontation, especially nuclear war with the U.S. and its allies. In this way China could "wage a war against the imperialists" and maintain a tough policy, without taking any of the risks.[25] Aid was thus a policy which substituted for military action.

Mao used aid to other countries similarly. Chinese aid to Pakistan, which also included considerable military aid, supported Pakistan against India. Although China has not been able to compete with Western or Soviet military aid, it has given weapons and other military equipment at crucial junctures and it has had significant impact. Pakistan was able to balance India's influence in South Asia, and Chinese aid, in some senses, offset Soviet aid to India. China gave valuable help to Pakistan in at least two direct confrontations with India. This not only balanced India's influence in the area, but also helped China to brand India an aggressor nation and sully its image as a leader of the neutral nations.

China has also given considerable military as well as economic aid to Albania and Tanzania. In these two countries China has a considerable investment in aid, and both represent for China beachheads in the region. Aid to these nations also mirrors an effort to deal with a real or perceived Soviet threat. In the case of Albania, China has an ally and may be able to establish a second front against the Kremlin in the event that their border fighting escalates into conventional war. Albania has already provided China with important military bases, especially naval bases. Tanzania affords China a staging area in East Africa and offers a means of dealing with the expansion of Soviet naval power in the area.

In addition to these cases of direct military aid, China has used aid to support wars of national liberation or conflicts of a less direct nature in a number of other areas of the world, most notably in the Middle East and Africa. Mao has provided financial help to rebel forces in Algeria, the Congo, and a number of other countries. China has given assistance to the Palestinian Liberation Organization. And Peking has sent aid recently to independence movements in the former Portuguese colonies and groups opposing the white-ruled governments in Africa. This aid has consisted generally of small arms and supplies of various kinds. Nevertheless, aid was and may remain vital to China's support for foreign revolutionary groups and movements.

China's foreign aid has also benefited its cultural diplomacy. During the mid-1950s China's aggressive and inflexible stance toward the neutral nations proved counterproductive, and Peking set out to change its image and establish contacts on a broad front with Third World countries, especially Afro-Asian nations.[26] This was called the "Bandung phase" of China's foreign policy. Since this time, China's foreign ministry has frequently emphasized informal, friendly contacts, especially with Third World countries. In carrying out its friendly diplomacy China sends cultural missions such as art, educational, and athletic groups.[27]

Since the funding of such missions must be done in an indirect way, economic aid is an integral part of China's cultural diplomacy. Frequently China provides funds so that the recipient can invite Chinese groups to their country. On other occasions China finances local groups that want to go to China. And in a number of countries China has promised or built exhibition halls, gymnasiums, etc.

China's foreign aid is so closely related to its Red Cross operations that it is frequently unclear which is which. Red Cross work often involves aid in the millions of dollars. And frequently, economic aid is clearly humanitarian or for disaster relief. For the purposes of this study Red Cross donations are generally not considered as aid unless they exceed $1 million, even though their relationship to China's foreign aid diplomacy may be intimate. The reader should thus keep in mind that much of Chinas humanitarian aid relates closely to its Red Cross work and vice versa.

China also finances considerable technical, medical, and agricultural aid. In some cases this is done directly out of aid funds. Sometimes it is done out of Red Cross budgets or other funds. The same goes for paying for exchange students and technical or other training in China. In recent years technical, medical and agricultural aid missions have increased in number. Peking is clearly using its aid missions, especially this kind, to spread good will. Many of China's aid personnel now receive instruction or training in cultural activities. China's aid missions to Africa have been the most active in this respect.

China also uses aid to win influence in a number of regional organizations. In some cases China simply buys a membership or gives monetary pledges to the organization. In other cases it gives money to influence the organization directly and to change the direction of the groups' interests and attitudes. Sometimes Peking has succeeded in buying the votes of members of regional or other organizations. China has been especially active in its intercourse with the Afro-Asian People's Solidarity Organization, the Organization of African Unity, and a number of other such organizations. Peking has also used aid to influence several conferences and has bribed nations to influence invitations and agendas. The Afro-Asian Conference scheduled to be held in 1965 in Algeria is the best case in point, and it is discussed at length in later pages.

Finally China's economic aid has been and is used to finance cultural contacts, which in turn lead to more formal diplomatic relations. As already mentioned, Peking has made promises or deliveries of aid virtually simultaneously with attaining formal recognition. This relationship is too close and can be demonstrated in too many cases to be coincidental. This has been most obvious in Africa, where in 1967 Peking was recognized by only 13 countries, while by the beginning of 1974 it was recognized by 30 countries. Since then even more African nations have set up formal contacts with China, and aid in recent cases has still served as a medium for establishing such relations.

A third instrument of China's foreign policy that relates closely to foreign aid is its propaganda.[28] Propaganda is readily seen as an important part of China's external relations from a variety of points of view. Since Mao's global perceptions are founded on Marxian economic theory, it is understandable that China's propaganda consists of many statements on economic issues, and often aid is a central one. It has already been noted that China contends that Western and Soviet aid is exploitive and in many ways harmful; Chinese aid, in contrast, is not. This, of course, is an important publicity theme. Many Chinese aid projects are designed specifically to demonstrate how Chinese aid is unique and generous.

More than this, economic aid has been utilized in a number of cases to influence or buy a Chinese presence in the recipient country that includes the right to station press agency representatives, sell books, set up exhibits, etc. These are more direct facets of China's propaganda diplomacy. In a number of specific cases offices of the Chinese news agency have been set up following aid promises. Other privileges in this realm have also been bought with aid. In addition Chinese aid has financed the building of radio stations in a number of countries, and they have been used to propagate Peking's foreign policy line.

In some cases Chinese aid has been diverted to local businesses or organizations that are sympathetic to Peking. This is notably true in Southeast Asia where aid funds have been provided to local pro-Peking newspapers, schools, etc. Here considerable aid money has also been expended to win over local Chinese and undermine or counter Nationalist China's goodwill and propaganda efforts.

All of China's aid personnel, even manual laborers, are instructed on how to behave in the country where they are to be working. They live at the standards of local residents, unlike aid personnel from many other countries; and they learn the language and spread Chinese Communist doctrines when they can. China's aid workers are intended to be models of good behavior. Generally China's aid personnel have made a good impression in the host country, especially because of their willingness to live at the local standard of living. Aid workers have also been called upon to disseminate propaganda leaflets, even against the will of the local government; and they have intentionally started rumors and whisper campaigns.

Finally, China's aid projects are usually simple show projects intended to help the local populace as quickly and as directly as possible. In almost all cases they are designed to produce a good impression of China in the minds of local citizens. This is a much more important consideration than helping economic development in the recipient country. Thus China's aid provides grist for the propaganda mill as well as complementing it in other ways.

In the following pages China's foreign aid program is analyzed on a bloc level, and by country. The style of analysis will vary from country to country. In the first two chapters more emphasis is given to the traditional tribute mission as a model for aid. In addition, in Chapter 2, on aid to bloc countries, ideology and the Sino-Soviet dispute are major themes. The military threat of the West plays a central role in explaining aid to North Korea and North Vietnam. In Chapter 3, on aid to non-Communist Asian nations, China's aid is related to its traditional diplomacy, an effort to create a sphere of influence, offset India's impact in the area, and ward off U.S. and Soviet intrusions. Aid to Middle Eastern countries marks a special effort to win diplomatic recognition and avoid being isolated by the U.S. and Soviet Union, to stimulate wars of national liberation and to solidify an Afro-Asian bloc. It is also the beginning of an effort to unify the poor nations against the rich. China's aid to African nations in the subsequent chapter reemphasizes these themes and adds to it Chinese efforts to decolonize the world and take advantage of unstable situations, racial turmoil, and hatred.

The reader's attention is directed to the various themes in China's foreign policy already mentioned. In some cases the quantitative evidence to support these claims is clear and overwhelming. In others it is merely suggestive. In all cases an effort is made to look at China's foreign policy from the vantage point of one tool—foreign aid.

2

China's Aid to Communist Bloc Countries

In 1949 after the takeover of mainland China was complete, Mao and his followers announced a policy of "lean to one side" or aligning with other Communist countries. The reasons for Peking's alliance with other Communist nations were myriad: Communist ideology was the foundation of the Communist revolution which vaulted Mao into power and it was also vital to Mao's mode of rule and his new government; Mao found an enemy complex useful in his endeavor to unify China; membership in the Communist bloc provided China with allies and protected Peking from being isolated by hostile powers.[1]

However, just as important, Mao realized that China needed economic aid. And he knew that this would not come from the United States or other Western countries. The alternative was the Soviet Union, which not only promised economic assistance, but also offered a military alliance and a model for economic development. Thus in February 1950, the Sino-Soviet Treaty of Friendship and Alliance was signed. China received protection against the United States, guaranteed by the Soviet nuclear arsenal. Cultural contacts, trade, and aid followed. Aid included the tools, blueprints, expertise, etc., to develop an industrial superstructure. It also included an immediate loan of $300 million. In April specific agreements were signed on commodity exchanges, the delivery of Soviet machinery to China, and joint stock companies. Moscow agreed to supply China with a total of 300 industrial plants, the whole spectrum of Soviet technology, and administrative and technical skills.[2]

With the cementing of Sino-Soviet relations, China became a member of the so-called socialist union. Although China's trade contacts with the Eastern European Communist nations were not important, ideological bonds were significant. Peking committed itself to Communist solidarity and established cultural and trade relations with other members of the Communist bloc. China's relations with the bloc were also furthered by the fact that the capitalist West controlled international trade. Western currencies were the medium of exchange, and capitalist business practices the mode of doing business. Therefore, China could not participate extensively in international business, even if it weren't for the post–Korean War boycott inspired by the United States.

Although China was obviously subservient to the Soviet Union in all matters relating to bloc affairs, Peking was different from the other members of the bloc that were small and not economically self-sufficient. Peking became a kind of junior partner and in some ways an equal with Moscow in Communist bloc affairs. For this reason Chinese leaders saw no contradiction in giving aid to bloc countries, while at the same time receiving aid from the Soviet Union. This was simply a manifestation of the economic nature of the socialist union. Peking assumed a Chinese sphere of influence in Asia which included the three Asian Communist countries—North Korea, North Vietnam, and Outer Mongolia.[3] These three countries formerly related to China as tribute bearers. China may have had such a relationship in mind when it initiated aid to these three Communist "fraternal" nations. In the cases of North Korea and North Vietnam, Mao was also moved by the threat that wars there presented to China. In the case of Outer Mongolia, Chinese aid was in large part used to develop transportation links which supported trade between China and the Soviet Union. China also provided Hungary with aid in the mid-1950s, but this can be seen almost exclusively as an effort to improve bloc unity. The amount of this aid was small, and it did not promote trade between the two countries or tie Hungary economically to China.

In all instances China's early aid supplemented or complemented Soviet aid. Sometimes geography made it easier for China to provide aid rather than the Soviet Union. This was especially true for the case of North Vietnam; but it was also true of North Korea and Outer Mongolia. Cooperative aid offered phychological benefits and gave the impression of a unified Communist bloc. Further, it tended to foster a division of labor in the bloc and enhance bloc trade.

However, as time passed increased specialization generally made the bloc nations more dependent upon Moscow. And as Soviet aid became an instrument of control over bloc affairs, China's role became uncertain. Would Peking become more dependent upon the Soviet Union, assuming a role like the other Communist countries—a satellite of the Soviet Union? Or would China improve its position and become an equal partner rather than a junior partner? Economic relations constituted a major source of friction between Peking and Moscow in the early 1950s and was the first sign of a Sino-Soviet rift.

By the late 1950s friendship and unity began to change into competition and distrust. Since aid was an important instrument in maintaining or altering ties within the bloc, it was a crucial factor in the change. In fact, economic aid became a major issue in the verbal exchanges between Peking and Moscow that made a serious rift apparent. In retrospect, it was an accurate barometer of Sino-Soviet relations; it indicated a dispute long before most observers believed it was serious.

Peking had cause to suspect Soviet leaders even in the early 1950s when relations were amicable. At a time when Mao had no other sources of aid and China desperately needed financial help, Soviet assistance to China was by no means generous. It was small in terms of what Moscow might have given, and what China needed. Moreover, it consisted of loans that had to be repaid, and the terms were not charitable.[4] Mao had other reasons to be upset with Moscow in regard to its aid policies. During the Korean War, Peking obtained large quantities of military equipment from the Soviet Union on credit terms. This equipment was used by Chinese forces in Korea or was given to the North Korean Army. Mao felt that Chinese troops were fighting in Korea in lieu of the Soviet Army and that Moscow should at least supply the equipment and weapons free.[5]

A further cause for disagreement was the aid that the Soviet Union gave to North Korea, North Vietnam, and Outer Mongolia during the late 1950s. The Chinese saw this as an effort by Khrushchev to bring these countries under Soviet control. Soviet aid at this time had political conditions attached, and Moscow seemed to be trying to undermine Chinese influence. Since Khrushchev had made tacit promises to Mao regarding a Chinese sphere of influence while he was struggling for power and denied it once his position was firm, Mao had cause to feel that he had been betrayed.[6]

Hence Mao embarked on a policy of self-reliance. This meant an economic independence from the Soviet Union and, in part, a rejection of the Kremlin's leadership in bloc affairs. In 1957 he launched the Great Leap Forward—an attemp to make China economically self-sufficient and to sustain the industrialization process based upon native and grass-roots efforts. It was an ideological insult to the Russians who had already tried such schemes and regarded Mao's plan as an effort to put China ahead of the Soviet Union on the road to socialism. In response, Moscow cut off new aid to China and in 1960 withdrew its aid officials, shut down projects that were not completed, and destroyed the blueprints for others. Open confrontation between Peking and Moscow followed.

Peking, however, did not change its policy of active participation in Communist bloc affairs; rather China began to compete with Moscow for leadership of the bloc. One means of doing this was aid. Hence, after 1960 China competed with the Soviet Union for the allegiance of other Communist bloc countries and for support on ideological and other issues, and economic aid was a major weapon. In some cases China won; in most it lost. When the Sino-Soviet dispute came to a head China clearly lost its bid to win support from Outer Mongolia. Hungary was also won over by Moscow; but this can hardly be considered a defeat for China due to its very small commitment of aid. Peking also experienced a temporary defeat in North Korea. That is, Pyongyang became reliant upon Soviet aid and Chinese aid was discontinued. Nevertheless it was not a permanent Soviet victory. North Korea has been quite independent of the Soviet Union in ideological matters and in many other ways. In the case of North Vietnam, China was able to compete with the Soviet Union, and Hanoi generally remained neutral in the Sino-Soviet dispute. At times Chinese aid and influence seemed to predominate. At other times the Soviet Union had the edge. In the last two or three years Soviet aid, and consequently Moscow's influence, has seemed to predominate.

Of the bloc countries that China has aided since the break in relations, Cuba went to the Soviet Union. Greater Soviet aid was the deciding factor. And, up to the present time, there is no evidence to indicate that this is not permanent. However, in the case of Albania, the victory belongs to China. Peking was able to supplant Soviet aid and win over Albania on ideological and other matters. In fact, Albania became a beachhead of Chinese influence in Europe.

China has also extended aid to Rumania. But at this time it is too early to assess the success of China's efforts. Peking has managed to entice Rumania to relax its close ties with the Soviet Union and accept help in breaking its economic dependence on Moscow. It may also be seen as a ploy to attract Soviet attention to Europe and away from the Sino-Soviet border; and it may dampen Soviet efforts toward détente with the West. If successful, Peking may aid more Eastern European countries.

Currently, competition characterizes Sino-Soviet relations. China continues to offer aid to bloc countries to win their friendship and allegiance. Although Moscow has the advantage of being able to offer more aid, China has by no means given up; nor is it defeated. However, China's world view has changed, and now Peking considers relations with other Communist nations less important. Hence more new aid is going to non-Communist countries. But the Kremlin has made similar moves.

Until recently, Peking's officially announced aid to bloc nations exceeded its aid to any of the following: non-Communist Asian countries, Middle Eastern countries, or African countries. In terms of aid actually given Communist nations have received much more than any of the other groups. This is primarily because China gave large amounts of unofficial or unannounced assistance to North Korea and North Vietnam during the conflicts there, and continues to provide aid to North Vietnam. If estimates of China's loans and grants which include vast quantities of unannounced aid are used, aid to bloc countries probably exceeds aid to other areas by three to five times. (See Table 2–1.) North Vietnam is certainly the single most important recipient of nations in all blocs; It has received several times more aid from China than any other country.

The predominance of aid to bloc countries may be explained in terms of China's concern for security, the desire to improve bloc relations, and now competition with the Soviet Union for leadership of the bloc. These vast quantities of aid were important to the recipients. But just as important, economic aid has constituted a major instrument of China's foreign policy vis-à-vis other Communist countries. Also, though China's aid to countries within the bloc has declined in relative terms, it has not decreased in absolute amounts. China's aid to several bloc countries remains considerable.

In addition to efforts to promote bloc solidarity and to compete with the Soviet Union for bloc leadership, China's aid to bloc countries was motivated by a desire to restore former economic, i.e., tribute, relations with neighboring countries. Aid to Asian Communist nations promoted trade relations just as the tribute missions did in the past. The tribute mission bolstered China's influence in the region; aid has done likewise. In neither case, however, can it be said that China's aid to bloc countries has been very successful. China's trade is primarily

Table 2-1
China's Total Aid by Area to December 1975[a]
(In Millions of U.S. Dollars)

Area	Aid Promised Official Aid	Aid Delivered Low Estimate	Aid Delivered High Estimate
Communist Bloc	1,352.25	3,110.00	6,340.00
Non-Communist Asian Nations	933.70	440.00	1,600.0
Middle East Nations	518.20	120.00	420.00
African Nations	1,488.50	400.00	1,000.00
Latin American Nations	162.00	10.00	50.00
Non-Communist European Nations	40.00	5.00	25.00
Total	4,494.65	4,085.00	9,435.00

[a]Aid totals cited here include recent donations, some of which have not been confirmed. See Addendum. The following charts do not include these figures, thus the totals are different.

with Japan and the United States; its natural trading partners are the developed countries. Furthermore, China has not been able to restore its historical influence in Asia, because of the influence of the superpowers and the competing regional powers such as Japan and India. This goes far in explaining why China's aid to bloc nations has occupied a smaller and smaller portion of its total aid. Peking's failures have engendered a broader world view. Or the reverse has occurred. Probably they are reinforcing trends. Nevertheless, bloc relations have been important and remain so. And there is little reason to think that Peking will abandon bloc relations altogether.

Looking at individual recipients, North Vietnam is by far the biggest recipient of Chinese aid. Hanoi has received nearly 35 percent of Peking's official aid to bloc countries or roughly one-half, if estimates of actual aid are used. (See Table 2-2.) North Korea has received a similar amount if official statistics are used, but certainly less in terms of real amounts. Pyongyang no doubt received much aid that was never announced; but it is likely that it did not receive some of the officially promised aid. Certainly it has not received as much aid as North Vietnam.

Albania accounts for a little over ten percent of Peking's official aid, but more if estimates of actual deliveries are considered. Tiriana has also received unannounced aid from China. Outer Mongolia follows as the next most important recipient in official terms, but a significant portion of this was probably never delivered. Cuba and Hungary are next in terms of published figures; but again they, especially Cuba, did not receive all of the aid they were promised.

It is uncertain how much official aid China has given to Rumania. Bucharest

Table 2-2
China's Aid to Communist Bloc Nations
(Amounts in Millions of U.S. Dollars)

			Aid Actually Given			
Nation	*Total Official*	*Percent*	*Low Estimate*	*Percent*	*High Estimate*	*Percent*
Albania	153.75	11.2	420.00	14.4	800.00	13.3
Cuba	60.00	4.5	40.00	1.4	60.00	1.0
Hungary	57.50	4.3	50.00	1.6	65.00	.9
North Korea	495.00	36.5	800.00	25.7	1,200.00	19.9
Outer Mongolia	115.00	8.6	100.00	3.2	115.00	1.9
Rumania[a]	–	0.0	200.00	6.4	300.00	5.0
North Vietnam	471.00	34.7	1,500.00	48.3	3,500.00	58.0
Total	1,352.25	99.8	3,110.00	101.0	6,040.00	100.0

[a]Aid was officially announced; however, no figures were given.

received an announced grant for flood relief of a size that probably should be considered foreign aid. In addition, formal aid has been announced, but the figures have not. In terms of aid actually received, Rumania no doubt leads Outer Mongolia, Cuba, and Hungary.

Following is an analysis of China's economic aid to each of the Communist bloc countries mentioned. Specific objectives in aid-giving in most cases are examined, as well as the unique aspects of China's aid and its significance relative to the Sino-Soviet dispute. Where appropriate, security, alliances, and trade will be given special emphasis as motives for Chinese aid giving.

Aid to North Korea

It is uncertain when China first gave economic assistance to North Korea. Immediately after Mao's regime established control over China, in October 1949, Peking held negotiations with the North Korean government on the joint construction of a dam project on the Yalu River. Apparently China paid more than its share for this project.[7] In any case, in 1950 at the onset of the Korean War, China provided the North Korean government with large quantities of equipment, supplies, and credits. Subsequently Peking sent "volunteers" who fought beside the North Korean Army. It is estimated that China supplied 2.5 million troops and suffered casualties upward of 1 million.[8] This kind of aid is impossible to estimate in dollar terms; the human sacrifice and cost to China cannot be counted. It certainly constituted a "debt" on the part of North Korea.

In terms of direct financial assistance to North Korea during the Korean

War, China provided outright grants totalling at least $75 million.[9] Considerably more aid must have been given, judging from the amounts of equipment, supplies, etc., China sent to North Korea. Furthermore, much of this equipment was purchased by Peking from the Soviet Union on credit. It is quite certain that had China not aided North Korea at its time of dire need, North Korea would have been defeated by the U.N. forces. It is also clear that China made human and economic sacrifices in aiding Korea both during and after the war. Peking needed its resources to develop its own economy; and inflation, which had just been brought under control, was restimulated by China's involvement in Korea.

In terms of official aid, China first extended promises to North Korea in November 1953. In fact, this marked the formal launching of China's foreign aid program. Peking cancelled trade debts accumulated by Pyongyang in the amount of $56.9 million. In addition, China promised $338 million in the form of a free grant to be used during the period 1954–1957 to help North Korea repair its war damage.[10] Although part of this grant may have been used to maintain Chinese troops in North Korea, they were probably supported by funds provided by China which never entered official aid statistics. Most of the grant was supplied in Chinese goods, the prices of which were set by the Chinese government; but the prices were not high and the goods made available were generally things that North Korea needed in rehabilitating the country after the war.

In September 1958 Peking negotiated two more aid agreements with North Korea. One was a non-interest-bearing loan in the amount of $10 million to be repaid over a 10-year period beginning in 1963 for North Korea's share of a jointly owned hydroelectric power station on the upper Yalu River.[11] The second was a loan in the amount of $42.5 million at an interest rate of 1 percent for the purchase of Chinese machinery and equipment to build a textile mill and two cement bag plants.[12] Both the large grant made in 1953 and subsequent loans were given by Peking to help North Korea rebuild after the war and to become a showcase of socialism. Mao also sought to integrate China's industrial heartland in Manchuria with North Korea's heavy industry. Both China and North Korea at that time were giving emphasis to heavy industry as the basis for economic growth. This accounts for the fact that almost all Chinese aid was in the form of equipment, machinery, and aid to build infrastructure projects such as railroads, dams, power plants, bridges, etc. It also explains the many joint projects financed by Chinese aid.

In October 1960 China extended another promise of aid to North Korea. A loan was made for $105 million, specified for the purchase of equipment from China and for factory construction and technical aid during the period 1961–1964.[13] The exact terms of this loan were not made public, and the vagueness of the agreement seems to suggest that Mao intended that it would be renegotiated. How much of this loan was used is also questionable. It was made at a time when China was experiencing economic problems as a result of the failure of the Great Leap and widespread natural disasters. It was probably granted to insure North

Korea's loyalty to China in view of the crisis in Sino-Soviet relations. It is note-worthy that this loan was made at almost the same time that the Soviet Union cancelled its aid commitments to China and ordered the return of its aid person-nel in China.

By 1960 North Korea had for some time outpaced China in economic development. Therefore, Chinese aid was less appropriate. Moreover, North Korea's continued rapid economic development necessitated aid from Moscow and broader economic ties with the Soviet Union. Pyongyang needed techno-logically advanced equipment and sophisticated military aid. Up to this time the Soviet Union had supplied North Korea with loans of $53 million, $250 million, and $75 million in the years 1949, 1953, and 1956 respectively.[14] Some grants may also have been made. In addition, North Korea had an imbalance in its trade with the Soviet Union, and no effort was made to change this. In the fall of 1960, Moscow announced further aid agreements with Pyongyang, including a $190 million debt cancellation and an extension of previous loans in the amount of $35 million. Also, the Kremlin promised assistance for the construction of several industrial plants in North Korea during the period 1961-1967; and an earlier agreement to provide goods in the form of a grant worth $21 million was formalized.[15]

Probably because of China's earlier aid, including Mao's commitment of manpower, etc., during the Korean War, Pyongyang did not take Moscow's side in the dispute with China. Rather North Korea tried to remain neutral regarding Sino-Soviet differences. In response, in 1963 Moscow suspended its aid to North Korea—including military assistance. The Korean government bitterly criticized the Soviet Union for this and publicly cited evidence of the harmful effects of Soviet aid. It also embarked on a policy of self-reliance which China had advo-cated.

Beginning in 1965, however, relations between the Soviet Union and North Korea began to genuinely improve. In part, this can be seen as the result of North Korea's disappointment with China's blundering in Indonesia. Events in China during the Cultural Revolution also alienated North Korea. At the same time North Korea began to feel the effects of the cutoff of Soviet military aid, and its economic development was being outpaced by South Korea's. Since China had not yet recovered from the Great Leap Forward and was unable to supply the kind of aid that North Korea needed, Pyongyang was forced to seek better relations with Moscow.

In February 1965 Premier Kosygin visited the North Korean capital and negotiations on military aid began. Pyongyang desparately needed military aid to relieve the loss to the government and to economic development caused by high expenditures for the military. Subsequently a North Korean military mission traveled to Moscow, and a joint military agreement was signed. Soviet military aid was apparently resumed at that time.[16] In 1967 another North Korean mili-tary delegation went to Moscow, and shortly after, North Korea began receiving large amounts of Soviet military equipment and hardware.[17] At the same time Soviet economic assistance was reactivated. During this period China made no new aid promises to North Korea, and there is no evidence that any of the earlier aid granted by Peking was delivered.

After the Cultural Revolution, in February 1970, a Chinese trade delegation visited North Korea, followed by a visit of Chou En-lai in April. Between the two visits Peking promised to send economic aid to Pyongyang.[18] In midyear military representatives from North Korea were invited to Peking, and China promised military assistance in the form of ships, fuel, and technical personnel. In October Mao asked a North Korean economic delegation to Peking, and a treaty was signed by which China committed economic and technical aid to North Korea.[19] Neither of these agreements, however, specified the conditions or amounts of aid. In fact, the wording was vague, suggesting that further negotiations should follow. Probably Mao made these promises with the intent of feeling out the North Koreans in terms of their relations with the Soviet Union and their stance on the Sino-Soviet dispute.

In the fall of 1971 Peking extended another promise of military aid to North Korea, but again no mention was made of the amount, conditions, or other details.[20] Almost at the same time North Korea signed an agreement with the Soviet Union for military aid. Perhaps Pyongyang wanted to gain some independence from Moscow by getting promises from Peking; or North Korea intended to use China's commitments to enlist more aid from the Soviet Union. In mid-1975 it was reported that China had again promised military aid to North Korea and that a list had been drawn up which included tanks, torpedo boats, destroyers, submarines, and fighter planes.[21] Subsequently Kim Il-sung made demands for Chinese assistance to renew the war against the South—being encouraged by events in Indochina.

In any event, there have been no reports of Chinese economic or military aid reaching North Korea following either of these promises. Commensurately, China has been unable to exert a significant influence on North Korean foreign policy in recent years. On the other hand, North Korea has maintained some semblance of autonomy and has not fallen into the Soviet orbit completely. This may be in part a result of Chinese aid in the past and, more recently, promises of future Chinese aid.

Aid to North Vietnam

China may have given some military aid to the Vietnamese Communists even before 1949. In any event, Mao provided Ho Chi Minh with weapons and supplies in considerable quantity beginning late in 1949. However, there were no formal aid agreements made until 1954, in order not to provoke the United States into granting aid to the French. Thus the amount of Chinese aid during this period is difficult to estimate. Chinese aid consisted primarily of supplies and weapons that had been captured from the Nationalists in the drive south. China also furnished guerrilla bases for Vietminh operations and some food and other necessities.

In early 1950 Ho Chi Minh went to Peking and asked Mao for aid of various kinds. Peking dispatched military advisors to Hanoi, and Vietminh officers went to China for training. An office was set up at Nanning in southern China to direct the transport of weapons and supplies to North Vietnam.[22] The level of Chinese aid increased markedly at this time because Communist control over South China was consolidated and transportation links were built or improved. In early 1950 the French reported that the Vietminh were using heavier arms, their morale was higher, and the Vietnamese People's Liberation Army had switched from guerrilla operations to conventional attack.[23] By late 1950 the French Commander in Chief stated that victory was now beyond the grasp of the French Expeditionary Corps.[24] Clearly by the end of 1950 there appeared to be a new war in Vietnam.

In the fall of 1951 Chinese workers completed a rail line from Liuchow in south China into North Vietnam. This became the largest supply route into North Vietnam and transported Chinese troops and advisors, reportedly numbering 4,000 to 6,000 in 1951.[25] After 1951, as the Korean War drew to a close, Peking further increased its aid to Hanoi. In 1953 Chinese trucks, cannons, and other heavy equipment were seen in North Vietnam. This aid was crucial in the defeat of the French forces at Dien Bien Phu in 1954.[26]

On the other side, American aid to the French more than matched the Chinese aid to North Vietnam. China did not, or could not, furnish aircraft and other weapons which might have given the Vietminh a final victory. Whether the Chinese limited their aid intending the conflict to end in a stalemate or not is unknown. Peking was represented at the Geneva Convention that followed and gained status as a major power in the eyes of the world. Certainly Chinese leaders had cause for wanting less than a complete victory for Hanoi, since Mao sought his own sphere of influence in Southeast Asia.

After the Geneva Convention, China put its aid to North Vietnam on an official basis. In December 1954 Peking concluded its first formal aid agreement with Hanoi in the form of technical aid, aid for postal and telecommunications facilities, and aid to improve civil aviation. Part of this aid was designated to convert the railroad between the Chinese border and Hanoi to the Chinese gauge.[27] But Hanoi needed even more aid to repair the damage done by the war, to compensate for the departure of French companies and technicians, and to make up the gap in food production caused by the division of the country. Thus in June 1955 Ho Chi Minh made another trip to Peking to ask for more assistance. At that time China signed an agreement to supply North Vietnam with nonrepayable aid in the amount of $338 million for national reconstruction during the period 1955-1957.[28]

From Peking, Ho went to Moscow and there received a promise of $100 million in economic aid. Subsequently Poland, East Germany, Czechoslovakia, and Outer Mongolia also made contributions, doubtless at Moscow's behest. However, no figures were made public on the extent of this aid.

Up to 1957 China probably provided more aid to North Vietnam than the Soviet Union and the other Communist bloc countries combined. North Vietnam's budget figures indicate receipt of most of the aid Peking promised. In addition, trade between the two countries increased rapidly. Mao also provided Ho with weapons during this period to continue the war in the South, and it is likely that this was not subtracted from China's official aid to Hanoi. The preponderance of Chinese aid to North Vietnam, when compared with that of the Soviet Union and other bloc countries, can be explained by Peking's overriding concern with events in Southeast Asia and its desire to gain a sphere of influence there. Moreover, physical proximity and the convenience of rail and road transportation made it easier for China to supply aid.

After 1957, however, Chinese aid declined in relative importance. During the period 1957–1961 China's official aid to North Vietnam totalled only about $100 million, and of this, three-fourths was in the form of loans rather than grants.[29] The major portion of this aid came in February of 1959 when two aid agreements were signed—a gift of $20 million and a loan of $61 million.[30] Interest on the loan was one percent and it was to be repaid in Vietnamese goods over a 10-year period beginning in 1967. Most of this aid was earmarked for building or expanding industrial plants. Soviet aid during this period totaled about $126 million, supplemented by about $25 million from the Eastern European Communist countries.[31] Thus Chinese aid was surpassed. Nevertheless the totals up to 1960 still showed that China had given more.

During this period Soviet aid became increasingly important for several reasons. After the Great Leap Forward, Peking was less able to supply aid, especially food which North Vietnam sorely needed. Also Hanoi adopted a strategy of rapid industrialization in order to defeat the South economically. To accomplish this North Vietnam needed the more sophisticated aid that only the Soviet Union could provide. China expanded its foreign interests at this time and began to offer aid to non-Communist countries; it simply could not afford to give more aid to North Vietnam.

Soon Mao became concerned about the Soviet influence in North Vietnam, especially as Sino-Soviet relations deteriorated. In late 1960 the cancellation of Soviet aid to China and the withdrawal of aid advisors forced Mao to decide whether China would continue to seek its own sphere of influence in Southeast Asia independent of Moscow—and whether to continue its foreign aid program. Mao decided in the affirmative, and in January 1961 China offered Hanoi another loan worth $157.5 million.[32] Neither the interest rate nor the conditions of repayment were announced, although the funds were specified for the purchase of technical aid and complete sets of equipment.

Undoubtedly Hanoi appreciated Peking's generosity as during 1961–1962 Moscow gave very little aid to North Vietnam. This was probably to demonstrate Moscow's coolness toward Hanoi's efforts to liberate the South by force and the close relations with Peking. In 1963 Hanoi publicly announced a policy of support for a national liberation struggle in the South—a policy advocated by Mao. It also took the Chinese line on the Nuclear Test Ban Treaty signed that year by the United States, the United Kingdom, and the Soviet Union. Through 1964 Peking managed to keep Hanoi on its side vis-à-vis the ideological dispute with the Soviet Union. China served as a model for North Vietnam in political and economic development and the guerrilla war in the South operated according to Chinese strategy.

However, after the Gulf of Tonkin incident in the fall of 1964 and the resulting U.S. escalation of the war this changed. Mao had not anticipated a change of events and had not extended Hanoi any new economic aid for some time. Also he had pushed the North Vietnamese into a more aggressive strategy with hopes of winning a quick victory without taking into consideration the U.S. escalation of the war. Furthermore, in January 1965 when the U.S. initiated the bombing of North Vietnam, Kosygin was in Hanoi. At that time he promised the necessary aid to cope with the U.S. threat.[33] Jet fighters and surface-to-air missiles were thereupon delivered to North Vietnam. Other aid was also given by Moscow; according to a Soviet source its aid in 1965 totaled $500 million.[34]

In midyear new talks were held between Chinese and Vietnamese leaders on economic assistance. Aid promises were apparently made. In December Peking announced that it had extended more aid, but no details were given.[35] Probably the main reason for not announcing the amount or conditions of this aid was that much of it was military aid. However, China probably could not match Soviet aid and did not want to make possible any comparison between its aid and Moscow's. In addition, at the close of the year the Cultural Revolution gripped mainland China and paralyzed transportation, production, etc. This doubtless had some effect on aid deliveries from China. Thus after 1965 Soviet influence began to predominate in North Vietnam.

Nevertheless, because of Mao's intense concern with events in Southeast Asia, aid to Hanoi was not discontinued. Aid was given in large enough quantities to preserve Chinese influence. And North Vietnam remained unquestionably the largest recipient of Chinese aid. In 1966 Western estimates put China's aid to Hanoi at between $150 million and $250 million.[36] Although no official figures were released, these or higher figures probably reflect Chinese aid in subsequent years until the war officially ended in 1973. On the other hand, probably seventy-five percent of North Vietnam's military aid came from Moscow.[37]

At one point during the height of the war it was estimated that China had sent 40,000 to 50,000 workers to North Vietnam.[38] During the U.S. bombing of North Vietnam, and after the mining of Haiphong, Chinese aid continued in spite of greater risks. In fact, according to some reports it increased—probably for a brief interval, giving the Chinese a slight edge over the Soviet Union in the rivalry to influence Hanoi. In early 1972 North Vietnam began construction of a pipeline to its northern border, with Chinese assistance.[39] This was to hook up with another pipeline in China to supply Hanoi with oil and other fuels. This no doubt enhanced Chinese influence. Other aid continued, but no official announcements of details were made.

In January 1973, at the time of the peace agreement, the U.S. government announced that it hoped that both China and the Soviet Union would suspend their military aid to Hanoi. Shortly after, Washington averred that it had an understanding with Peking and Moscow, that they would limit their aid to North Vietnam to between $600 million and $700 million annually.[40] United States aid was promised to North Vietnam at this time. But shortly thereafter, Hanoi announced that it was asking China for more aid, since it had not gotten any aid from the United States. In November the yearly aid pact was signed between China and North Vietnam, but again no details were given.

The importance of Chinese aid up to 1973 can hardly be questioned. North Vietnam's survival was dependent on Peking's largess. Much Chinese aid was given in the form of grants; other assistance was in the form of loans that had low rates of interest and generous repayment conditions. Probably many of the loans will never be repaid.

China, however, also benefited from its aid to North Vietnam. By 1954 Chinese aid to North Vietnam had helped win Peking the tacit recognition of various world leaders. Since then it has gained Peking a reputation of global power. China gave enough assistance to counter U.S. aid to South Vietnam, allowing Hanoi to prosecute a war that caused unrest and economic problems in the United States. It was in part the reason the United States was forced to seek a negotiated settlement of the Indochina conflict and détente with China.

On the other hand, it is questionable if Peking's aid will continue to be so generous or vital to North Vietnam. In 1970 an Aid Indochina Organization was set up in China to aid North Vietnam, Cambodia, and Laos. Before, China had aided the Viet Cong and the Pathet Lao primarily through Hanoi. Clearly, Peking and Hanoi did not see eye-to-eye on the role each played in Southeast Asia. Furthermore, the importance of Chinese aid to North Vietnam diminished when the Paris Agreement was signed in January 1973. With the halting of U.S. bombing Haiphong Harbor was cleared, and Soviet aid increased, since it did not have to be shipped by rail through China. Peace favored the Soviet Union since it can supply more assistance of the kind that Vietnam needs. This will be more true as time passes.

In addition, Hanoi's victory is more a credit to the Soviet Union than to China since it was attained in the final stages with Russian military equipment and supplies. Thus in recent months Hanoi has shown a slight tilt toward Moscow. This may explain the appeals that North Vietnam has made to China for more aid. Apparently Peking is reluctant to continue aid to Vietnam in view of its tilt toward the Kremlin. This may also explain some disparaging remarks Mao allegedly made concerning Hanoi's requests for aid.

If it turns out that Vietnam becomes a Soviet satellite, China's immense investment will have been in vain. Recent estimates have put Soviet and Chinese aid to Vietnam since the beginning of the conflict there at $7.5 billion, and as much as 40 to 50 percent of that could be Chinese aid.[41] This puts Chinese aid to Vietnam at $3 billion or more. Certainly most of it won't be recoverable. If Peking intended to buy Hanoi and create a puppet regime, it clearly made a bad deal. On the other hand, Hanoi may pursue an independent line and not succumb to greater offers of Soviet aid. This could explain why North Vietnamese leaders seem anxious to establish relations with the United States and have asked for aid from Japan and other Western countries.

The future of China's economic aid to Vietnam is uncertain. Peking may decide that continued aid will be worthwhile in keeping Hanoi out of the Soviet orbit. Or it may perceive that its money can be better spent elsewhere, and that it should use its economic aid to win influence directly in neighboring countries.

Aid to Outer Mongolia

In the early 1950s China and the Soviet Union began construction of the Trans-Mongolian Railroad, and as part of this project Peking sent Chinese laborers to Outer Mongolia. Agreements were signed between China and the government of Outer Mongolia on the use, living conditions, etc., of the Chinese laborers. However, there was no transfer of money. In 1954 an agreement was signed between Peking and Ulan Bator on the exchange of goods, which provided for the sending of Chinese products to Outer Mongolia.[42] This was the beginning of Chinese aid to Outer Mongolia, though there was still no formal agreement as such.

In 1956 the first official aid agreement was signed, and Peking agreed to provide nonrepayable economic and technical assistance to the government of Outer Mongolia in the amount of $40 million.[43] Included in this agreement was a provision for paying for the Chinese laborers already in Outer Mongolia—which by this time numbered up to ten thousand. It is likely that some of the aid was allocated to pay for goods already sent via the 1954 agreement. China gave aid to Ulan Bator in order to improve Sino-Soviet transportation links. Peking also sought to amplify bloc relations. And Mao wanted to bring Outer Mongolia into the Chinese sphere. Khrushchev had suggested in 1955 that Outer Mongolia should eventually come within the Chinese sphere of influence.

Soon, however, Khrushchev changed his attitude—if indeed he ever meant what he said. In 1956 Outer Mongolia was granted admission to the United Nations following Soviet maneuvering and pressure. And in 1957 Moscow announced that it had already given $225 million to Outer Mongolia and promised a new grant for $61 million.[44] The Kremlin did not want to be outdone by China.

Mao apparently felt that China could compete, and in 1958 offered more aid in the form of a $25 million loan to be used during the period 1959–1961.[45] This loan was designated for the building of power stations, bridges, housing, and other small projects. In 1960 Peking announced still another loan in the amount of $50 million for building industrial enterprises, water conservation projects, and public utilities.[46] Several months later more Chinese workers were sent to work on aid projects, and it was reported that their numbers had reached 20,000 to 40,000.[47] Mao and other Chinese leaders ostensibly felt that the injection of large numbers of Chinese workers would give Peking a fifth column in Outer Mongolia and perhaps a permanent hold over the country. However, the sending of such a quantity of laborers was necessitated by the kind and size of Chinese aid projects, since Outer Mongolia was underpopulated and there was a scarcity of labor for construction and building.

The Soviet Union became concerned about this, and as Sino-Soviet differences became more acute Moscow made special efforts to reduce Chinese influence in Outer Mongolia. In late 1960, shortly after the Chinese aid agreements, the Soviet Union promised $500 million in aid to Outer Mongolia to be used during the period 1961–1965.[48] At the same time Moscow put pressure on Ulan Bator and the Mongolian Communist Party to follow Soviet ideological initiatives. In 1961 the Outer Mongolian government announced that restrictions were being placed on the Chinese workers living there. Chinese workers were not allowed to leave construction sites, and most were moved to camps outside the cities where armed guards were stationed. In 1962, as a result of the Soviet pressure, about two-thirds of the Chinese laborers were sent home; and by the late 1960s there were almost none remaining.[49]

By 1963 Moscow had forced Outer Mongolia into its orbit, and Chinese–Outer Mongolian relations began to decline rapidly. Soviet trade ties with Outer Mongolia increased, and in 1964 a $733 million loan was granted by Moscow, perhaps to help offset the loss of Chinese aid.[50] The Soviet Union continues to provide extensive aid to Outer Mongolia. Chinese aid has ceased entirely.

Chinese aid did not prove sufficient to keep Outer Mongolia from falling under Soviet control, or at least Peking lacked other means of preventing such an eventuality. Thus Outer Mongolia is a case of the failure of Chinese aid. On the other hand, Peking's aid to Outer Mongolia does not compare in amounts to its aid to North Korea or North Vietnam. Much of the initial aid was in the form of Chinese laborers, and probably most of the 1960 loan was never used. Outer Mongolia is a defeat for China's aid diplomacy, but not a costly one in terms of the amount of aid given.

Aid to Cuba

In July 1960, following the takeover of the Cuban government by Castro, Peking signed a trade and payments agreement with the new regime. By this agreement China pledged help to train Cuban technicians and apparently promised to supply economic assistance. In any case, by the end of the year 10,000 tons of Chinese rice had arrived at Havana harbor and other goods followed.[51] In November, after Che Guevara made a trip to Peking, Mao promised economic assistance to Cuba amounting to a total of $60 million in the form of noninterest loans to be used during the period 1961-1967.[52] Part of this money was designated for the payment of Chinese technicians—giving Peking a presence in Cuba, some of it was to pay for equipment, the rest was unspecified—perhaps for arms.

Mao apparently felt that Castro was a real revolutionary and that he had used Chinese experience and tenets of Maoism in coming to power. Therefore, Mao felt that China might win some influence in Cuba despite the fact that the Soviet Union could give more aid. Also, Chinese leaders may have perceived an opportunity to push Moscow to a more revolutionary stance vis-à-vis the West or to embarrass the Soviets for not doing so.

During 1961-1962 Peking did not extend any new aid, probably because of economic difficulties in China. In addition, Mao may have wanted to observe Cuba's stance on the Sino-Soviet dispute. However, earlier aid that China had promised to Cuba was delivered. In 1962 relations between Peking and Havana improved as a result of Castro's more militant stance toward imperialism and his ideological statements in support of the Chinese position on wars of national liberation. Relations even improved during the period when the Soviet Union was sending missiles to Cuba. Subsequently, when the missiles were taken out, Peking criticized the move as a "Munich policy," and Castro could hardly disagree.

Perceiving that relations between Havana and Moscow were deteriorating and that Peking could support Cuba economically, Mao made another promise of aid to Cuba in February 1963, the amount and conditions of which were not made known.[53] However, Mao misjudged Cuba's needs and its ability to diversify its economy away from reliance on sugar production. He was probably equally unaware of Cuba's financial problems. In the same month Moscow negotiated a credit to Cuba of $403 million, though this deal was not finally approved until December.[54] In addition, Soviet negotiators agreed to buy more Cuban sugar at a price above the world market price. Thus in April Castro went to Moscow, and, to the disappointment of Mao, publicly accepted the Soviet interpretation of the missile crisis and peaceful coexistence.

In early 1964 Castro made another trip to Moscow for the purpose of getting economic aid. This time he conceded to the Soviet policy line regarding other Communist Parties and bloc unity. At the same time he criticized Chinese efforts to split Communist Parties in other Latin American countries. Castro needed more aid than the Chinese could or would provide and thus had to turn to the Soviet Union. Mao had overestimated Cuba's willingness or ability to follow a policy of self-reliance. Moscow clearly won another aid battle.

In February 1966, at exactly the time another Soviet loan was announced and just a month after the first Chinese credit expired, Castro assailed Peking for not accepting 800,000 tons of sugar that China had agreed to purchase and for not delivering 250,000 tons of rice.[55] He further accused the Chinese of breaking a protocol agreement and of "brutal reprisals" of an economic nature for purely political reasons. In reaction, Peking attempted to appeal directly to the Cuban people. Castro then accused Mao of distributing antigovernment propaganda in Cuba and of using tactics and methods formerly employed by the U.S. Embassy. An almost complete break followed and trade decreased to nearly nothing. Needless to say, Peking offered no more aid. This situation has remained.

Thus Cuba represents another defeat for China's aid diplomacy. The Soviet Union could consistently make bigger offers than China, and this turned out to be more important than ideological affinities or missions of good will. Mao learned another lesson about the effectiveness of foreign aid. Nevertheless, China had not promised much and delivered even less aid to Cuba. Mao was undoubtedly aware of his handicap from the beginning, but apparently he felt that it might be overcome. He gambled and lost.

Aid to Albania

Peking first extended aid to Albania in 1954, when in October that year it presented $2.5 million as a gift to the Albania government to "commemorate its 10th Anniversary."[56] Immediately thereafter China shipped 20,000 tons of wheat, 100,000 meters of silk, 2,000 tons of rice, 2,000 tons of sugar, and other goods to Tiriana. In December Chinese leaders signed another agreement providing Albania with a $12.5 million loan at 0.5 percent interest for goods to be provided during the period 1955-1960.[57] Chinese aid came at a time when Albania suffered economic hardship due to a drop in agricultural productivity caused in large part by collectivization. In December 1956 another aid agreement was signed, though no details were made public by either side.[58] It may have been merely an agreement on the use of aid previously promised. In any case it expressed a continued interest on the part of China in good relations with Tiriana.

After the revolt in Hungary in 1956, however, the Soviet Union became much more generous toward the Eastern European countries, and in 1957 extended two loans to Albania worth $8 million and $40 million.[59] The Albanian government was also released from paying for joint stock companies there that were partly owned by the Soviet Union—according to Moscow worth $90 million. The Kremlin also urged some of the Eastern European countries to assist Albania economically and aid was forthcoming from these countries.

Political differences still existed between Tiriana and Moscow, so friendship with China was not hurt. Thus in 1959 China doubled its aid to Albania with a new loan for $13.75 million earmarked for the purchase of equipment and industrial projects during the period 1961-1965.[60] This loan was important to

Albania because it allowed Tiriana to preserve its flexibility vis-à-vis Moscow. It also provided Mao with an ideological ally when challenging Soviet leaders. Both countries were practicing Stalinist methods of internal political control and economic development.

Mao wanted to keep Albania from falling completely into the Soviet orbit, and since Albania was a small country lacking a common border with the Soviet Union this seemed possible. China may also have had an interest in Albanian chromium, which is needed in the production of the type of steel used in nuclear weapons, or Albanian oil. Peking also sought a base from which to operate in the area and more specifically a transit point for its shipments of arms and other aid to revolutionaries in Algeria. Albania was one of the few countries on the Mediterranean with which China had good relations.

Albania's trade with the Soviet Union and the East European satellites, however, increased to 40 or 50 percent of its total trade by 1960, and in that year Moscow extended another loan for $40 million.[61] The Soviet Union made special efforts to get Albania to specialize and integrate its economy with the bloc. And it kept Albania's wheat reserves low. Nevertheless, ideological differences between Moscow and Tiriana escalated at the Bucharest Conference held in June 1960 and at the Moscow Conference held in November. After the first meeting Moscow stopped its aid to China and put pressure on Albania to change its ideological position. After the second meeting Moscow's representatives negotiated with Albanian leaders in an attempt to patch up differences. Meanwhile Albanian representatives were in Peking negotiating more aid.

In April 1961 Peking signed an economic agreement with Albania which included a $123 million loan for Albania's new Five-Year Plan.[62] This was one of the largest loans China had made up to this time and it overshadowed the aid which it had given to Tiriana up to that time—a total of $25.8 million. This loan included capital goods, agricultural machinery, and other commodities, and it provided for the building of twenty-five plants in the areas of chemicals, metallurgy, and light industry. China also agreed to send technicians. In addition, Peking sent 2.2 million bushels of wheat that had just been purchased from Canada. The amount of this loan equalled what Albania was receiving from other sources, namely, the Soviet Union and several Eastern European countries. In short, by this agreement Albania obtained enough aid from China to make up for the loss it would suffer as a result of breaking ties with Moscow. Why was Peking motivated to provide such aid?

First, Mao was incensed by the cutoff of Soviet aid and the withdrawal of Soviet technicians as retaliation for China ruining the conferences held in 1960 and escalating Sino-Soviet ideological differences. Albania was likewise considered a rebel by Moscow. Therefore, the Kremlin also used economic pressure on the Albanian government to force it to come to terms. In short Peking and Tiriana were in agreement on ideological differences with Moscow and both were being threatened with economic reprisals. China did not want to be isolated, nor did it want to see Moscow's economic pressure force Albania to change its ideological commitments.

Second, Moscow's economic pressure and grant-in-aid donations had reduced Chinese influence in North Korea, Outer Mongolia, and Cuba and in general threatened China's foreign aid program. Chinese leaders had to decide whether or not to bow out of the economic aid game. If its foreign aid efforts could be overshadowed by larger Soviet donations resulting in continued foreign policy defeats, then bowing out would be a reasonable solution. But it was one that Peking rejected.

Third, the dispute had implications for China's policy vis-à-vis the Third World. China was a model for economic development and revolution among developing countries. Furthermore, Peking had already shown an interest in the Middle East and Africa. Mao could not succumb to Soviet pressures at this point and still pursue independent goals in these areas of the world.

When the Chinese loan agreement was finalized Moscow cancelled its aid to Albania, severed trade relations, and even stopped tourists from going there. China provided aid as it had promised and sent in technicians as Soviet technicians left. In short, China filled the gap.

During the period 1962–1964 Peking made yearly agreements with Albania on the use of aid. Chinese aid was fully drawn, and from all indications supplanted Soviet aid without difficulty. In June 1965 Peking granted another loan to Albania; however, neither the conditions nor the amount were made public.[63] In 1966 an agreement was signed on assistance to Albania's petroleum industry, but again no details were revealed.[64] In 1967, after the Middle East War, China put two radio stations into operation that had been built in Albania to broadcast to Eastern Europe and the Middle East. In February a nitrogen fertilizer plant built with Chinese aid was opened, and in October construction was begun on a $30 million textile factory.[65]

Following the Soviet invasion of Czechoslovakia in August of 1968 Peking announced that it would assist Albania in the event of a Soviet military threat. This was subsequently backed up with an agreement on military aid.[66] At this time China leased four naval bases in Albania for 66 years and brought in a number of ships. It was also reported that China had started construction of missile bases in Albania and had equipped the Albania military with jet fighter planes and submarines.[67] The missiles may have been intermediate-range missiles capable of hitting Soviet cities with atomic warheads.

During 1969 several more Chinese aid projets were completed in Albania including a thermoelectric plant, a petroleum processing plant, a textile combine, and an electric bulb factory. In addition it was reported that another aid agreement was signed between the two countries and China promised new assistance in the amount of $200 million.[68] China apparently wanted to demonstrate that its ability to grant aid had not been impaired by the Cultural Revolution. Or Mao wanted to guarantee Albanian support in the event that Sino-Soviet hostilities escalated further; serious border clashes were occurring at this time. Peking may even have sought to open up a second front in the event of an escalation of the conflict.

In early 1970 an Albanian delegation went to Peking to discuss economic and military aid, and at the end of the talks another aid agreement was signed. No details were published, though thirty industrial installations were mentioned.[69] In October another agreement was signed. Later an Albanian press release said the loan was interest-free and would assist Albania's fifth Five-Year Plan. Another source estimated the value of the loan at $400 million.[70] In any case Chinese aid continued to flow to Albania.

In July 1975 China signed still another aid agreement with Albania in the form of a long-term, interest-free loan.[71] The talks mentioned complete sets of equipment for projects, goods, and materials. However, no mention was made of the size or terms of the loan. Since it was allocated for use during the period 1976–1980, and considering the good relations between the two countries, it was probably considerable.

Chinese aid to Albania has not been without rewards. Albania was one of the few countries to support the Cultural Revolution in China. Tiriana proposed the resolution in the United Nations whereby Peking was seated and Taipei expelled. Albania also serves as a center of Chinese propaganda and a base of operations in the area. Albania may even be expected to serve as a second or diversionary front for China in the event that hostilities escalate with the Soviet Union. Perhaps even more important, China has been able to keep Albania from kneeling to Soviet pressure, and it has demonstrated that it can give aid and support its own causes. Albania has taken Peking's side on all important foreign policy and ideological issues and can be expected to continue to support Mao in the near future. China has, in a sense, bought a satellite.

Aid to Hungary and Rumania

In addition to the bloc countries already mentioned, China has given aid to Hungary and Rumania. Donations to these two countries, however, may be seen as isolated cases of aid for specific purposes. These countries may not be aid recipients in the real sense. This is especially true of Hungary.

Following the revolt in Hungary in the fall of 1956 China made a nonrepayable grant to Budapest for $7.5 million.[72] This was followed in 1957 by a $50 million loan at 2 percent interest to be used over a two-year period.[73] The revolt and the events which followed led to considerable economic dislocation in Hungary. The Soviet Union and all the Eastern European Communist countries made aid donations. Peking's first donation may thus have been merely a token gesture. However, it may have expressed approval of Moscow's hard line policy toward Hungary. The second and much larger promise suggests that China may have had other motives. Mao feared a similar revolt in China and wanted to insure that no more trouble would occur in Hungary, since it might set a dangerous precedent. There were dissidents within the Chinese Communist Party that observed events in other Communist countries and related them to China. Peking may also have seen events in Hungary as endangering the Warsaw Pact and, indirectly, the Sino-Soviet Alliance. Likewise, Mao might have been fearful of the breakup of the Communist bloc. Alternatively China may have sought at this time to gain more influence in bloc affairs, especially ideological decisions. Events in Hungary fostered considerable rethinking on ideological matters, and China began to play a somewhat more important role at this time.

Nevertheless, Sino-Soviet differences soon dominated the ideological sphere and Hungary was forced back into the Soviet economic union. Thus China did not give any further aid to Hungary and to date has expressed no interest in doing so.

China's first aid went to Rumania in early 1970. A total of $21 million was extended to aid flood relief—obviously more than was needed to assist flood victims.[74] The real reasons behind Peking's largess probably relate to the announcement of the Brezhnev Doctrine after the invasion of Czechoslovakia and growing antagonisms between Bucharest and Moscow. More specifically, Moscow had put economic pressure on Rumania to make changes in its ideological views and the floods made this pressure even more effective.

In November Peking signed another aid agreement with the Rumanian government.[75] No details were provided, but Premier Chou En-lai, Vice Premier Li Hsien-nien, and Deputy Chief of Staff Ch'ou Hui-tswo were all present at the signing ceremony. Subsequent protocols mentioned "complete plants and technical aid." Several sources put the amount of this grant at between $200 million and $300 million.[76] China's motives are uncertain. Subsequently, there was speculation that Rumania had helped arrange President Nixon's trip to China. China may have sought better relations with Yugoslavia and may have hoped to expand its relations with other Eastern European countries in an effort to balance Soviet threats on its northern border. Rumania may have been viewed as a go-between. Mao also may have sought some assistance from Rumania in the realm of oil exploitation in return for aid that was forthcoming.

In any case this aid improved relations between the two countries. China's aid diplomacy may be seen as temporary, however, since Rumania's level of economic development is far above China's. This may become a point of embarrassment as China continues to seek a role of leadership among the underdeveloped countries. On the other hand, if Sino-Soviet differences continue to affect China's decisionmaking—and there is no evidence to suggest otherwise—Mao will probably try to weaken Moscow's hold on the Eastern European countries. The same may be said of détente in Europe: Peking does not want Soviet military units released to be sent east. Thus Mao wants to preserve tension in Europe and can do so by undermining Moscow's influence over its satellites. Close Sino-Rumanian relations may continue, and aid may play some part in this. At minimum Peking can give Rumania a kind of economic insurance.

3

China's Aid to Non-Communist Asian Countries

In the years immediately after the takeover of mainland China, Mao's primary concerns were to consolidate power and increase bloc relations. This explains Peking's overriding attention to bloc affairs and the limiting of foreign aid to Communist countries. With this accomplished, Mao sought to establish a sphere of interest in Asia and to restore China's position in the world community. Thus only three years after China officially launched its foreign aid program with aid to North Korea, Peking expanded its aid diplomacy to include non-Communist Asian countries.

Much of Asia had once been an Imperial Chinese sphere of influence. Historically, China had dominated East and Southeast Asia. Tribute missions that were sent to China paid obeisance and recognized this fact. The coming of the West destroyed this system of international relations and Peking's position of primacy. Although in the 1950s Chinese leaders probably did not seriously consider reestablishing the ancient mode of diplomatic relations, many Asian countries still related to China as a country that would play a dominant role in Asia. Others felt that China would be able to help them develop economically; and China thought likewise.[1]

Thus Asia became the arena where Peking sought to expand its influence, establish a sphere of influence, and play the role of a big power. At first China envisioned exerting its power in Asia with the concurrence and help of the Soviet Union. Mao may have had an understanding with Khrushchev to the effect that China would have a sphere of influence in Asia comparable to that of Moscow in Europe. But if so, Mao was soon disappointed. However, other factors were also important in Mao's design. Asia was an area where poverty was commonplace and Communism had a strong appeal. Much the Asian continent, especially Southeast Asia, was a power vacuum. Nationalism was a growing force in Asia. Chinese leaders also saw the East as the weak link in America's imperialist designs. Finally, there were local Communist Parties or insurgent groups with whom China could build contacts and offer aid. Hence, Mao perceived Asia as fertile ground for expanding Chinese influence. Mao's theory of revolution fit the situation in many Asian countries; certainly the nations of Southeast Asia seemed to resemble China during Mao's rise to power. In short, Asia was seen as a staging area for the application of Maoism.[2]

Peking soon found that economic aid was a useful tool of foreign policy in dealing with non-Communist Asian countries. Most of these nations were poor and trying desperately to develop. They faced many of the problems that China faced. Chinese aid and advice were seen by Asian countries as valuable. Many felt that they could not follow Western models for economic growth because their situations were quite different. But they could follow the Chinese model. Chinese leaders were likewise ambitious to become a major industrial power. China's economic planners pushed development of heavy industry while Mao envisioned China becoming the industrial center of Asia.[3] In the Chinese view, this would lead to the kind of extensive trade relations with the less industrially developed nations of Asia that the Western countries had with their colonies. Aid would initiate such relations. Peking failed in this effort; nevertheless, the attempt influenced China's foreign policy and aid diplomacy for several years.

Asia is also an area where China's geographical proximity is an advantage. In the 1950s, Peking did not have a large merchant marine, but it could establish trade links in Asia based on land transportation. By doing this it could reestablish some traditional trade routes. Relatively small amounts of aid would advertise Chinese products, get the people of the area accustomed to Chinese goods, and further trade. Asia was likewise an area where Chinese propaganda efforts were effective. Many Asian countries were poor and susceptible to the appeal of Communism. More than this, China understood the problems of the Asian nations and their ways of thinking. In many cases Peking could work through the local Chinese in spreading its influence.

Finally, Chinese decision-makers were frequently at a loss concerning a general policy toward non-Communist Asian countries.[4] Peking could not decide whether to treat them as antagonists or as friends. Its policy line frequently changed. Whenever Mao moved toward a more friendly stance or put into effect a soft line policy, aid donations proved to be an effective policy instrument. Aid projected an image of friendliness, reasonableness, and generosity.

When China initiated its foreign aid diplomacy to non-Communist Asian countries, America was China's major competitor. Thus aid was given primarily to keep neutral nations out of the U.S. camp. Specifically, Peking used aid to persuade several South and Southeast Asian nations not to join SEATO. Also, China used economic aid to obtain favorable border settlements. China's borders were generally not natural land forms and were therefore difficult to defend. Moreover, they were not demarked and constituted a source of fear and tension in adjacent countries that the U.S. could exploit.[5] Finally, Mao sought to break out of the embargo placed on China during the Korean War. Neutral Asian nations were favorably disposed to trade with China and U.S. influence on them was not great.

During the late 1950s Peking began to perceive a threat from Japan. Tokyo had built significant trade ties with other Asian countries, and its aid, in the form of reparations, was successful in introducing Japanese products to many Asian countries. Peking reacted to this threat in the late 1950s by using its aid and economic power to challenge Japan.[6] Peking failed in part because other more important concerns brought an end to the endeavor. But Japan remains a growing force in Asia and one that concerns Peking. Japan is now an industrial giant—a role which China once envisioned for itself. Moreover, Japan is the source of considerable foreign aid which undoubtedly will compete with China's. In short, more serious competition between these two Asian powers will very likely develop in the future.

India's growing influence in Asia also became a challenge to China in the 1950s, and this situation remains. India is a regional power and a competitor for influence in Asia, especially Southeast Asia.[7] New Delhi is a leader of the neutral, or nonaligned, nations, which include many Third World nations. Finally, China has a territorial dispute with India. Initially Peking employed aid to woo countries on India's borders. China has also endeavored to preserve a balance of power in South Asia. China's massive aid to Pakistan, including military equipment, can only be explained as concern about Indian expansionism and its threat to the power balance in South Asia. Its aid to Nepal, Sri Lanka, and, to a lesser extent, Burma can also be explained in terms of India's challenge.

Beginning in the late 1950s and early 1960s China used economic aid to constrain Soviet influence in Asia and to counter Moscow's growing military strength. Sino-Soviet differences in Asia were particularly related to aid-giving: When Khrushchev cancelled Soviet aid to China in 1960, he diverted these aid funds to non-Communist Asia. Mao was embittered and strove to increase China's influence there without Moscow's help and independent of the Kremlin's goals for the international Communist movement. Aid-giving became for Mao a means of demonstrating that Soviet aid was neither generous nor vital to China's economic development. It was also for China an important vehicle in reducing fears of Chinese irredentism and expansionism. Because of U.S. and Soviet efforts to win influence in the area, China could not continue a hostile policy toward neighboring Asian countries. China's historical influence, geographical proximity, and greater understanding of Asian problems proved to be an advantage. The generally smaller amount of aid that China had to offer was a handicap.

China's aid to Southeast Asian countries also related closely to its aid to North Vietnam—and this is still the case. Mao sought his own sphere of influence in Southeast Asia and was frequently at odds with Hanoi concerning relations with Communist movements in the region as well as official state-to-state relations with non-Communist governments. And Peking was always suspicious of Soviet influence in Vietnam. In the past two years as Moscow's aid to Hanoi and, commensurately, its influence there have increased, China has looked to Cambodia, Laos, and the other nations in the area—and sent aid. Its recent aid to Cambodia and Laos can be seen in the light of differences with Hanoi and as an effort to establish a Chinese sphere of influence, if not satellites, in the area with or without Hanoi's concurrence.

Mao's recent concern in Asia (and this again reflects the thrust as well as the level of Chinese aid) also relates to Soviet naval expansionism and perceived Russian efforts to "surround and contain" China. Aid to Pakistan and Sri Lanka are particularly motivated by fear of the Soviet Union. Likewise, aid to several Southeast Asian nations currently seems to reflect opposition to Moscow's Asian Security Plan. This alarm over Soviet presence in the area certainly helps explain the willingness of the Chinese to aid nations that also receive aid from the U.S. without competition or friction occurring between the two donors.

Undoubtedly China still regards Asia as an area of prime concern, despite its expanded interests and increased aid to Middle Eastern and African countries. Asia is China's "backyard." And China is still a regional power—not an international one. With the decline of U.S. power in the area following the fall of the three Indochina states, Mao is even more anxious to play a central role. Competition will likely increase with the Soviet Union, India, and Japan. And without a doubt this will involve economic aid rivalry.

Another motivating factor in Chinese aid-giving to non-Communist Asian countries is the fact that China's economic assistance relates closely to other tools of policy. Compared to other geographical areas, aid particularly complements and supplements China's military policies in Asia. It serves to extend China's military influence when used to support guerrilla movements. It complements it when it is given to relieve anxieties in local countries regarding a Chinese military threat. And aid strengthens Peking's military stance, particularly through its road-building efforts. In Laos and Nepal, and to a lesser extent in Burma, the construction of roads makes these countries more susceptible to the threat of the Chinese army. Adjacent countries are similarly affected.

Aid has also been closely tied to China's cultural diplomacy, propaganda, and trade. In a number of countries, Chinese aid has financed cultural projects. Nepal, Burma, and Sri Lanka are good examples. In others it advertised China's foreign aid program and its economic model for development. It also has adduced to China's reasonable foreign policy stance and its flexibility. And generally it has been more effective in promoting trade than in other areas.

In terms of China's aid commitments by regions, non-Communist Asia is second to the Communist bloc in amounts of aid actually delivered. Peking has delivered more aid to non-Communist Asian nations than to Middle Eastern nations to African countries. (See Table 2-1.) If some of the aid China has given to Hanoi is connected to China's goals in non-Communist Asia, the difference would be even greater.

Peking initially gave aid to countries that were former tribute bearers, poor nations, small nations, or border nations. These nations could be influenced more easily, and it was less likely that they could be attracted by larger U.S. or Soviet aid offers. Cambodia was the first nation in the non-Communist world to receive Chinese aid, and it fits into all of the categories listed except the latter. Nepal was the second recipient and it fits into all of them. Burma, Laos, and Afghanistan later received aid from China; they also fit into all of these categories. Sri Lanka is a small and poor nation. Indonesia and Pakistan are exceptions. They are large nations, and they were never tribute nations in a meaningful sense. In

Table 3-1
China's Aid to Non-Communist Asian Nations[a]
(Amounts in Millions of U.S. Dollars)

| Nation | Total Official | Percent | Aid Actually Given | | | |
			Low Estimate	Percent	High Estimate	Percent
Cambodia	97.50[b]	10.4	40	9.1	90	6.1
Nepal	44[b]	4.7	40	9.1	70	4.8
Indonesia	126[b]	13.4	30	6.8	60	4.1
Sri Lanka	130.70	13.9	70	15.9	100	6.8
Burma	86.20	9.2	30	6.8	70	4.8
Laos	32	3.4	15	3.4	80	5.4
Pakistan	342	36.6	200	45.6	950[c]	64.6
Afghanistan	75.50	8.1	15	3.4	50	3.4
Total	933.90	99.7	440	100.1	1,470	100.0

[a]This chart does not include aid given to the Maldive Islands, the amount of which is unknown. Cambodia and Laos are included here as non-Communist nations even though their governments are now Communist.
[b]Official aid may be slightly higher than this figure. In the case of Cambodia it may be many times higher. See Addendum.
[c]Includes estimates of extensive military aid.

the case of the former, Peking sought to influence internal events there and win a co-partner in gaining a position of dominance in Southeast Asia. Aid to Pakistan was specifically designed to preserve a balance of power in South Asia blocking the growth of Indian influence. This remains the goal of Chinese aid to Pakistan.

Pakistan ranks first among recipients of Chinese aid in non-Communist Asia both by official promises and by estimates of aid actually received. (See Table 3-1.) Much of China's aid to Pakistan has been costly military aid. Moreover, Pakistan is a large country and can absorbe large amounts of aid. Chinese assistance certainly helped win Pakistan's friendship; nevertheless, in 1971 India succeeded in dismembering Pakistan by creating the nation of Bangladesh from what was formerly East Pakistan. Pakistan remains China's ally, and needs Chinese assistance—especially military aid—even more. And since the balance of power in South Asia has been upset in India's favor, China must make even greater efforts to stop Indian expansion.

Sri Lanka is the second largest recipient of Chinese aid to non-Communist Asian countries, both officially and in terms of aid actually received. China's motives for aiding Sri Lanka relate to India, to internal events in Sri Lanka, and to Sri Lanka's leadership role among the nonaligned nations. Generally, Peking's aid diplomacy has been successful. Like Pakistan, China's aid to Sri Lanka has increased markedly in recent years.

In terms of officially announced aid promises, Indonesia is Peking's third largest donee in non-Communist Asia. But all of China's aid to Indonesia was given in the late 1950s and early 1960s. Peking did not realize its objectives, and much of the promised aid was never delivered. No new aid has been given.

Cambodia (until a very recent aid promise), Burma, Afghanistan, Nepal, and Laos follow in that order as official recipients. When Sihanouk was ousted, Cambodia was a failure for China's aid diplomacy. But China's aid to Cambodia had not really been extensive and most of the aid promised was never delivered. Now the situation is quite different: China is making new aid deliveries to Cambodia and its influence there is predominant. Nepal also seems to be a clear case of success for Chinese aid. Peking has managed to keep Nepal from falling into the Indian orbit and has built trade and other ties. Burma, Afghanistan, and Laos are uncertain, though China has attained limited objectives with the donations to these countries.

In the country-by-country analysis which follows, recipients are taken up in order of the first to receive Chinese aid. Again, more specific objectives, aid techniques, and results will be discussed. Some direct comparisons are made with aid to Communist countries and to other non-Communist Asian countries.

Aid to Cambodia

In June 1956 Chinese foreign ministry officials signed an agreement with the Cambodian government promising aid in the form of a $22.5 million free grant designed to facilitate Cambodia's development plan for 1956–1957.[8] Funds were specified for the purchase of construction materials, equipment, and technical assistance. Later Peking signed a protocol agreement stating that it sought no control over Cambodian affairs and that no Chinese laborers or technicians would be sent to Cambodia. By the end of the year, mixed Sino-Cambodian commissions were set up, and some of the grant was used. Shortly thereafter, it was decided that most of the aid would go to build four factories.[9]

Peking was ostensibly motivated by a desire to alter its hard-line policy toward non-Communist countries and by Cambodia's neutralist stance. Mao may have likewise been impressed by Prince Sihanouk's perception that China would eventually dominate Southeast Asia and by his friendly attitude toward China. In addition, Cambodia was strategically located in relation to the Communist effort to take over South Vietnam. On the Cambodian side, Sihanouk felt that Chinese aid would offset part of the aid he was receiving from France and allow Cambodia a more genuinely neutralist foreign policy.

In 1958 a second aid agreement was signed and a $5.6 million grant was mentioned.[10] However, the protocol of this agreement also stated that the 1956 agreement was being extended. So this grant may have been in part or in total an extension of the earlier grant. That agreement had expired and evidently not all of the aid promised had been used. In any case, some new projects were started, and shortly thereafter Peking sent a number of technicians to Cambodia.

Chinese decision-makers may have been motivated to make this second agreement by the fact that Cambodia had granted diplomatic recognition to Peking. This occurred in July; the promise of aid was made in August. Also at this time Cambodia was locked in dispute with Thailand over the marking of their border and the ownership of an ancient temple. The dispute had become heated when Thailand sent troops into the area allegedly pursuing Viet Cong. Thus, it was an opportunity for China to demonstrate its anti-imperialist stance to Cambodia as well as other nations in the area. Peking likewise sought some influence in the Chinese community in Cambodia. Four or five Chinese newspapers in Phnom Penh received financial help through Chinese aid personnel, and some of them subsequently adopted a more clearly pro-Peking orientation. It was also reported that Peking attempted to influence Chinese schools in Cambodia and that aid funds also were given to unemployed Chinese there.[11]

Peking combined extensive propaganda efforts with its aid. Claims were made that Chinese aid projects built an economic infrastructure and led to considerable employment of the local work force. China used some of its aid funds to build a radio station in Cambodia—the most powerful in Southeast Asia at the time.[12] Thus China's propaganda machine attained a base of operations in Southeast Asia. Some projects, however, demonstrated poor planning. A plywood factory was built in an area where trees could be cut only during the dry season and therefore had to be stored until rains came and the river could carry them to the mill. The mill operated only a few months a year. The locally produced glue was of poor quality and the plywood fell apart in the humid climate.[13]

In December 1960 Peking signed another agreement with Phnom Penh promising $26.5 million more in nonrepayable aid.[14] This grant was probably related to the treaty of friendship with Cambodia that was signed at the same time. The treaty stipulated that neither could join an alliance against the other—precluding Cambodia from joining the Southeast Asia Treaty Organization. However, not all the earlier grants had been used, and this promise did not increase the flow of Chinese aid. Even by 1964 most of China's aid to Cambodia had not been used and was apparently renegotiated and changed to military aid.[15] Military assistance may have been intended to compensate for the fact that Hanoi had stepped up its efforts to win in South Vietnam, and North Vietnamese soldiers were using Cambodia as a supply route and sanctuary. Peking may also have sought a more direct influence over events in Southeast Asia, since it may have perceived the imminent collapse of the Saigon government.

In any event, Peking made considerable propaganda mileage on the aid it did deliver, and its promises caused tangible changes in Cambodia's foreign policy. After the 1960 donation Cambodia supported Mao's policy on the "Taiwan Question," and voted for Peking's admission to the U.N. In 1963 Sihanouk requested that the United States aid mission leave. Cambodia subsequently supported China's position on the Nuclear Nontesting Agreement in 1963 and its atomic test in 1964. In 1965 diplomatic relations with Washington were severed.

At no time did Chinese aid constitute more than twenty percent of the total aid received by the Cambodian government. Up to 1964 Peking had promised less than ten percent of the aid the U.S. had given to Cambodia and had delivered even less.[16] Therefore, Peking made considerable gains with its aid to Cambodia without making a large investment. But closer relations with China proved costly to Cambodia. Soviet and Eastern European aid declined, and with the cutoff of U.S. aid, serious economic problems arose. Scarcities, deficits in the budget, and inflation of the local currency resulted.

China came to Cambodia's rescue, and in early 1966 another aid agreement was signed whereby Peking promised an additional $43 million.[17] No details were given about the kind of aid or conditions of repayment. However, this was just when the Cultural Revolution started in mainland China, and Mao could not, or did not choose to, make aid deliveries to Cambodia. Perhaps he felt promises would suffice; or the radicalization of ideology in China caused Chinese decision-makers to see Cambodia in a different light: namely, that Cambodia could be won by revolutionary force. By late 1966 there were incidents in Cambodia involving Chinese Embassy connections with Red Guard organizations and their activities among local Chinese. Also, Chinese arms were found in the hands of Khmer Rouge forces.

These developments notwithstanding, in 1967–1968 Peking made more promises of military aid to Phnom Penh. And in 1968 China delivered significant quantities of military equipment, including aircraft and antiaircraft guns.[18] Mao apparently wanted to assuage Cambodia's concern about the use of its territory by North Vietnamese troops. Perhaps Peking also expected a coup and wanted to have some ties with the Cambodian military.

In early 1970 when Prince Sihanouk was abroad, his government was overthrown. The U.S. immediately announced arms aid to the new government, and Cambodia joined the International Monetary Fund and the Asian Development Bank to get loans to support its faltering economy. Sihanouk took up residence in Peking, and in August 1970 the Chinese Foreign Ministry announced an aid agreement with the Cambodian government (in exile).[19] China subsequently increased the level of its arms, equipment, and supplies to rebel forces in Cambodia. However, there is no information available on the amounts or details of this aid. It was probably not large in terms of amounts, but was vital to the Communist victory there. And since the guerrilla movement succeeded in the initial stage without significant Soviet aid, the Chinese gained a predominant position in Cambodia vis-à-vis the Soviet Union. Policies adopted by the Khmer Rouge in the wake of its victory reflect Chinese advice.[20]

After the fall of Cambodia to Communist forces and the establishment of a new government China sent new official aid and a sizeable number of Chinese advisors. In the fall of 1975 China announced a huge donation of aid to Cambodia (see Addendum). This makes it possible to speculate that Cambodia may be financially supported by China in coming years, like Albania has been since 1961. It also suggests the possibility that Cambodia will become a Chinese satellite. Clearly China appears to have the upper hand in Cambodia, over either Moscow or Hanoi.

Aid to Nepal

In September 1956 Peking signed an agreement to give the government of Nepal a loan worth $12.7 million to be used over a three-year period.[21] The stated purpose of the loan was budget stabilization. The motive behind this loan was evidently Peking's desire to normalize relations with Nepal. At this time an old treaty which gave Nepal special rights in Tibet was cancelled and trading posts and consulates were exchanged. Peking also endeavored to reduce Indian influence in Nepal. Nepal's foreign relations were handled through the government of India, and Nepal was in essence a satellite of India. Therefore this aid agreement may be seen as a faint recognition of Nepal as an independent nation and as an indication of China's new friendly policy line toward the neutral nations established at Bandung.

However, very little of this aid was drawn. In 1957–1958 Peking's attitude toward the noncommitted nations changed. A hard line was reestablished. In 1958 China laid claim to territory in Nepal and, to bolster its case, claimed that a Chinese mountain-climbing expedition had reached Mt. Everest, within territory that was disputed. Relations between Peking and Katmandu soured.

Nevertheless, a turnabout occurred in 1960 when Peking became locked in dispute with both India and the Soviet Union. Thus Mao again sought better relations with Nepal and more specifically a settlement of their disputed border. In the spring of 1960 negotiations began on a border treaty, at which time Peking made an additional promise of aid worth $21.2 million.[22] An extension was also provided for the two-thirds of the 1956 grants that had not been used. A provision in this agreement allowed for sending Chinese technicians and workers to Nepal, giving Peking a foothold there. It also stated that Chinese aid personnel would live at the same standard of living as people of equal rank or status in Nepal. This impressed the Nepalese and became a usual provision in later aid agreements, providing a basis for Chinese propaganda claims about its aid. This was aimed at India, since Indian aid officials were living in Nepal at standards considerably above their counterparts.[23] Peking also won diplomatic recognition from Nepal, which gave prestige to Mao's regime and helped in the struggle with Taipei to represent China in world affairs. Perhaps even more important, diplomatic ties repudiated India as suzerain of Nepal.

In the fall of 1961 Peking promised more aid; this time it granted $9.8 million in free aid for the construction of a road between Lhasa and Katmandu to be completed by 1966.[24] This project promised to further China-Nepalese trade and wean Nepal away from India. The road also had military implications—especially since it was later reinforced to hold vehicles weighing 60 tons, the weight of the heaviest Chinese tank.[25]

After China's border conflict with India in 1962, Peking gave even greater emphasis to its road-building efforts in Nepal. Other planned projects were dropped or scaled down. Roads served military objectives by providing China more direct access to the Indian border in the event of further hostilities, and justified the presence of Chinese workers in Nepal, many of whom were intelligence or propaganda agents or trained soldiers. China's aid personnel also helped to reduce Soviet influence in the area—perhaps directly. The Soviets accused the Chinese of damaging some of their projects, and Chinese aid officials apparently did start an effective whisper campaign against a Russian-built hospital.[26] Since the Soviet Union does not have a common border with Nepal, Soviet aid tended to enhance Chinese-Nepalese trade, and probably for this reason was not continued at a high level.

By 1964 Peking's presence in Nepal was considerable, and the Nepalese government began to fear that Chinese influence might become excessive. Previously it had been viewed by Nepalese officials as a balance to Indian influence. Now Katmandu invited the United States and the United Kingdom to provide aid—in spite of Chinese protests. And the Nepal government placed some restrictions on the building of new roads.[27]

Nevertheless, in December 1964 Peking signed another agreement to extend earlier aid promises not fulfilled. A total of $43 million in aid had been promised, and not much had been used—perhaps as little as $5 million or $6 million.[28] On the other hand, Peking probably paid for much of the road-building costs itself without drawing on aid funds. During 1965–1966 two more aid agreements were announced, but it was uncertain if they involved new aid or merely the extension of earlier aid. They may have provided more funds for road projects. The talks held in 1965 cited $28 million for a road to extend east from Katmandu.[29]

Aid continued to be drawn, even during the Cultural Revolution. In 1966 an agreement was signed whereby China converted its aid to British currency; previous aid had been in Indian rupees, which had just been revalued downward.[30] In 1967 China made a delivery of rice and promised to construct electric power lines in Nepal. Peking also agreed to extend a road completed earlier and delivered $1.25 million in machinery, medicine, cement, and metal goods.[31] During 1968–1969 Chinese leaders renegotiated several old aid agreements and extended new ones—one including a $2.5 million donation in cash.[32] More technicians were sent to work on the roads and surveying began on a power plant.

In 1972 an electric station on one of the Chinese-built roads was completed, reportedly valued at $14.4 million. Also, a 125-meter expansion bridge was finished.[33] In addition, Peking made a new promise of aid that included another highway and a textile mill.[34] No further details of this agreement were made public, so it is uncertain if this was a promise of more credits or merely a renegotiation of earlier ones. The timing of these agreements and announcements suggests that Peking was concerned about events in South Asia—the dismemberment of Pakistan and the creation of the state of Bangladesh. These negotiations paralleled increased tension on the Sino-Indian border and a strengthening of India's position vis-à-vis Nepal, as a result of its victory over Pakistan.

Since 1972 China has made no new promises of aid to Nepal. But earlier aid is being drawn, and China's presence in Nepal is still legitimized by road building and other aid work. In December 1975 a trolley-bus system linking Katmandu and a nearby city was opened, having been constructed by 100 Chinese technicians over a two-year period at a cost of $4 million.[35] It represents ongoing aid contacts and the continued Chinese interest in Nepal.

China's aid diplomacy to Nepal has been generally successful. Peking was able to tear Nepal away from India and make it a truly independent state. Trade relations also developed. In addition, China has accrued military advantages with its sizeable road-building projects, while demonstrating its capabilities in this area. In fact, China was probably encouraged to offer road projects elsewhere based on its success in Nepal. Peking has been able to outdo the Soviet Union in Nepal, although factors other than aid donations are important. Currently, Sino-Nepalese relations are good, and China's aid diplomacy is to a large extent responsible.

Aid to Indonesia

China's first aid to Indonesia was negotiated in November 1956 in the form of a $16 million moratorium loan to make up for the imbalance in trade between the two countries.[36] China had increased its exports to Indonesia, largely accounting for the situation. However, Mao also sought broader trade relations to enhance China's influence in Indonesia and to gain some control over the growing Communist movement there. In 1957 the trade imbalance between the countries changed, and apparently Indonesia repaid the loan.

In April 1958 Peking offered another loan to the Indonesian government; this one for $11.5 million at an interest rate of 2.5 percent.[37] This loan was extended to help Sukarno deal with political and military opposition on the islands of Sumatra and Celebes. The rebels demanded a new government and greater regional authority; Sukarno charged that they had received outside aid from the United States and Taiwan. The Chinese viewed Sukarno as an anti-imperialist and anticolonial leader and may have perceived that together with Indonesia, China could dominate Southeast Asia politically and economically.

In 1959 Peking extended more aid, also as a loan, worth $30 million.[38] This loan carried an interest rate of 2.5 percent and was repayable over a period of fifteen years. It was designed to finance the building of six textile factories and a spare-parts factory.

Unlike China's aid to Communist bloc countries and most of its aid to non-Communist nations up to this time, all of its aid to Indonesia was in the form of loans; and these loans carried interest. Probably Chinese decision-makers felt that China had no hope of appreciably increasing trade with Indonesia or supplanting aid given to Djakarta by various Western countries. Peking may have perceived that it could not afford enough aid to such a large country as Indonesia to have much influence. Thus Mao was probably testing Chinese-Indonesian aid relations. Also Peking faced competition with the Soviet Union. Moscow had an intense interest in Indonesia due to the growing size and influence of the Indonesian Communist Party. In 1956 when Peking granted its first credit to Indonesia, Moscow offered a loan worth $100 million; another, worth $250 million, was proposed in 1960. Besides these loans several Eastern European countries made offers at Moscow's behest totalling close to $200 million. Finally, Moscow supplied a considerable quantity of military aid, possibly putting total Soviet aid to Indonesia as high as $1 billion.[39]

Mao continued to view Indonesia as a revolutionary force nevertheless. And he may have held high hopes for Indonesia in terms of supporting leftist revolutionary movements in the area. Mao was no doubt impressed with Sukarno's self-reliant proclamations and his efforts to "liberate" West Irian—which caused considerable dissension with the NATO alliance due to Holland's intransigence on the matter. Thus in October 1961 Peking made another promise of aid, again in the form of a loan, valued at $30 million.[40] No details on the use or conditions were provided. However, it was revealed that it was in cash, suggesting that it may have been for budget support; the Indonesian budget showed a serious imbalance of payments.

The next year Indonesia mediated the Sino-Indian conflict as a member of the Colombo Conference and refused to condemn China as an aggressor. In 1963 Djakarta took China's stand on the Nuclear Nontesting Treaty, and in 1964 backed Peking's atomic test. Peking supported Indonesia's confrontation with Malaysia, and when Indonesia withdrew from the U.N. as a result of Malaysia being voted a temporary member of the Security Council, Chou En-lai proposed that another world body be established—a "revolutionary one." Relations seemed to be improving steadily.

In January 1965 Peking promised another loan to the Indonesian government in the amount of $50 million.[41] This reflected more optimism on Peking's part regarding its ties with Sukarno and its ability to gain further control over the Indonesian Communist Party. However, it was probably also intended to sway Sukarno vis-à-vis the Sino-Soviet feud and Moscow's role in a second Afro-Asian Conference. The first conference had been in Djakarta, and Indonesia seemed to have considerable say on plans for the second one. In addition, U.S.-Indonesian relations had deteriorated as a result of Washington's support for

Malaysia. Sukarno refused U.S. aid and closed U.S. businesses in Indonesia. At the same time, Indonesia experienced difficulties getting aid from the World Bank and other Western sources. The Indonesian government was sorely in need of financial assistance and could not count on help from the West.

Talks had just been held on the implementation of China's aid when, in September 1965, an army-led counterrevolution against the Indonesian Communist Party occurred, resulting in a bloodbath. Thousands of Communists and Chinese were killed, arrested, or removed from positions of importance. Peking was implicated in the attempted Communist coup and diplomatic relations were severed. Subsequently, Djakarta restored relations with the U.S., and Western aid in significant quantities became available to Indonesia. Because of this, Chinese aid was discontinued. Little if any of the January loan had been used, and perhaps a good portion of the 1961 loan remained untouched.

Indonesia is thus a defeat for Chinese aid diplomacy. However, not much was invested and certainly little of the aid Peking promised was actually delivered. China's aid to Indonesia can be seen as a gamble that Peking lost. Since 1965, relations between China and Indonesia have remained cautious, if not cool. Also, since vast amounts of aid are available to Indonesia from other sources and potential profits are available from the sale of its natural resources and oil, it seems unlikely that China will again offer aid.

Aid to Sri Lanka

China's first formal aid to Sri Lanka, then called Ceylon, was given in 1957. However, prior to this date Peking had signed trade agreements with Colombo, which in essence constituted an aid relationship. An agreement in 1952 involved the exchange of 50,000 tons of rubber for 270,000 tons of rice.[42] Peking paid Ceylon a price for the rubber above the world market price and sold its rice at less than the market price. Similar barter deals advantageous to Ceylon were negotiated in subsequent years. In mid-1957 Peking promised Ceylon aid in the form of a free grant, worth $15.8 million, to facilitate economic development during the period 1958–1962.[43] Most of this was designated to improve rubber plantations. China's aid was apparently given to win recognition or as a reward for giving it.

In 1958 Peking made a second grant of aid to Ceylon for $10.5 million.[44] This was in the form of a loan with interest (though it was later changed to an interest-free loan), given for flood relief and rehabilitation. Peking sought support for a second Afro-Asian Conference. Mao was also apprehensive about India's expanding influence in South Asia and among nonaligned countries. Differences existed between Ceylon and India, which hurt New Delhi's image as a leader of the nonaligned nations.

In 1960 Mrs. Bandaranaike became prime minister of Ceylon and pushed politics to the left. Not long after this, China extended another aid donation, probably in the form of a nonrepayable grant, for approximately $10.5 million.[45] In August 1961 an agreement was reached between the two governments on the construction of a cotton mill. And in May of the following year China's 1957 aid commitment was extended for five more years. In August the loan for flood relief was also extended.

In June 1964, the 1958 loan was converted into an interest-free loan, and another loan was announced for $4.2 million.[46] This brought China's total commitment to Colombo to about $41 million, slightly more than the commitment of the Soviet Union and the Eastern European Communist countries combined.[47] Chinese aid amounted to only about one-half of American assistance to Ceylon, but U.S. aid had been cut off in 1963 following the nationalization of U.S. oil companies in Ceylon. Peking sought to compensate for this loss of aid. Also Chinese leaders wanted to preserve friendly relations with Ceylon in view the border war with India in 1962 and the potential for further hostilities. Ceylon was a possible ally and, in the eyes of Chinese decision-makers, might even provide a potential site for a second front against India. In addition, Peking still sought Colombo's backing for an Afro-Asian Conference in competition with India, which supported a Nonaligned Nations Conference.

As a result of the 1964 loans, Chinese goods flowed to Ceylon and trade figures increased commensurately. However, in 1965 Colombo agreed to compensate U.S. oil companies for the nationalization of their property and U.S. aid was resumed. With Washington's guidance, an aid consortium of Western countries and Japan was formed that extended $250 million to Ceylon in the form of a long-term loan. This completely overshadowed Peking's aid. After this, China extended no new donations, and there probably was only a trickle of old aid delivered.

In 1970 Sino–Sri Lanka relations once again improved. The Cultural Revolution had ended, and a new leftist government was back in power in Colombo. Aid began to flow in February 1970 as a result of an agreement by Peking to supply equipment and materials for the construction of a textile factory.[48] In September another agreement was reached by which China sent 100,000 tons of rice and some other goods worth a total of $8.3 million.[49] It was not made clear whether this was new aid or merely a renegotiation of earlier grants. In any case, a joint shipping company was established at this time to handle increased trade and aid shipments.

In 1971 economic problems continued to plague the Colombo government, and China came to the rescue with a long-term, interest-free loan for $31.5 million given in convertible currencies.[50] Peking was moved by Sri Lanka's difficulties with socialist development schemes. Also there was some concern over growing hostilities between India and Pakistan. Chinese leaders were no doubt equally apprehensive about the Soviet-Indian alliance and Moscow's growing naval presence in the Indian Ocean.

In May 1972 China extended another loan for $5 million to help Colombo resolve its foreign exchange deficit.[51] The next month Mrs. Bandaranaike visited Peking, and Mao promised $52 million more in the form of an interest-free loan designated for the construction of an integrated textile mill and other development projects.[52] This loan was repayable over a period of twenty years with a grace period of ten years. Shortly thereafter a joint shipping agreement was signed between the two countries, and China agreed to send Sri Lanka two cargo ships on credit worth $1.7 million.[53] Again this credit was interest-free, and was repayable over a period of fifteen years. At almost the same time it was reported that China gave Colombo five patrol boats for coastal defense.[54] Obviously, these boats were sent for use against India.

In October 1973 Peking agreed to send more rice to Sri Lanka, to be paid for with 1974 rubber shipments. Shortly after, 40,000 tons of Chinese rice arrived in Colombo.[55] During 1974 China provided more than one-half of the food aid that Sri Lanka received. Also, China became Sri Lanka's number one trading partner.[56] Thus Peking's aid relationship with Colombo became unique in two ways: China supplied significant food aid, which it had done for no other country, and aid succeeded in fostering significant trade ties. The food aid may be temporary, and the trade relationship may be natural. Nevertheless, China's aid diplomacy stands out in both respects. During 1975 aid deliveries continued though no new agreements were concluded.

To date, Chinese aid to Sri Lanka totals approximately $130 million. Including military aid it might be ten to twenty percent more. Peking's aid exceeds Soviet aid plus Eastern European aid. Yet it is questionable that it is all that Colombo needs. The U.S. is also providing aid, and it is perhaps ironic that there is little or no suspicion on either side. Both are concerned about Soviet naval expansion in the area. Peking also stands to benefit in its efforts to contain Indian expansionism. Peking likewise has Sri Lanka's support in attempts to neutralize the Indian Ocean and in other issues of mutual concern, such as relations with the other developing countries. So far, China's aid diplomacy to Sri Lanka is a success.

Aid to Burma

Peking's first aid promise to Burma came in 1958. However, as with Sri Lanka, China gave aid to Rangoon indirectly before this. In 1954 a trade agreement was signed between the two countries, and China subsequently purchased 150,000 tons of Burmese rice at a price above the world market price.[57] U.S. food aid in rice had caused the value of rice to drop on the world market, thus engendering bad relations between Washington and Rangoon. Peking did not follow this up with direct economic assistance to the Burmese government, probably because it was furnishing arms, training, and other kinds of support to the White Flag Communists (pro-Peking) in Burma.[58] They were engaged in guerrilla activities against the government.

In 1958 Mao apparently changed his mind about the chances of success of the White Flags. Possibly aid given to the Burmese government by India, Japan, and the Soviet Union turned the balance in the favor of Rangoon. At any rate, China felt the need to secure its borders. The Sino-Burmese border was not yet demarked, and Mao may have believed that he could build meaningful ties with the Burmese government while negotiating a border settlement, particularly in view of the difficulties Rangoon was experiencing at the time with Nationalist Chinese troops still in the area. Thus, in January China joined the other aid donors and offered a $4.2 million loan at 2.5 percent interest to the Burmese government.[59] This loan was designated to assist Burma's textile industry. However, relations did not improve appreciably. This was due in part to Burmese concern for the way China handled events in Tibet, especially its treatment of the Tibetan Buddhists. In addition, the U.S. made renewed efforts to improve relations with Rangoon, and Moscow continued to make attractive aid offers. Finally, China's aid offer was not big.

During 1960, border negotiations were again sought by both sides and a tentative agreement was reached, along with a treaty of nonaggression. When the formal treaty was ratified by Burma in January 1961, Peking announced an aid grant of $84 million in the form of a noninterest loan for sets of equipment, technicians, and technical training.[60] This loan was the biggest China had extended to a non-Communist country up to this time and had a marked effect on Sino-Burmese relations. However, it was probably not in any sense compensation for a border settlement favorable to China. The marking of the border seemed fair in view of both historical and current claims. Prime Minister U Nu and other high Burmese officials remarked at the time that it was a settlement generally beneficial to Burma. Mao probably wanted to advertise the border settlement and give an impression to the world of his reasonableness and generosity—which indeed he did. This was aimed at the Soviet Union and India where border problems remained unsettled.

Chinese leaders may also have been alarmed at the rise of Japanese influence in Southeast Asia. Japan had been the largest source of aid (in the form of reparations) for the Burmese government. The reparations agreement had just expired, and was renewed in the form of economic aid for another twelve years. This stimulated trade between Tokyo and Rangoon and enhanced Japanese influence in Burma. Meanwhile Peking was selling rice abroad and competing with Burmese rice; Chinese aid may have been in part compensation for this. Finally, this loan was made in the context of a crisis in Laos. A right-wing-led coup overthrew the Laotian government a month before and threatened to throw the country into turmoil. Peking may have thought that Burma would play a role in Laos if the conflict expanded.

However, the situation in Southeast Asia, including Burma, soon changed; or at least, Chinese leaders perceived a change. Also the aftermath of the Great Leap Forward and poor harvests began to be felt in China. Thus Mao made available very little of the aid he had promised Burma. Up to 1964 Rangoon had drawn probably less than five percent of the loan—less than any nation China had aided in Asia.[61] No Chinese project of any size was built, nor was Chinese aid visible in any other way. Mao apparently felt that other policy instrumentalities were more effective in managing China's relations with Burma. Or he may have thought that China could not compete with U.S. or Japanese aid in view of economic straits at home. China certainly had interests elsewhere and other places to put its foreign aid. Mao may also have been disappointed or even displeased with Burma's role in the Sino-Indian border conflict in 1962. Rangoon favored India and offered to mediate the conflict.

At this time instability was on the rise again in Burma, and Mao, for this reason, or to take revenge against the Burmese government, began aiding the White Flag Communists again. The rebels did not want Peking to aid the Burmese government, since this aid could have been used against them. Also it would have helped cope with rural problems, which the guerrilla movement fed on. Thus, in 1962 when General Ne Win overthrew the government and established a military regime, he nationalized a number of foreign banks, among them two Chinese banks that had been instrumental in financing local Communist operations and had given help to local Chinese loyal to Peking. He also sent 200 Chinese advisors home, saying that they could be replaced by Burmese personnel.[62] China's aid presence in Burma thus waned.

Nevertheless Peking did give some military aid to Burma—specifically marked to help eliminate Nationalist Chinese forces from Burmese territory.[63] The amount of aid China gave to the Burmese army, however, is uncertain. Although Peking and the Burmese government stood together on this problem, China could not guarantee how its aid would be used and was thus cautious.

From 1964 to 1967 relations gradually improved with the Burmese government. China made some aid deliveries, and helped Burma build a number of small factories, including a machine works, a sugar mill, a paper factory, a plywood mill, a tire factory, and a textile mill. During this period China again became one of Burma's most important trading partners and sources of investment. Increasing political stability, failures of the White Flags, and continuing bad relations with India and the Soviet Union probably motivated Peking. Soviet aid had not done well in Burma, and the Burmese government seemed to favor Peking's position on the planned second Afro-Asian Conference.[64] Also Rangoon leaned toward the Chinese brand of Socialism and China's model for economic development.

But in 1967 another reversal in relations occurred. The excesses of the Cultural Revolution spread to Burma. There were serious incidents and mutual accusations. At this time Chinese advisors, numbering about 400, left Burma.[65] Shortly after, some of them appeared among rebel groups in northern Burma, and Peking began to supply arms and supplies to these groups again. Border clashes occurred during 1968, and in 1968–1969 trade and aid almost ceased.

In 1971 Sino-Burmese relations returned to normal, and in August Chou En-lai informed the Burmese government that the 1961 aid grant for $84 million that had been suspended in 1967, would be renewed.[66] Over $56 million had not been delivered, and this was extended in the form of a ten-year, interest-free loan. Later, six industrial plants were planned, and construction started with the use of this aid. This was a product of China's new soft-line foreign policy and Peking's efforts to win a leadership role among the underdeveloped countries. More specifically, China was apprehensive about events on the subcontinent and sought some influence with the Burmese government. Mao was particularily concerned about Burma's relations with Bangladesh.

More recently China has once again given assistance to rebel groups in Burma, and there is little activity on its aid projects. The renewed pledges of aid are apparently in cold storage for a while. Nevertheless, Burma has been able to buy Chinese products on credit, as its trade balances show. Apparently, Peking is buying insurance in the event the rebels fail.

Frequent change has characterized China's relations with Burma, including China's aid policies toward Rangoon. Aid has been responsible for some specific gains but has not produced a long-term friendly relationship. Perhaps it was not supposed to. Considering how much aid Peking has promised to the Burmese government, it has given little. And it has had little, if any, effect on Burma's economic development. The future of China's aid diplomacy vis-à-vis Burma is uncertain.

Aid to Laos

China gave aid to Communist forces in Laos during the 1950s, though much of this assistance was given indirectly—transferred through North Vietnam. The first official grant to the Laotian government was made in 1961 in the context of the Second Geneva Conference on Laos. Peking sought to build closer relations with the neutralist government of Prince Souvanna Phouma and wanted to gain a role in peace negotiations independent of Moscow. This grant was made in April, just one month before the Conference, and was specified for building a road linking the two countries.[67] No further details were released on this agreement, not even the amount. While the Geneva Conference was in progress, Peking made another promise of aid to build a second road. Again, no details were released except that this aid was nonrepayable.

In December 1962 Prince Souvanna Phouma traveled to Peking, and at that time China made another promise of aid in the form of a long-term credit.[68] No further details were made available. However, subsequent to this agreement the Chinese government reported that the Laotian government had requested that a road be extended further south to the northern border of Thailand. Reports notwithstanding, Chinese workers and engineers assigned to the road-building project were soon withdrawn. Chinese aid to Laos and the presence of its workers and engineers violated the Geneva Convention on Laos signed in 1962. Peking may have feared American retaliation if Chinese road-builders got too close to Thailand. Or Peking decided against helping the Laotian government and instead once again opted to supply aid to the Pathet Lao. Thus little or none of the December 1962 credit was used.

Peking nevertheless found it advantageous to continue with road projects in the north, mostly in territory held by the Pathet Lao. These roads gave the Chinese Army a logistical advantage in the event of further hostilities and offset the fact that other supply routes favored armies moving from the south in Laos. The new roads also amplified China's contacts with the Pathet Lao independent of Hanoi. Thus through 1962–1963 progress on the roads was slow and intermittent, but continued. Peking probably did not want to alarm the West to its penetration of Laos, although it could justify this violation of the Convention because of a Thai military presence there. Yet China wanted to preserve a presence in northern Laos and deal with the Pathet Lao directly, rather than through North Vietnam.

In 1963 one stretch of road from Phong Saly to Meng La was finished. In April of the following year Chinese roadguards were captured following a right-wing coup, thus openly implicating Peking in a violation of the Geneva agreements.[69] Then due to events in Vietnam following the Gulf of Tonkin incident, Peking chose not to aggravate the situation in Laos. Work on aid projects, especially roads, almost stopped. Mao may have hoped that slowing down aid would encourage the Soviets to step in leading to a direct confrontation with the United States.

After a period of caution, however, Peking began work on the roads again. In 1968 it was reported that 3,000 Chinese workers were working on nine roads in Laos.[70] In addition, China provided training for Pathet Lao troops at bases in China and recruited minority nationalities in China to help the Pathet Lao. Chinese engineers also established a radio network for broadcasting from southern China to Laos.[71] How much Peking spent on all of this is unknown. The $4 million figure which constitutes official aid is in any case irrelevant. This was aid promised to Vientiane when there was peace in Laos. China certainly gave much more than this to the Pathet Lao.

In 1971 it was reported that the number of Chinese laborers working on roads in Laos had increased from something over 6,000 to nearly 20,000 in two years.[72] At that time Peking's engineers had just finished a stretch of concrete road and were working on the construction or repair of more than nine other roads. In early 1973 one of these roads was being extended further south than any agreement with the Laotian government allowed, almost to the Mekong River.[73] A few months later it was said that China had 20,000 to 26,000 personnel in Laos. In addition, considerable military aid was given to protect these roads, including radar-controlled antiaircraft guns, making this one of the most heavily defended areas in Indochina.

During 1974 progress on the roads continued, and China provided additional aid to the coalition government of Laos. Although this aid was not formally announced, the total for 1974 was put at $25 million. Probably most of the aid was for reconstruction, especially in the northern part of Laos.[74] Peking apparently perceived that the Pathet Lao were gaining ground and might soon dominate the government of Laos. When it did, China wanted to help. In addition, during 1974 the Soviet Union gave no aid to Laos; thus the Chinese did not have to face competition from its chief rival in aid-giving.

In early 1975 aid talks were held between Chinese and Laotian delegates in Vientiane, and it was reportedly decided that China would extend interest-free loans for the extention of a road to the ancient capital at Luang Prabang, dwellings for 500 people, a police headquarters, and a meeting hall and hospital.[75] The road was to be a two-lane, all-weather road capable of carrying 60-ton tanks. Subsequently a trade agreement was signed between the two countries, and in it China promised credits for the purchase of Chinese medicine, lorries, canned food, textiles, building materials, and oil. In May the Laotian government announced that it had obtained Thai rice purchased by China, and that it was sending an economic delegation to Peking to negotiate more aid.[76] In June the Laotian government stated that it had made agreements with China for aid in the amount of $20 million for road building and $8 million for other goods.[77]

Chinese efforts, however, recently have been challenged by Soviet aid promises. Moscow delivered considerable military equipment to the Vientiane government as the American presence and aid declined in mid-1975, and it has made plans to help in reconstruction. These plans include building entire cities, setting up transport facilities, etc.[78] Soviet weapons have been used by Laotian soldiers in skirmishes with the Thai military, and a sizeable assemblage of Soviet military and economic aid advisors has been seen in Laos recently.

Moscow's advantages lie in its ability to give more aid and military assistance of the kind that Laos needs if it is to engage in more hostilities with Thailand. The pullout of U.S. aid caused a collapse in the Laotian economy and a vacuum that perhaps only the Russians can fill. Also Vietnamese influence in Laos seems to favor the Kremlin. On the other hand, China has a longer, meaningful commitment to Laos and is deeply rooted in the countryside. The roads are important not only as trade outlets for landlocked Laos, but also strategically for China. Also, China has a geographical advantage. At present another aid battle seems to be in progress, and it is difficult to predict who will emerge the winner.

Aid to Pakistan

Peking's first financial assistance to Pakistan was granted in July 1964 in the form of a $60 million interest-free loan.[79] According to the talks held at that time, the loan provided funds for the purchase of industrial equipment and commodities, one half for each, and it was to be repaid in Pakistani goods over a period of twenty years beginning in 1966. The publicizing of this aid deal coincided with a border treaty between China and Pakistan, which involved disputed Kashmir. Peking's aid conveyed the image of reasonableness and generosity. In addition, it may have been designed to force India into a border settlement— especially one favorable to China.

This $60 million loan may also have been used to pay for the military equipment that China sent to Pakistan a year later. In late 1965 Chinese-made T-34 and T-59 tanks and MIG aircraft were seen in Pakistan.[80] Peking also sent military advisors and provided training for Pakistani pilots in China. And some guerrilla training centers were set up in Kashmir, apparently with Chinese assistance.[81] Mao wanted to compensate Pakistan for the cut of U.S. military aid in 1965 and help bolster Pakistan's defenses against India. Peking announced at the time that it would provide "resolute assistance" to Pakistan to defend its sovereignty and territorial integrity. Mao may even have sought to provoke Pakistan into initiating hostilities with India. Confrontation between India and Pakistan would have brought to question culpability for the 1962 Sino-Indian conflict and would have made India appear an aggressor nation. It also would have sullied New Delhi's reputation as a leader of the neutral bloc of nations. Finally, it might have undermined the whole concept of neutrality and thus lent support to Peking's stand for an Afro-Asian bloc rather than a neutral bloc.

China's warmer relations with Pakistan also gave Peking added contacts with the outside world during a time when, at least according to the perceptions of Chinese leaders, the Soviet Union and India were attempting to isolate China. At nearly the same time that China announced its aid to Pakistan an agreement was reached on radio and telephone communications. A civil aviation agreement had been signed earlier. In March 1965 Foreign Minister Ch'en Yi declared that efforts to isolate China had been unsuccessful because of China's peaceful relations with Pakistan. Chinese aid may also have been given with the intent of influencing Pakistan's foreign policy on several key issues. Islamabad issued a statement favoring China's first nuclear test (this came just after aid had been promised), and Pakistan gave support to Peking on the Taiwan issue, condemning the so-called two-Chinas scheme. Islamabad's role in arranging events that led to a rapprochement between the U.S. and China may also have been the product of Chinese foreign aid. Pakistan was an ally of the U.S., and the Pakistan government arranged Henry Kissinger's first trip to Peking.

Peking, however, made a serious mistake in getting Pakistan embroiled in a conflict with India (if indeed Peking's role was instrumental in engendering the confrontation) and then not helping Pakistan during the actual fighting. At any rate, this is the way it appeared, since hostilities occurred between Pakistan and India soon after the delivery of Chinese arms. Peking was intimidated by the superpowers during the fighting, and Moscow ended up arranging for a peaceful settlement of the conflict at Tashkent.

In spite of this setback, Peking continued to supply Pakistan with weapons and economic aid after the brief war. In November 1965 an agreement was reached on the construction of plants, factories, and workshops. In June 1966 Peking agreed to help build an industrial complex in Pakistan.[82] And more weapons were delivered. Probably most of the $60 million granted in 1964 was used by the end of 1966, and maybe more. In January 1967 Peking signed an agreement on food aid and promised 100,000 tons of wheat and 50,000 tons of rice. This was estimated by foreign reporters to be worth $7 million and was said to take the form of an interest-free loan.[83] Later in the year Pakistan sent an economic mission to Peking that was offered a noninterest-bearing loan for commodities and equipment to build heavy industrial projects. No figures were announced, suggesting that it was small or was part of a loan already given. In any case, Pakistan refrained from participating in SEATO and CENTO meetings that year—perhaps a quid pro quo.

But China faced stiff aid competition. In April Premier Kosygin traveled to Pakistan and promised new aid to build a steel mill and an atomic power plant. Shortly thereafter Moscow announced a $60 million loan; and at about the same time it was reported that the Soviet Union would also provide arms to Pakistan.[84] It was later reported that the Soviet steel mill was worth $200 million. A few months after, loans were made to Pakistan by West Germany, Japan, and the United Kingdom, and the Aid Pakistan Consortium promised $450 billion.[85]

Peking was not discouraged. In December 1968 the Chinese foreign ministry announced another loan to Pakistan, interest-free and worth $42 million.[86] The stated purpose of this loan was to pay for sets of equipment, commodities, and technical assistance. In July 1969 talks were convened on the construction of another road. China also continued to deliver military aid and supply training for Pakistani pilots and special forces. In November 1970 Peking extended the largest donation of aid yet to Pakistan and one of the largest it had made anywhere: a $200 million interest-free loan.[87] The agreement was not announced in the Chinese press, suggesting that Mao did not want to let the Chinese people know about his largess in view of the need for investment funds at home. Perhaps he intended to draw Pakistan further into the Chinese orbit before actually delivering the aid, or the money was earmarked for military aid.

During 1970 Pakistan received two or three submarines from China. Also it was reported that Peking sent Pakistan some fast patrol boats fitted with 37mm guns and torpedo tubes, which would make it possible to turn them into missile carriers.[88] Smaller Chinese arms were also seen in Pakistan. During 1971 relations deteriorated between the two sections of Pakistan and there weapons were put to use. Although a "war of national liberation" seemed to be brewing in the eastern section, Peking supported Islamabad and tried to preserve Pakistan's unity. Mao sought to preserve a balance of power on the subcontinent at all costs and prevent the spread of Indian influence in South Asia.

In February the opening of a Chinese-financed road connecting China and West Pakistan was announced. This was an all-weather road and made possible the flow of more Chinese military equipment. Islamabad apparently timed the announcement (with Peking's concurrence) to let rebel forces in the East know that it had access to additional military supplies.[89] In May 1971, however, Peking dispatched a plane carrying powdered milk to Dacca to ease the food shortage there.[90] Mao hoped to mediate the conflict. But Peking's effort to stop the war did not succeed. China also failed to come to Pakistan's rescue by opening up another front against India when New Delhi's army entered the war. Mao could do nothing in view of increasing tension on the Sino-Soviet border and threats coming from Moscow.

After Islamabad's disastrous military defeat, Peking once again came to the rescue. In February 1972 China announced that it was writing off four previous loans to Pakistan totalling $110 million and tht it would defer payment of the $200 million loan for twenty years.[91] Also, Peking promised more military aid, and in June delivered sixty MIG-19 fighters, one-hundred tanks, and an unspecified amount of small arms.[92] Mao apparently sought even more aggressively to preserve a power equilibrium in South Asia, which of course was now more difficult. Perhaps China's strategy could more aptly be described as an effort to contain India. Regardless of what its strategy is called, it did seek to reduce the impact of India's victory and limit the expansion of its influence. With a new situation in the area, Pakistan became even more vital to China than before.

During 1973–1975 Chinese aid to Pakistan continued to flow, even though no new grants were offered. Peking has first to fulfill the $200 million granted of 1970. In the latest aid talks, held in February 1975, earlier Chinese loans to Pakistan were extended. New projects were also mentioned, such as a fertilizer plant and a heavy-engineering complex.[93]

Chinese aid to Pakistan to date has been considerable; in fact, Pakistan is the second largest recipient of Chinese aid among non-Communist countries, surpassed only by Tanzania. In military aid Pakistan is the largest recipient among non-Communist countries. China's aid, both military and economic, has been delivered promptly—probably more quickly than any aid China has promised to a non-Communist Asian country. And by most standards it is generous. Some of the Chinese projects in Pakistan, such as the steel mills, are more modern than China has at home. And although loans have been the chief form of aid, some have already been written off and others probably will be.

China has attained several important foreign policy objectives through its aid to Pakistan. Islamabad has sided with China on most foreign policy issues and has supported Peking's stance on Sino-Soviet differences. Pakistan has been a useful link to the Arab world, where China has important interests. China's ties with Pakistan have also helped Peking avoid being "contained" by the Soviet Union and India. Finally, Islamabad helped engineer contacts between China and the United States.

Although two or three years ago it appeared that China's efforts to preserve a balance of power in South Asia had failed and that Pakistan would have to come to terms with India, this has not been the case. Pakistan has managed to resist Indian pressure, and now that relations between India and Bangladesh have soured, Pakistan will probably continue to serve as a balance or at least a partial balance to India's influence in the area. Pakistan may have remained subborn in the face of India's threats and pressure because of China's friendship and foreign aid. This says much for Chinese foreign aid diplomacy.

On the other hand, it is unlikely that Pakistan will fall into the Chinese orbit, since it is so reliant upon other sources of aid. China is by no means the only donor and is far from the largest. Pakistan remains very much dependent upon U.S. and other Western aid. Thus China's influence over Pakistan must be seen as largely political and temporary, since its aid is supplemental. Nevertheless, China's aid diplomacy to Pakistan has been and remains a success.

Aid to Afghanistan

Peking's first aid offer to Afghanistan was made in March 1965 in the form of a noninterest-bearing loan for $28.7 million.[94] No information was provided on the use or conditions of the loan. There were no projects started at that time and no visible transfer of funds. China's promise of aid to Afghanistan was rather puzzling since Afghanistan had received, and was still receiving, hundreds of millions of dollars of aid from both the Soviet Union and the United States. In fact, Afghanistan had more aid than it could use effectively. And when Peking made this donation, it totaled less than 5 percent of Soviet aid delivered up to that time and less than 3 percent of combined Soviet and U.S. aid.

Chinese decision-makers may have perceived that the Afghanistan government sought a greater degree of independence from Moscow and that in view of increasing U.S. aid Kabul might reduce its economic ties with the U.S.S.R. Also, at this time Peking wanted to get support for a second Afro-Asian Conference, with the Soviet Union excluded, and backing to give the conference precedence over a Nonaligned Nations' Conference. Chinese aid may likewise be seen in the context of a border agreement between the two countries. Peking may have sought to convey the image of reasonableness in view of continuing hostilities with India and the Soviet Union over territorial settlements. But the border between China and Afghanistan is very short, and reaching a settlement was more in the interest of Kabul than Peking.

In any case, by the beginning of 1966 no aid had actually been delivered. In August further talks were held on the use of the aid and six projects were specified.[95] Nevertheless, in early 1967 talks were still going on, and no aid funds had been transferred. Then in mid-1967 China sent some aid. Several fish ponds, a water conservation works, an experimental tea planting farm, and some other projects were built. In March 1970 agreements were signed whereby China would help build a textile mill and an engraving plant. Chinese aid was being implemented, albeit gradually.

In November 1971 another loan agreement was signed, Peking promising an additional $2.7 million.[96] At about this same time Peking sent shipments of grain to help relieve a shortage caused by drought. The value of Chinese grain shipments was estimated at $2 million and probably constituted the fulfillment of most or all of this agreement.

In early 1972 it was reported that Peking had offered another loan worth $44 million to assist Afghanistan's fourth Five-Year Plan.[97] This marked a dramatic change in the amount of aid that China provided to Afghanistan. However, there were no official announcements on either side to confirm this loan. New projects were started, and this together with other indications, suggests that an aid donation was made.[98] Mao apparently felt that there was considerable benefit in maintaining good relations with Afghanistan. It sealed a part of China's border in an area where minority groups frequently crossed, and at a time when China had serious problems in this regard with the Soviet Union. Moreover, Kabul had been seeking better relations with Pakistan. Chinese decision-makers may have perceived that improved relations between those two countries would be in its interest, since it would allow Pakistan to devote more of its energies to coping with India. Chinese leaders may even have felt that bonds with Afghanistan would directly help contain the spread of Indian influence in the area. Mao may also have perceived that a presence in Afghanistan would serve as a diversionary tactic against the Soviet Union and aleviate growing tension on the Sino-Soviet border.

While Peking cannot hope to supplant Soviet and U.S. aid, it has won tangible gains with its aid, and may continue to do so. Reports of its projects in Afghanistan suggest that they have been built quickly and efficiently and that they have been useful. At this point, Chinese aid to Afghanistan may be said to have offered China some diplomatic possibilities, and this situation remains.

4

China's Aid to Middle
Eastern Countries

Although Peking made its first aid commitment to a Middle Eastern country shortly after it gave aid to a non-Communist Asian country, China's interests in the Middle East were not as intense, and its diplomacy was based on quite different objectives and perceptions. Historical connections between China and Middle Eastern countries are minimal, and certainly in 1949 were of little importance. Past tribute was not a factor. Nor could China's military strength threaten countries of the Middle East. Finally, there was little hope for trade with Middle Eastern countries.

Nationalism, however, was strong in the Arab world, and it was something which Mao understood well. The Chinese Communists welded it into a powerful force against the West and expected the Arab countries to do likewise. Some regard it as the strongest political force in the Arab world and the common ground on which China bases its relations with Middle Eastern countries.[1] Chinese and Arab nationalism alike were and still are directed against Western colonialism, neocolonialism, and imperialism. Both perceive that they had a common past and a common goal: disengaging themselves from Western control, economic and otherwise.

Another basis for understanding and building mutual bonds was socialism. The Arab countries espoused a kind of socialism which despite Western origins found many ideals in common with the Communist countries, including China. Thus Chinese leaders seemed to envision the Arab countries as being the first to join the World Socialist Union.[2] Chinese decision-makers also observed that there was considerable instability in the countries of the Middle East. Some were very poor. Most could be considered revolutionary. Certainly it was an area of the world that evidenced much discontent. Mao saw the area as a revolutionary zone where there was an intense desire to change the status quo—a desire that matched Peking's.[3] And as Sino-Soviet differences increased, Mao apparently perceived that the Soviet Union could not deal with the intense nationalism and anti-imperialism present in the Middle East.[4] To do so, Moscow would have to become more revolutionary, as China had admonished. Finally, the Middle East was an area where the Chinese might make inroads, even though Moscow had more to offer in terms of foreign aid.

Peking furthermore viewed America's support for Israel as a sore spot and one that it might exacerbate. Certainly Israel provoked hatred and radicalism among the Arabs. For this reason when Israel offered diplomatic recognition to Peking, Mao declined to reciprocate. He sought purposely to make Israel an enemy. And after the early 1950s China consistently took the Arab side in the Middle East conflict. Mao gave various kinds of support to Middle Eastern countries, including economic and military aid. China also sent arms and aid to the Palestinians.

One of Peking's early goals in the Middle East was the winning of diplomatic recognition. Mao probably felt that setting up embassies in some Middle Eastern countries might influence the rest: China could win diplomatic recognition from an entire bloc of nations. Equally important, Mao may have perceived that winning diplomatic recognition from Middle Eastern countries would influence African countries as they became independent. Certainly the Middle East offered China the best prospects of any area of the world in the late 1950s and early 1960s to attain greater diplomatic support.

Another objective of Chinese foreign policy in the 1950s and later was to undermine the Western alliance system in the Middle East, namely the Baghdad Pact. Chinese diplomacy, initially with Soviet cooperation, endeavored to prevent Middle Eastern nations from joining this alliance system.[5] This foreign policy aim, like China's interests in the Middle East in general, was based on a broad concept of security and a more global foreign policy. It also reflected a realization that Sino-Soviet differences placed limits on China's diplomatic prospects with other Communist countries and with non-Communist Asia. Thus, at first China's aims were anti-Western; but later Peking sought to reduce Soviet influence in the area, and this is still the case. China's aid-giving in the area has been motivated by both, with an emphasis on anti-Soviet efforts in recent years.

Finally, Chinese decision-makers may have been influenced by Middle East oil and by trade prospects. In the 1950s Peking did not know about China's own petroleum reserves and may have felt that China would need to import oil. Certainly Mao may have wondered how he would obtain energy for China's vast industrialization. Peking also sought sources of raw materials, such as cotton, and may have perceived that the Middle East could become a market for Chinese goods, since their relations with many Western companies was fragile. These factors no doubt influenced Chinese decision-makers in their willingness to extend aid to countries in the area.

Recently Peking has come to regard the Middle East as a geographically strategic area. It links Europe, Africa, and Asia. It is in some senses the center of world trade. A foothold in the Middle East is important for China in relation to its expanded interests in East Africa. Last but not least, the Middle East is a vulnerable link in the Soviet Union's naval expansion. Since 1969 Sino-Soviet confrontation on their common border has stalemated, and the conflict has shifted to other areas. Clearly, Peking perceives that Moscow's naval growth is intended to encircle and contain China. China's maritime trade is unprotected, and Moscow can compensate for Peking's geographical advantages in Southeast Asia with its naval power. Likewise, Chinese missile and atomic bomb sites have been moved south away from the Soviet border, but now are vulnerable to attack from the Indian Ocean. Soviet bases in the Middle East, the free use of the Suez Canal, and control of the Red Sea will greatly facilitate Soviet naval forces in Asia.

Also, China seeks to cooperate with the Middle Eastern countries to control the price of petroleum. Petroleum has become an important political weapon, and the need for oil has become a weakness of the industrialized countries. And China has oil for sale. If the price can be kept high, China will continue to reap considerable profit from its exports of petroleum. In 1974–75 the sale of petroleum was Peking's largest foreign exchange earner. China may want to join the oil exporting group of nations. This would possibly give Peking a leverage over Japan, the United States and Western Europe. China needs the industrial countries to help it with its own development. It also needs capital for its development—and for aid.

Peking's first aid to a Middle Eastern country went to Egypt. Egypt was a leader of the Arab nations, and through Cairo China won diplomatic recognition from several other Arab countries. Chinese leaders also viewed Egypt as the most revolutionary of the Arab countries and an excellent base of operations. Mao sought to influence Arab and African regional organizations from Cairo and in some measure was successful. The early date of aid to Egypt suggests that Peking began to develop a global foreign policy in the mid-1950s. China may have perceived at that time a decline in Soviet support for revolution and lessened any expectations of influencing Soviet foreign policy in areas other than Asia.

However, the Soviet Union commited large amounts of aid to Egypt just when Sino-Soviet differences came into the open. And China could not compete with Soviet aid. So Peking sought to shift its base of operations. When revolution broke out in Algeria, China rendered support to the rebels and continued to aid them when they became the legitimate government. China wanted to use Algeria as a springboard to extend its influence southward into sub-Saharan Africa. Once again, however, Peking was rendered a defeat at the hands of Moscow's bigger offers of aid. And almost the same thing happened in Syria. Syria was a more radical country and the Communist movement there larger, but the Soviet Union's greater amounts of aid overshadowed Chinese efforts.

Thus Mao turned southward to aid smaller countries in the southern part of the Middle East—where revolution was also in progress. Peking found smaller amounts of aid effective in Yemen and Southern Yemen. It also found these countries strategically located in terms of China's growing interests in Eastern Africa and in terms of controlling the southern entrance to the Red Sea. At present China may hope to limit Soviet naval expansion by retaining some influence over the nations in this area. The same is true of Sudan, which has been the most recent of China's aid recipients in the area. The Sudan is seen by Peking as both revolutionary and strategically located.

In terms of blocs, Peking has given considerably less to Middle Eastern countries than to the other blocs. (See Table 2-1.) But fewer nations are involved, and the area is smaller. Also China's aid diplomacy in the Middle East has suffered three defeats by Soviet aid efforts. This, however, does not mean that China's foreign aid program has been a failure in this region. Nor does it signify a diminishing thrust in aid-giving to Middle Eastern countries. This remains to be seen. The successes and losses must be examined in greater depth.

Chinese aid was generally successful in establishing contacts which led to diplomatic recognition. Egypt and Algeria, the first two important recipients of Chinese aid, had an impact on other countries in the Middle East and Africa. Their recognition of Peking was a way of demonstrating anti-imperialist and anti-Israeli feelings. Most countries in the region now have diplomatic accords with China. Six Middle Eastern countries co-sponsored the Albanian Resolution which admitted Peking to the United Nations. China had aided all of them.

However, Chinese assistance had little economic impact on Egypt, Syria, or Algeria. These countries did not become dependent on China, and their economic development was furthered very little by Chinese aid. This may help explain the failures of China's aid diplomacy to these countries, as well as a switch to several other countries in the area. This is not true of the three most recent recipients. Chinese aid to these countries—Yemen, Southern Yemen, and Sudan—has been considerable, given their size and the aid they have received from other countries. Thus China's economic impact recently has been more meaningful.

Chinese aid helped initiate trade ties with countries in the Middle East, including Egypt. But these trade ties were generally weak and depended on continued aid deliveries. China bought Egyptian cotton, and some Chinese products were seen in Egyptian markets. There is potential for trade with the Sudan. China currently buys Sudanese cotton and sells textiles there at competitive world market prices. Though its trade with Egypt was short-lived and its trade with the Sudan is only beginning, there seems to be some potential for continued trade with these two countries. The Sudan may also offer China an alternative source of grain. China's trade with Syria has been considerable at times, but has not been consistent. The prospects for trade with other Middle Eastern countries is less.

The weak economic impact of China's foreign aid must be seen in light of the fact that Peking has used much of its aid to support liberation struggles. This was the case for most of the aid China gave to Algeria, and is currently the case for aid to Yemen and Southern Yemen. China won a reputation for supporting liberation struggles with its aid to Algeria—even though when peace was attained, the Soviet Union won a position of predominant influence pushing China out. In the case of Egypt, Peking still has representation there and has important contacts with Arab and African regional organizations. The story remains to be finished in Yemen and Southern Yemen, where due to geographical conditions and size, China may be able to give sufficient aid and maintain some control. Whether Peking has gained a permanent base in the region is still uncertain. The prospects seem a little better than the first two times that resulted in failure. But, the area remains one where sudden change can be expected and where the Soviet

Table 4-1
China's Aid to Middle Eastern Nations[a]
(Amounts in Millions of U.S. Dollars)

Nation	Official Aid	Percent	Aid Actually Given			
			Low Estimate	Percent	High Estimate	Percent
United Arab Republic	110[b]	25.1	25	20.8	50[c]	15.6
Algeria	70[b]	15.9	15	12.5	50[c]	15.6
Syria	16	3.6	10	8.3	30[c]	9.4
Yemen	47[b]	10.7	30	25.0	60[c]	18.8
Southern Yemen	78	17.8	20	16.6	60[c]	18.8
Sudan	117.2	26.7	20	16.6	70	21.9
Total	438.2	99.8	120	99.8	320	100.1

[a]This chart does not include aid to Iraq or Morocco, which has been promised very recently. See Addendum.
[b]Estimates based on varying announced figures.
[c]Includes military aid.

Union is trying to push the Chinese out. Events since the end of the October 1973 War also suggest it possible for the United States to once again exert influence in the area.

Following is a country-by-country survey of China's aid diplomacy in the Middle East. Aid was first given to Egypt, and to Syria as part of the United Arab Republic, and then separately to both after the union broke up. Then Algeria became Peking's focus of interest. Since then Yemen, Southern Yemen, and the Sudan have been the important recipients of China's aid in the region. (See Table 4-1.) In the former three, Peking has failed. In all three cases, greater Soviet aid was the cause. In the latter three China has succeeded—so far.

Sudan is the largest recipient in the area, followed by Egypt. Neither, however, have received all of the aid promised: Egypt because China was outdone by the Soviet Union; and the Sudan because there has not been time for China to fulfill its promises. Southern Yemen, Algeria, Yemen, and Syria follow in that order as the next largest recipients. In perhaps all of these national China has not fulfilled its promises, either because its objectives could not be attained as a result of Soviet interference, or because it has not had time to deliver the aid it has granted.

Aid to Egypt

Peking extended aid worth $4.7 million to Egypt in November 1956 in the wake of the Suez Crisis.[6] This loan was made in foreign currency and was designed to help the Egyptian government overcome the shock caused to its economy by the severing of contacts with several Western countries. The purpose of the loan was to demonstrate Peking's anti-imperialist stance and to establish contacts with "progressive" countries in the Middle East. Also, Peking had obtained diplomatic recognition from Cairo only a few months before; perhaps this aid donation can be seen as a reward. Cairo, in addition, advised other Arab countries to grant Peking diplomatic accords, and many were influenced by Egypt's precedent.

After this aid grant Egypt took Peking's side on a number of foreign policy issues: Taiwan, colonialism and imperialism, etc. The Chinese embassy in Cairo became a base of operations from which Peking could seek contacts with other countries in both the Middle East and Africa. This was done in large part through regional organizations that had their headquarters in Cairo. Mao's revolutionary theories and radical stance on many issues had considerable appeal in the area. Also China's small aid donation helped increase trade between the two countries, which had some potential. China began to purchase Egyptian cotton, and Egypt in turn bought various goods from China. Trade increased steadily from 1956 to 1959.[7]

But at the same time Cairo acted to restrict Chinese influence. Nasser on several occasions suppressed leftist movements in Egypt, some of which were pro-Chinese, and he outlawed the Communist Party. Nasser likewise opposed leftist and progressive movements in other Middle Eastern countries, which he could not control. In fact, the creation of the United Arab Republic by a union of Egypt and Syria was to stem the influence of Communism in Syria. In 1958 Peking and Cairo were directly at odds over the course of the revolution in Iraq. Also, relations between Peking and Cairo cooled over Peking's interest in Algeria. In the late 1950s the Chinese turned to Algeria as the most progressive country in the area and sought a base of operations there.

Anyway, China's aid efforts in Egypt were outdone by those of the Soviet Union. In 1958 Moscow accepted the Aswan Dam project and committed $335 million to it. The Soviet Union and the East European Communist countries also financed other projects in Egypt. China could not afford to compete with these much larger offers. Moreover, Cairo was commited to the Soviet Union both politically and economically after the Aswan Dam project was finalized.

Yet Mao could neither ignore Nasser's successes in dealing with the West nor substitute for his influence among revolutionary forces in the area. Cairo remained a center of various regional organizations in Africa and the Middle East. Mao could also see that Cairo and Moscow were not always on good terms, despite the magnitude and importance of Soviet aid. Thus, Peking maintained its diplomatic ties with Egypt and sought to keep Nasser neutral vis-à-vis Sino-Indian differences and the second Afro-Asian Conference. Thus in December 1964, just a few months after Moscow had extended another credit to Cairo, Peking announced an $80 million credit.[8] This loan was without interest, and repayment was not to begin until 1970. Subsequently China announced that its aid would be used to purchase equipment for building textile mills, sugar refineries, and other light industrial projects. Peking also sent 250,000 tons of corn to Egypt when U.S. food aid was cut off, at the same time Moscow made a delivery of wheat in a like amount.[9]

Mao may have specifically hoped to influence Cairo's stance on the Afro-Asian Conference. If so, he failed. Although the conference was not held, it appears that Cairo unequivocally backed Moscow. Mao may also have expected that the war in the Congo would go on and that Cairo would serve as a base of operations for China. But the conflict in the Congo ended soon after this. Thus, although there is evidence that some of the loan was drawn immediately, probably very little of it was ultimately used. Shortly thereafter, the Cultural Revolution broke out in China and aid funds were no longer made available to Egypt. Cairo had plenty of Soviet aid anyway.

Nevertheless, during the height of the Cultural Revolution, when the June 1967 War broke out, Peking announced that it was sending 150,000 tons of wheat to Egypt and promised a $10 million loan in hard currency with no set date of repayment.[10] This was no doubt a Chinese effort to win over Egyptian sympathies and to appeal to other Arab countries during a time of crisis. It was supplemented by loud propaganda support for the Arab cause. But the amount of this loan was small compared to what Cairo needed, and can be regarded primarily as a gesture. Moreover, the earlier loan had still not been used and during 1968-1969 Sino-Egyptian trade declined. Moscow continued to give large quantities of aid to Egypt; and the Soviet Union provided military assistance in huge amounts—in the billions. Peking simply could not compete.

Since 1967 Peking has offered no more economic aid to Egypt. And it is unlikely that any will be forthcoming in the immediate future. Egypt received huge amounts of military aid from the Soviet Union before, during, and in the wake of the October 1973 War. More recently Cairo has obtained loans from several Western countries. In addition, Arab oil money is available to Egypt. In this context Chinese aid could not have much impact.

In summary, China managed to win diplomatic support from Egypt and made considerable propaganda mileage on some small donations of aid. Egypt as a leader in the Arab world helped Peking make inroads into other Arab countries. Cairo still finds Peking's support useful and wants to preserve formal relations. Nevertheless, there seems little cause for greater expectations regarding China's foreign aid diplomacy vis-à-vis Egypt.

Aid to Algeria

In late 1958 the Algerian National Liberation Front sent a small delegation to Peking apparently to seek arms and other aid. They were met by Mao and

Chou En-lai and probably received assistance or a promise of aid.[11] In the spring of 1959 another mission was sent, and it was reported that China gave them weapons and aid. Chinese aid to the Algerian rebels was estimated at $10 million up to this time.[12] Subsequently, Peking provided military training for Algerian guerrillas, and Chinese arms and equipment were observed in use in Algeria. In fact, this was true up to March 1962 when Algeria won its independence. On the other hand, the Algerian National Liberation Front was cautious in accepting too much Chinese help since it could see what had happened in Vietnam. Rebel leaders were afraid of U.S. intervention. Thus they maintained a degree of self-reliance and tried to balance Chinese assistance with help from other sources, even though there were few willing donors.

China nevertheless improved its image as a revolutionary country by aiding the Algerian guerrillas. Mao's writings served the guerrillas well, and their revolutionary strategy followed the Chinese model. Most important, it suggested the applicability of Chinese-style revolution in the rest of Africa. In short, Algeria was in Mao's eyes the beginning of "People's War" in the area. Algeria also presented a situation where the Chinese could argue that the Soviet Union was not aggressive enough and did not support revolution. Moscow did little to help the Algerian rebels. Finally, Algeria gave Mao an alternative to Cairo as a base of operations in the Middle East and Africa.

When independence was granted, the new government forthwith accorded Peking diplomatic recognition. Mao may have requested that the Algerian government try to influence other nations in the area to recognize his regime. Tunisia was one specific case. After independence, Peking continued to send military aid to Algeria, reportedly used to establish guerrilla centers where revolutionaries from Angola, Mozambique, Portuguese Guinea, and South Africa could be trained and equipped.[13]

Nevertheless, it was not long until the new Algerian government shifted its concern to economic development, and as a consequence sought aid from the West and from the Soviet Union. Large amounts of Western aid were forthcoming. During the period 1962–1965 Algeria was the third largest recipient of Western aid—absorbing a total of over $1 billion.[14] The Soviet Union sent food and military equipment and in September 1963 offered a $100 million loan. This was followed in May 1964 by another loan valued at $128 million.[15] The Eastern European satellites also gave aid, obviously at Moscow's prodding.

Peking joined the competition in October 1963, one month after the first Soviet donation. China extended an interest-free loan for $50 million repayable over a 20-year period beginning in 1970.[16] This loan was used for small industries, land reclamation, and for building roads across the Sahara to link Algeria's port cities with several of the landlocked sub-Saharan nations. In 1964 Peking provided the Algerian government with a commercial ship and four transport planes.[17] Presumably this was part of the aid agreement of the previous year.

China's motives for aiding Algeria must be analyzed in context with the large amounts of aid that Algeria was receiving from Western countries and the Soviet Union. Peking probably sought to preserve the ties built up during the period of the revolution and felt that aid afforded some leverage. Much of the Chinese aid was used to finance guerrilla centers and thus did not have to compete with Western and Soviet aid that was given primarily for economic development. Mao probably felt that with the cooperation of the Algerian government—despite the influence that came with Western and Soviet aid—he could spread revolution throughout the continent. In fact, in 1964 guerrillas reportedly trained by the Chinese in Algeria tried to overthrow the government of Morocco.[18] China also sought to influence the course of events in the Congo at this time. Algerian leaders called for a more aggressive policy in the Congo and the overthrow of Tshombe; their stance was almost identical to Peking's. Chinese weapons and equipment were shipped via Algeria to the Congolese rebels.

Peking also sought to win Algeria's support for its proposals on the second Afro-Asian Conference scheduled to be held in Algiers in late 1965. China gave a number of grants of aid at this time to influence those nations going to the Conference. (See Table 4–2.) This was probably one of the more important reasons for the October 1963 grant to Algeria, and it also explains why the loan was drawn in following months in spite of aid Algeria was receiving from other donors. Since the Algerian government was to sponsor the conference, it had considerable influence over who would be represented at the meeting and what the agenda would be. Peking sought to bar the Soviet Union from the Conference for the alleged reason that it was not an Asian country. Mao also intended to use the Conference as a stage for venting his anti-Soviet feelings. In short, China endeavored to win a position of leadership of the so-called Afro-Asian bloc, as it had to some extent at Bandung a decade earlier.

In June 1965, however, the Algerian government was overthrown, and the new regime was less pro-Chinese and more pro-Soviet. This marked the end of warm relations between Algeria and China, at least for a while. In June 1966 China made an offer to build an exhibition hall.[19] But this was only a gesture and it was unsuccessful. Probably Chinese leaders hoped to rescue something in terms of relations with Algeria and the Afro-Asian Conference. Meanwhile the Cultural Revolution absorbed the attention of Chinese decision-makers.

It is uncertain how much of the 1963 Chinese loan was used. Certainly not all of it. Thus in 1971, after events of the Cultural Revolution had been pushed into the background, Peking signed an agreement with the Algerian government to provide experts and equipment to build water works, under the 1963 loan agreement.[20] A loan agreement was announced by China at this time, but this was probably the renegotiation of the unused aid.[21] In late 1972 another agreement was concluded whereby China would provide aid to agricultural and industrial projects in Algeria.[22] Probably Mao felt that in view of the situation in the Middle East good relations with Algeria were worthwhile. Peking also sought support for its bid to lead the underdeveloped countries and perceived that Alger-

Table 4-2

**Chinese and Soviet Loans to African and Asian Nations prior to the
Scheduled Afro-Asian Conference in Algeria
(Amounts in Millions of U.S. Dollars)**

	China		Soviet Union	
Country	*Amount*	*Date*	*Amount*	*Date*
Afghanistan	$28	March 1965	$ 39	June 1964
Algeria	51	October 1963	100	September 1963
			128	May 1964
Cambodia	5 to 10	November 1964	12	November 1964
Central				
African				
Republic	4	September 1964		
Ceylon	4	October 1964		
Congo				
(Brazzaville)	3	July 1964	9	December 1964
	20	October 1964		
Ghana	22	February 1964		
Indonesia	50	January 1965		
Iran			39	July 1963
Iraq			140	March 1965
Kenya	20	May 1964	3	May 1964
Mali	8	November 1964		
Pakistan	60	October 1964	11	June 1964
	60	February 1965	7	November 1964
Senegal			7	November 1964
Somalia	20	August 1963	30	1963[a]
Tanzania	42	June 1964	42	August 1964[b]
			168	April 1964
United Arab				
Republic	80	December 1964	280	May 1964
			60	September 1964
Uganda	12	April 1965	16	November 1964
Yemen	29	May 1964	39	March 1964

[a]This was a loan for military equipment.
[b]Combined aid given by the Soviet Union, Poland, and Czechoslovakia.

ia could exert considerable influence among the poor countries. All of this notwithstanding there has been only minimal Chinese aid activity in Algeria and
there is little likelihood that Chinese aid will play a major role in Chinese-Algerian
relations in the future.

Aid to Syria

In 1958 when China sent aid to Cairo, Syria was part of the United Arab
Republic and may have received some of the aid. However, it is doubtful if Syria

received very much. Nevertheless in February 1963, the Chinese Foreign Ministry extended aid directly to the Syrian government in the form of a $16 million loan.[23] No details were released about the loan except that it was interest-free and was to be repaid over a 10-year period. It was probably given by Peking with the intent of finding another base of support in the Middle East as an alternative to Egypt. There was a strong Communist movement in Syria that had certain ideological affinities to China. Moreover, Syria was one of the most radical and anti-status-quo countries in the area and of all the Arab countries was probably the most hostile to Israel. Mao also may have seen signs that the Syrian government was disappointed with the Soviet Union and could be weaned away from Moscow. Certainly Syria was displeased with Moscow's weak stance toward Israel. China's aid may also have been given to influence Syria's stand on the upcoming Afro-Asian Conference. Syria conceivably might have demonstrated its opposition to Soviet policy in the Middle East by supporting Peking at the Conference.

In view of the fact that the Syrian government was overthrown the month after Peking made its promise of aid and the new Baath regime was hostile to Communism, it is unlikely that any of this loan was drawn. One report indicates that by late 1965 none of it had been used.[24]

In 1966 there was another coup in Syria and another new government. Peking reacted by immediately dispatching an aid team to lay the groundwork for construction of a textile mill. And in early 1967 more projects were planned.[25] It is unlikely, though, that any of these projects were started, or if they were started, they were certainly not completed. The June 1967 War was fought partly in Syria and had a profound effect upon economic development plans. Also damage from the war was extensive, amounting, according to some estimates, to nearly $2 billion, almost a year's gross national product. After the war the Soviet Union offered to replace all of the weapons lost during the war and to provide more sophisticated equipment. Moscow also delivered extensive nonmilitary aid.

Apparently Peking delivered some of its promised aid during 1968–1969, since trade increased significantly. There were also reports that Chinese weapons had arrived in Syria. In 1969 the Syrian Army overthrew the Baath Socialist Party. At the time there was speculation that the army had used Chinese weapons to enhance its strength beyond the weapons which the Soviet Union provided for use against Israel. According to one report, Mao had given the Syrian army a $15 million gift of weapons.[26]

In June 1971 China signed an aid agreement with Syria mentioning a loan of approximately $36 million.[27] In January 1972 Peking made another aid offer to Syria in the form of a $40 million loan designated to build two yarn factories and expand one already under construction.[28] Mao also promised to build a stadium in Damascus. No other details were made available on either of these loans. It seems likely that the second was merely a confirmation or formalization of the first rather than a separate donation. Probably this aid was given with the intent of supporting Syria's tough stance toward Israel and to demonstrate Peking's support for the Arabs in the event of renewed fighting. As a corollary, it may have been given to undermine Moscow's more moderate foreign policy goals in the area. However, it may have been given to sustain a high level of trade between the two countries; Syria was China's number two trading partner in the region.

In any event there is little evidence that much of the aid was actually used. The next year another Middle East conflict broke out. The war enhanced the influence of the Soviet Union and the United States and reduced China's presence in the area. Syria again suffered serious economic dislocation and was forced to seek more aid than China could afford, meaning Soviet aid.

More recently Syria has turned to the West for aid. In January 1974 Damascus asked France for aid, and a few months later the country was opened to American tourists. It is possible that Chinese aid will also be used if Peking decides to allow its early donations to be drawn. But Chinese leaders can hardly expect to exert much control over politics in Syria and will have to contend with Western influence and Western and Soviet aid in much vaster amounts than China can afford. Thus, again prospects for China's foreign aid diplomacy are limited.

Aid to Yemen

In January 1958 Chinese negotiators signed a treaty of commerce with the government of Yemen and at the same time promised a loan worth $16.3 million for the construction of a road, a cigarette factory, a glass factory, and some other projects.[29] This agreement also included a provision for technical assistance and the use of Chinese laborers. Most of the projects were started immediately and within a few months there were more than 800 Chinese aid personnel of various kinds in Yemen.[30] Shortly after, it was reported that there were more Chinese in Yemen working on aid projects than in any other Middle Eastern country.

Peking's primary motive in aiding Yemen was to gain some influence over the revolutionary situation there. This explains the nature of the aid projects—those which required Chinese personnel. There was a guerrilla war in progress in Yemen that gave Mao an opportunity to prove the Chinese model of People's War. It also gave China a chance to force the Soviet Union into a more aggressive stand against the West and against the conservative forces in nearby Middle Eastern countries. Peking also may have given aid to Yemen as a gesture against colonialism. Yemen received its independence after a violent revolutionary struggle and needed financial assistance to preserve its independence and prevent it from altering its anti-Western position. In addition, Yemen was a poor country where Chinese aid might have an immediate impact and a country that had not received significant aid from either the West or the Soviet Union.

Also Mao may have sought another base of operations in the Middle East, knowing that he could not rely on Egypt. If this was not true in 1968, it certainly was later. Chinese leaders were cognizant of this regional importance Yemen had played under British rule and the fact that Yemen might still be critically situated in terms of political developments in the area. Located at the southern entrance to the Red Sea, Yemen could provide a site for controlling maritime traffic to and from the Suez Canal.

In 1959 China sent more aid to Yemen in the form of 10,000 tons of wheat and flour to alleviate food shortages.[31] This aid went to the side Peking favored in the civil war and gave China considerable leverage over the revolution. However, Peking's aid was met by Soviet competition: Moscow promised fifty aircraft and a $20 million loan to be used to build an airport ten miles from the capital.[32] The Soviet Union also undertook the construction of a port that could be used by the Soviet navy. Moscow, as well as Peking, seemed to recognize Yemen's geopolitical importance. In March 1964 the Soviet Union offered another credit to the government of Yemen, this time for $72 million.[33] This loan was designated for the building of a road, obviously in competition with Chinese road-building, and some other projects.

Just two months after this loan was made Peking promised the Yemen government another $28 million to build yet another road and to purchase consumer goods from China.[34] No details were made public on the conditions of this loan; probably part of it was for military aid. This loan was extended to preserve China's toehold in Yemen in view of continuing instability and increased Soviet influence there. Probably the government of Yemen sought to retain Chinese influence and thus refused to take Moscow's side in the Sino-Soviet dispute. Both the Soviet loan and the Chinese loan can also be related to the upcoming Afro-Asian Conference. Yemen represented another vote in support of the proposals of one or the other. China's second loan may also be seen in connection with the change of government in Yemen and an effort to establish close relations with the new regime. The new Yemeni President visited Peking at this time, and a second Treaty of Friendship was signed. Both countries had just upgraded their missions to embassies.

In late 1964 various Chinese aid projects were seen in Yemen, confirming that this aid was being drawn. In March 1965 construction on a textile mill was started. Later Peking promised to keep Chinese road workers in Yemen to repair the first Chinese-built road.[35] These workers probably remained to enhance China's influence in view of Egypt's troop withdrawal after the June 1967 War and the stalemate in the revolutionary struggle in Yemen. It was reported that the number of Chinese in Yemen at this time totaled 3,300.[36]

In 1969 Royalist forces in Yemen reported that Chinese technicians were repairing bridges blown up by their troops.[37] This was offered as proof that Chinese aid personnel were directly involved in the fighting there. In addition, it was said that Peking sent arms directly to Republican forces, though this probably did not involve sizeable financial outlays. That same year it was reported that a $10 million textile mill offered by China as a 30-year loan was finished. It is uncertain whether this represented an unannounced loan, or whether this was a part of the aid that Peking had already extended to the government of Yemen. At this time some other smaller projects were also started, some wells were dug, and some medical teams appeared in the countryside.

In 1970 Peking sent 5,000 tons of wheat to alleviate the effects of a drought. More arms were also sent.[38] During 1971 and 1972 two Chinese-built roads were finished, one with fifty-five bridges. In 1972 China reportedly extended a new loan to the government of Yemen worth $20.2 million.[39] This was not, however, confirmed. Assuming this loan was granted, Chinese aid surpassed Soviet aid. It may, in fact, have been given to compensate for the expected loss of Soviet aid. In midyear the government of Yemen allegedly asked the Soviet Union to remove its base and people. It is also possible that this loan may have been given to keep Yemen from falling under Western influence. After 1970 the Yemeni government made repeated efforts to reconcile its differences with Saudi Arabia and the West. The United States promised to reinstate its aid program. Finally, Peking may have given this aid to balance the effect of its aid to Southern Yemen in view of the growing seriousness of the conflict between these two countries. It may have been intended to preserve good relations with both since discussions were being held between the two countries concerning a merger.

In any case Chinese aid to Yemen has generally been successful. As in Nepal and Laos, road-building projects have been done quickly and efficiently and have provided for the presence of Chinese in the country. Other Chinese projects have been carried out quickly, have employed some of the local workforce, and have made a good impression on the people. In short, Peking's aid projects to Yemen up to this point have been successful. Aid has given Peking a foothold in the area, which in view of Soviet naval expansion in the area, China's commitments to several East African countries, and the opening of the Suez Canal is a vital one. In view of Yemen's conflict with Southern Yemen, however, China's influence is somewhat tenuous. And the Soviet Union and the West cannot be counted out.

Aid to Southern Yemen

In September 1968 Peking agreed to provide the government of Southern Yemen with a loan worth $12 million for the building of a road and for wells along the road.[40] The People's Republic of Yemen had been formed from the Aden and Aden Protectorate a year before, and immediately civil war ensued. In addition, with the break of colonial ties, Britain ended its yearly $60 to $70 million in aid. Peking's economic assistance was given to help the new government through a financial crisis and, probably much more important, to support the leftist elements in the Southern Yemen government.

Peking also hoped to gain some influence over the revolution there. The civil war in Southern Yemen bore some resemblance to Mao's "People's War." Moreover, it offered some hope of becoming a revolutionary situation, which the Soviet Union could not cope with and which might spread to other countries in the Middle East. It was for this reason that Peking stipulated in the aid agreement that Chinese technicians be sent to design the road project. Mao wanted a presence in the country in view of the intense turmoil and instability.

The Soviet Union had already provided some military aid to the government of Southern Yemen. But it criticized "ultra-left-wing politics" there and declined to give any purely economic assistance. China's loan, however, prompted Moscow to increase its military aid. In mid-1969 it was reported that the Soviet Union promised the government of Southern Yemen a new loan for $48 million.[41] Nevertheless Soviet leaders held out on food and other assistance, knowing that the West would not come to the aid of the new regime and that China probably could not because of the Cultural Revolution.

In July 1970 Peking extended another loan to Southern Yemen for $43 million to build three more roads.[42] This loan probably was intended to compete with Soviet aid and to preserve Chinese influence. It justified sending more technicians and personnel, thus amplifying China's physical presence in Southern Yemen. By early 1971 it was reported that there were more than 400 Chinese aid workers in the country.[43] It was also rumored that Chinese arms had been seen in the hands of leftist forces in Southern Yemen in considerable quantity and that Chinese officers were assisting in the training of the Southern Yemen Army. In addition, Chinese aid included consumer goods, causing imports from China to increase 71 percent during 1971.[44]

Mao sought to control the course of the revolution in Southern Yemen and had advantages in doing so. Moscow was on good terms neither with the Southern Yemen government nor with the forces on the left. Also the Soviet Union and Egypt were at odds concerning the revolution in Southern Yemen and how to influence it. And after the June 1967 War, the Suez Canal was closed, making it difficult for the Soviet Union to deliver aid to Southern Yemen. Finally, after mid-1967 the Arab countries were in turmoil over their defeat by Israel and were at odds concerning their postwar strategy.

Peking also may have regarded its presence in Southern Yemen as crucial to the protection of its growing commitments in Eastern Africa. This was especially true after Peking made the decision to build the Tan-Zam railroad through Zambia and Tanzania. China also made significant aid promises to Ethiopia and Sudan at this time, suggesting that it sought a broad base of influence in this area. Mao was obviously concerned as well about growing Soviet naval presence in the area. Moscow seemed to be increasing its naval strength in the Indian Ocean to bolster its Asian security plan—which Chinese leaders interpreted as an attempt to contain China. This was certainly more meaningful after Moscow concluded a defense pact with India.

After 1971, Chinese aid missions were even more active in Southern Yemen.

The Soviet Union extended no new economic aid, and Southern Yemen could not get assistance from the West or the other Arab countries. In fact, Saudi Arabia, Kuwait, and Iraq supported Yemen, which was less Marxist, when conflict broke out between Yemen and Southern Yemen. Since Peking was also active in aid-giving to Yemen, Chinese leaders may have thought that they could play a role in mediating the conflict or that they might influence the terms of union, which were also being discussed at this time.

In January 1973 Peking offered another loan to the government of Southern Yemen worth \$22.7 million.[45] This loan was without interest and for the purchase of Chinese goods. No other details were provided. No doubt some of it was earmarked for military equipment and weapons. This brought China's commitment to Southern Yemen to \$78 million—the second largest of any country in the region. It also represented one of the largest amounts of aid Peking presented to any small country. In addition, this loan confirmed a change in China's aid policies: granting more aid to favored countries to insure that Peking's influence can not be erased by larger promises of aid by the Soviet Union.

Southern Yemen remains one of Peking's most important aid recipients and is an important base of operations for China in the area. It is a small, underdeveloped country where Chinese aid can have an economic effect, thus in part explaining China's large commitment. Southern Yemen is crucially located in terms of controlling traffic to and from the Suez Canal. It is thus important in China's efforts to stop Soviet naval expansion in Asia. It is also tied to China's interests in Eastern Africa. So far China's aid efforts here must be placed on the success side of the ledger.

Aid to the Sudan

In June 1970 a delegation from the Sudan visited Peking and upon its return home announced that China had promised a loan of \$42 million for the purchase of textiles, farm equipment and fertilizer, as well as road construction and other projects.[46] This agreement was not announced in Peking, perhaps because it included military aid. Mao apparently perceived that the internal situation in the Sudan afforded China an opportunity to increase its contacts and exploit the revolutionary situation there. Leftist groups and the Sudan Communist Party had gained considerable following as a result of bad economic conditions and civil strife. Chinese leaders also may have regarded the Sudan with more concern due to events in nearby Yemen and Southern Yemen, and in Ethiopia, Uganda, and Kenya. By 1970 the situation in the Congo was clearly unfavorable for revolution, and Peking's focus of concern in Africa had turned to Zambia and Tanzania, where Chinese aid personnel were at work on a large railroad project. Therefore aid to the Sudan may be seen in the context of Peking's plan to establish a larger base of operations and its new geopolitical concerns in the area. It may also be connected to Soviet naval expansion which was evident at that time.

The following year the Sudan Communist Party and a faction of the army cooperated in an attempt to overthrow the government, but failed. Moscow was implicated in the plot, and Soviet-Sudan relations deteriorated quickly. Peking immediately criticized the attempted coup and continued amicable relations with the government of the Sudan. Then, in October 1971 Peking made a second promise of aid to the Sudan. This took the form of a loan for $35 million specified to be used for the construction of another highway.[47] This aid was probably given to compensate for the loss of Soviet aid. In any case, it put Peking slightly ahead of Moscow in terms of aid commitments to Kartoum. Two months later a Sudanese military delegation visited China, and an agreement was apparently reached on military aid. However, this may have been part of the October loan. Subsequently, it was reported that China had given the Sudan eight MIG fighter planes and enough tanks to supply an armoured division.[48] Chinese medical teams were also observed in Kartoum at about this time.

Mao obviously felt the situation in the Sudan warranted further concern—and aid. Civil strife had become serious, political power having gravitated into the hands of the army and President Numeiry, with whom Mao had good relations. Many people were homeless and near starvation. The Sudan was seriously in need of economic assistance. The United Nations gave aid and several Western countries sent relief, but this was not enough.

In December 1972 Peking signed its third major aid agreement with Kartoum in as many years. This agreement was for $40.2 million in the form of a loan.[49] No conditions were specified, though the funds were earmarked for various projects, including a textile and yarn factory, an agricultural machinery and equipment project, fisheries, workshops for boat repairs, and a cold storage plant. This brought Chinese aid commitments to the Sudan to a total of $117 million—more than to any other Middle Eastern country. Indications are that the aid is being drawn and will be fully utilized. Various Chinese projects have been started in the Sudan in recent months and road-building continues. Chinese weapons have also been sent to the Sudanese army.

The last donation further confirms China's growing interests in the Sudan. Mao may expect the Sudan to serve as a base of operations for China and a means of blocking Soviet influence in the area. Peking seems to be trying to control the Red Sea from two sides in order to impede or in some way influence maritime and naval traffic. This aid donation also gives further evidence of a change in Peking's aid policies in the direction of more extensive loans to selected countries where China can gain a real foothold and where the Soviet Union cannot wipe out its influence with larger promises. Peking may also have an interest in Sudan's cotton. China has been importing cotton and appears to want to increase its textile production. In 1971 trade between China and the Sudan increased by 63 percent, and since then additional commercial ties have been made. There seems to be considerable potential for trade between the two countries. The Sudan also has considerable land that can be put into use for cereal production. This could be important in the future of East African politics. And grain could be used to repay Chinese loans. The Chinese-built roads will help link the agricultural area of the Sudan with city markets.

At present, it is too early to predict the success of Chinese aid diplomacy in the Sudan. So far Peking has made inroads, and there seems to be promise for more meaningful ties. Chinese aid projects have been both successful and useful. The Sudan could well become an even more important recipient of Chinese aid in coming years and an important friend of China's in the area.

5 China's Aid to African Countries

Prior to the early 1960s Peking showed little interest in Africa. The African countries, with only a few exceptions, were still colonies or were controlled by anti-Communist regimes. Between 1960 and 1965, however, China's view of the African continent changed. Many of the former colonies won or were about to win independence. At the same time Peking became disillusioned with its ties with the Soviet Union. After Moscow withdrew its aid personnel in 1960, competition between the two Communist countries began.[1] Contention for influence in Asia was keener; so Africa offered greater hopes for Mao and his colleagues. In Asia, besides U.S. influence, China had to cope with Japan's growing economic strength and the political influence of the Soviet Union and India.

Peking's formost goal in giving aid to African countries was to win diplomatic recognition.[2] Mao was still shut out of international affairs, and China was not recognized as a world power. And because there are more nations in Africa than in any other region of the world and since most had no commitment to Taipei, Africa held out glowing prospects for China to increase its diplomatic ties. Mao was successful in winning diplomatic recognition. Many new African countries accorded Peking the diplomatic nod. It is obvious that the dates of formal relations and of China's aid promises or deliveries to a number of African countries are closely related. (See Table 1-3.) African countries also supported Mao when he made a bid for membership in the United Nations. Twenty-seven African countries voted for the Albanian Resolution, which seated Peking and expelled Taipei. (See Table 1-4.) Eleven of the twelve African countries to which Peking had given aid voted for Mao's regime. In fact, it may be said that Peking's diplomatic efforts in Africa, which were to a large extent based on aid-giving, made the difference in the U.N. vote.

Many African countries also supported Peking on other issues. Mao garnered considerable backing from African countries when he opposed the nuclear non-testing agreement in 1963. He also received support for China's atomic test in 1964. Peking won concurrence with other tenets of its foreign policy: the question of Taiwan, Afro-Asian solidarity and opposition to a nonaligned bloc, neutralization of the Indian Ocean, etc. African countries to date remain favorably disposed to China's foreign policy aims and give support to Mao in a variety of ways.

Peking found black Africa receptive to Socialism and to China's brand of Communism. African leaders associated capitalism with imperialism and thus opted to avoid the development of a capitalist economic system. Many of the

85

new African countries also sought to eradicate tribal, class, and educational differences, and found socialist ideals helpful. Finally, many African nations adopted
one-party systems to avoid social disintegration and turmoil. Hence in a variety
of ways China served as a political and economic model.

Mao, moreover, was able to take advantage of racial feelings in Africa.
Africa was and still is receptive to anti–United States propaganda due to the
racial problems in the U.S. and Washington's association with the era of imperialism and colonialism.[3] Washington's support for the white-ruled countries of
southern Africa is also a sore point. The United States has not condemned
Rhodesia as adamantly or as loudly as black African countries demand. Furthermore, the U.S. trades with the white African governments and sells them arms.
Although China also trades with South Africa and other white-controlled governments in Africa, its stated policy is clearly in opposition to them. Peking has
made a major issue of this and has given aid to insurgency groups to prove its
sincerity. The Tan-Zam Railroad project is specifically intended to free Zambia
and Tanzania from economic control by the governments to the south. This has
won for Mao considerable sympathy from the rest of black Africa.

Mao, in addition, realized that he could use racial sentiments as well as the
potential for revolution and unrest in Africa against Moscow. Peking tried to
force Soviet leaders to become more revolutionary, to accept Mao's theories,
and to apologize for insults to China. China has also tried to outdo the Soviet
Union and win a role of leading Africa's revolution. In many cases China has
been able to attract African leaders with its revolutionary and anti-white policies
at Moscow's expense.[4] Likewise the Russians have experienced a number of
failures with their foreign aid projects in Africa. The Chinese have proven more
than willing, when Soviet aid projects were closed or proved useless to the recipient, to supplant Soviet aid.

Also, Africa is an area where China can compete easily with Japan and
India. Both have advantages over China in dealing with Asian countries, but this
is not true in Africa. The former African colonies are at a low level of economic
development and need to construct an economic infrastructure—which China can
assist as well as Japan. And there are few Chinese in Africa, and certainly no fear
of Chinese migrants as in Southeast Asia. This is one of India's problems in
Africa.

Finally, Mao found that his theory of people's war had particular application
in parts of Africa. Though many countries were given their independence wil-
lingly by their former mother countries, most demanded it and many had to
fight for it. Now, many of the new governments are led by African leaders who
were trained or educated in European countries, and they are frequently at odds
with local leaders. A number of scholars have observed that Africa in the 1960s
was the most revolutionary area of the world.[5] This situation remains. Due to
the low level of economic development, the gap between Western educated and

locally educated Africans, unnatural borders, tribal problems, etc., causes abound for unrest and revolution.

In the early 1960s Mao perceived that revolution would spread from the Congo to other parts of Africa. For this reason he endeavored to influence events in the Congo and aided the revolutionary forces with guns, supplies, and some funds. It was some years before guerrilla movement was stopped; meanwhile Mao had made inroads elsewhere. At this time West Africa seemed to be the most anti-imperialist and the most revolutionary. Furthermore, the first nations to gain independence were in West Africa. Thus this area was most promising to Mao who sought diplomatic recognition and revolutions to support.

More recently Peking has found that although Africa is a region of unrest and turmoil, China also experiences difficulties in securing a foothold or base. Thus its victories are ephemeral and China is vulnerable to "counterrevolutionary efforts" by the U.S. or the Soviet Union or simply the vicissitudes of African politics. For this reason Peking's geographic focus has changed from West Africa to East Africa.[6] In addition, Peking has been more selective in its aid in recent years, has switched to bigger projects, and has concentrated its grants in regions where China might attain a sphere of influence.

China has also expressed some interest in Africa's plentiful natural resources.[7] By the time Peking took an active interest in events in Africa, it had given up its rapid industrialization plan. Yet Peking sees Africa as an area which might be a weak link in the economic strength of the West. At the same time, Africa possesses certain metals and resources which China needs. It is hardly a coincidence that the Chinese-financed Tan-Zam Railroad will provide a shipping route for Zambia's copper. China has to import copper and several other metals that are exported by African countries. Also, China buys cotton, which Ethiopia and other African nations have for sale.

Peking now endeavors to win a position of leadership of the underdeveloped countries. In fact, this is currently one of the major tenets of Chinese foreign policy. Most of the countries of black Africa are poor. Greater unity with other developing countries in the control of export prices and the guarantee of steady markets would be beneficial to them. Peking seeks to lead the poor countries by exploiting the dichotomy between the rich and poor nations. So far, it has experienced some success. Therefore Africa is of continuing interest to Mao. China's recently announced aid policies and guidelines clearly reflect this thinking. Peking wants to make it appear that aid from the rich countries is not generous and aid is compensation for unfair economic relations that are part of the capitalist world market. Demonstrating this while forcing the developed countries to give more aid—which China's foreign aid program has done effectively—justifies China's claim to leadership of the poor African nation, at least in Mao's eyes.

In terms of total aid received from China, Africa ranks above the Middle

East, but below the Communist bloc and non-Communist Asian countries. However, the African bloc received little aid from China before the last ten to fifteen years. In terms of growth of aid receipits, African nations outrank all others. Africa now exceeds non-Communist Asia in official aid, and later probably will in actual aid drawn.

Tanzania and Zambia have been by far the largest recipients of Chinese aid in Africa because of the large and expensive railroad project that Peking has undertaken there. This is China's largest project to date and is a test of Peking's abilities in planning, and engineering. At present it seems to be a success. Thus, China has succeeded with its aid diplomacy to these two countries. Relations with both countries remain good, especially with Tanzania that ranks fourth behind only North Korea, North Vietnam, and Pakistan in terms of officially promised aid.

China's aid diplomacy has also been successful in the Congo, Guinea, and Mauritania. These nations remain on good terms with China and may be regarded as supporters of China's policy line and general activities and interests in Africa. But none can be regarded as a Chinese satellite. Until very recently Ethiopia was clearly building close ties with China, and Peking's aid promises were extensive. But the fall of Haile Selassie has changed this.

Kenya and the Central African Republic clearly appear as failures of Chinese diplomacy. However, not much aid was promised and much less was actually delivered. In Mali and Somalia, China experienced temporary setbacks. It is uncertain what China's relations with these nations will be in the next few years. The same is true of Uganda and Ghana; there Mao failed to attain his immediate objectives and China's influence waned for a while. But now, cordial relations have been restored.

A number of other nations in Africa have received aid from China, but the donations were too small or too recent to be analyzed in terms of their significance or China's motives. These aid donations are cited in the addendum that follows Chapter 6. These recipients of Chinese aid in Africa are considerable. In fact, this can be offered as further evidence of Peking's escalating interest in Africa. (See Table 5-1.)

Following is a country-by-country analysis of China's aid to individual African countries. The Tanzania-Zambia Railroad project is considered separately due to its importance.

Aid to Guinea

In 1958 China reportedly sent rice-growing experts to Guinea. And a year later when China's ambassador to Morocco visited Guinea, he promised 5,000 tons of rice as a "gift of the Chinese people." It was also rumored that he agreed to a $500,000 loan at this time.[8] However, Peking first gave official aid to Guinea

Table 5-1
China's Aid to African Nations[a]
(In Millions of U.S. Dollars)

Nation	Official Aid	Percent	Aid Actually Given			
			Low Estimate	Percent	High Estimate	Percent
Guinea	26	2.5	25	5.2	70	8.3
Ghana	42	4.1	15	3.1	35	4.2
Mali	22.4	2.2	15	3.1	30	3.6
Somalia	131	12.6	25	5.2	85	10.1
Tanzania[b]	410.8	39.7	300	61.9	400	47.6
Kenya[c]	17.8	1.7	0.5	0.1	4	0.5
Zambia[b]	212.8	20.5	60	12.4	120	14.3
Congo (B)	46	4.4	25	5.2	40	4.3
Central African Republic	4	0.4	0.5	0.1	2	0.2
Uganda	15	1.5	0.5	0.1	5	0.6
Mauritania	24	2.3	8	1.7	20	2.4
Ethiopia	84	8.0	10	2.1	30	3.6
Total	1,035.8	99.9	484.5	100.2	841	99.7

[a]This chart does not include aid to the following nations: Equatorial Guinea, Sierra Leone, Burundi, Rwanda, Togo, Nigeria, Dahomey, Cameroon, Zaire, Mauritius, Malagasy Republic, Niger, Upper Volta, Chad, Mozambique, Gabon, or Angola. See Addendum.
[b]This includes funds allocated for the Tanzania-Zambia Railroad.
[c]This does not include aid which was allegedly given to local politicians or to rebel groups in Kenya.

in 1960, after diplomatic relations had been established and in conjunction with a treaty of friendship—the first with a black African country. Mao gave the government of Guinea a $25 million noninterest loan to be drawn immediately and usable through 1963.[9] This loan was to be used for sets of equipment, Chinese technicians, technical training, and commodities. China agreed to pay for the transportation of Chinese technicians and guaranteed Chinese aid personnel would not live at a level above Guinean technicians and workers. Later in the year China gave Guinea 10,000 tons of rice, apparently as a gift.[10] Peking also invited Guinea to send ten students to study in China at the expense of the Chinese government.

Mao probably gave aid to Guinea primarily to win diplomatic recognition. This explains the aid donations reported before relations were established. The formal donation was then a reward for recognition. Guinea was the first nation in the area to attain independence, and was ruled by a radical regime. Setting up diplomatic relations was a good precedent for Peking to set. In addition to opening an embassy, China also sent cultural and commercial representatives to

Guinea and set up an office of the New China News Agency and a book store to sell Chinese books and periodicals.

Mao may also have sought to compete with Moscow in Guinea. The Soviet Union had already given aid. But Russian equipment did not work in the hot climate, some projects could not be finished, and others were too big. Russian aid projects produced surpluses that had to be exported to Western countries. In addition, the Soviet Union was charged with instigating "subversive activities" in Guinea with its aid projects.[11] China may have been awaiting such an opportunity: The break and the pullout of Soviet aid technicians from China occurred only one month after China's promise of aid to Guinea.

Soviet influence, however, was largely supplanted by American influence. In 1962 Washington inaugurated an aid program to Guinea, and by 1966 had given between $45 million and $60 million. Much of this was food aid, which Guinea desperately needed. The rest involved small projects; the U.S. apparently learned from the Soviet's mistakes. Thus China went slow on delivering aid to Guinea. By 1964, of the nine projects China had promised with its 1960 grant, only a small cigarette factory and a match factory had been finished. The worth of these two projects was estimated at only $3 million.[12] Aid work continued; but at the end of 1965 it was still estimated that only one-fourth of China's aid to Guinea had been drawn.[13]

Probably Peking did not pull out completely because Soviet aid personnel were still leaving. Also Mao sought support for his atomic test and for China's position on the Afro-Asian Conference scheduled for 1965. Further, Chou En-lai planned a trip to Africa at this time. Guinea supported China's nuclear test; in fact, it welcomed it. Guinean leaders lauded Chou when he came and Guinea seemed to take China's stand in preparation for the second Afro-Asian Conference.

From 1966 Guinea's relations with the West worsened, while Sino-Guinean relations improved. This was presaged or accompanied by deteriorating relations between Guinea and its neighbors: the Ivory Coast, Ghana, the Congo, and Mali. Coups in the latter three countries directly threatened President Toure's left-leaning government and forced him to rely on Peking for aid. Meanwhile, political instability in Guinea engendered economic problems, food shortages, etc. In this milieu several Chinese aid projects were started or were given higher priorities. In January 1967 a hydroelectric station was opened. Subsequently a dam, a sugar refinery, a nut oil factory, and a steel mill were started. And it was reported that China was providing the government of Guinea with arms, part of which were being used in nearby Ghana.[14]

In late 1967 Peking signed an agreement with the governments of Guinea and Mali to build a railroad linking the two countries.[15] This represented a major Chinese commitment to Guinea and an effort to help Toure spread his political influence in the area. Mao may have perceived that Guinea could become a Chinese base of operations in Africa. Since the project was not feasible from the economic point of view, China's motives were obviously political. In August of the following year a Chinese survey team completed its work, but a week later the Mali government was overthrown and the project was scrapped.

In October 1969 Peking signed another aid agreement with the government of Guinea promising to assist Guinea in solving its balance of payments problem and its general economic crisis.[16] No details were provided on the conditions or amount of this aid. A few months later it was reported that Peking had given Guinea $10 million for budgetary support. In March 1970 an agreement was signed whereby China agreed to send medical workers to Guinea.[17] And in November a pact was signed on economic and technical cooperation. Though no aid was mentioned in this agreement, Chinese aid projects were under construction, and the flow of aid from China appeared to continue uninterrupted. At this time Guinea also received a grant for $1.5 million from Tanzania.[18] Since Tanzania was receiving huge amounts of Chinese aid, this was probably in reality a grant from China.

In December 1972 an agreement was signed between the Chinese government and the government of Guinea on financial credits.[19] This may have constituted another promise of aid, but it was not announced as such. In any case, Chinese aid continued to flow. In 1973 a farm tool plant and some smaller projects were completed.[20] During 1974–1975 other Chinese projects were started and some earlier projects finished.

Guinea remains friends with Peking and supports China on a number of foreign policy issues. Guinea is, in a sense, a Chinese outpost in Western Africa. On the other hand, it is questionable whether China can or will provide all of the aid Guinea needs. This is especially true of food aid. Guinea was hit by the recent African drought and had to request food aid from the West. Also, Guinea has large reserves of bauxite, which China cannot develop or market. It has already made an agreement with a Western consortium to develop its bauxite resources. This may foster changes in Guinean politics not conducive to closer relations with China. In addition, a Canadian firm recently signed a contract with the government of Guinea to build a $555 million railroad. Construction began in 1975 and is to be completed in 1981. Finally, the Soviet Union cannot be counted out. Moscow has continued its aid deliveries to Guinea, recently in larger amounts. The Kremlin has also provided military aid and has been using a base in Guinea for reconnaissance of NATO forces in the area.[21]

Nevertheless, China's aid diplomacy has been successful in Guinea, and Guinea remains, at minimum, a close friend. This may be more important now that China's relations with a number of other countries in West Africa are less cordial and as Peking makes a more serious bid for leadership of the developing countries. However, China's future aid relationship with Guinea, in view of increased Western and Soviet aid, is an unknown.

Aid to Ghana

In August 1961 Mao invited Ghana's President Nkrumah to Peking and gave him a lavish welcome. He also extended Nkrumah a promise of $19.5 million in aid in the form of a noninterest loan repayable over a ten-year period beginning in 1971.[22] This aid was to be used to purchase sets of equipment, technical training, and Chinese experts. Mao may have given this aid in payment for diplomatic recognition, which Ghana had extended one year prior. On the other hand, since the agreement did not provide for the drawing of the funds until 1962, it was probably a way of testing Ghana's reaction and an effort to evoke certain changes in Ghana's foreign policy. It also provided China an opportunity to establish another base of operations in Western Africa. Ghana's was more revolutionary than Guinea demonstrated by its support of guerrilla movements in nearby Portuguese colonies, the Congo, and elsewhere. Perhaps Mao hoped to establish his own guerrilla bases or anticipated that he could send arms to African guerrillas through Ghana.

Peking, in addition, may have sought to exploit problems the Soviet Union experienced in Ghana and hoped to keep U.S. aid out of Ghana. Moscow had picked out Ghana as the most progressive country in the area and had extended considerable economic aid. By the end of 1960 Soviet aid promises totaled $82 million. But much of this was not used. Three million dollars was spent on surveying for a dam project which was never started, and Soviet planes were returned because they were too costly to operate. Moscow also took a considerable portion of Ghana's cocoa and other products resulting in a foreign exchange crisis.[23] The United States was considering a dam on the upper Volta River in Ghana and may have planned to supplant Soviet aid to Ghana. Some American politicians, however, were opposed. Chinese decision-makers may have perceived that their aid and their presence would cause the U.S. Congress to disapprove the project. Indeed this was the case.

Alternatively, Mao may have wanted to build trade ties with Ghana by using economic aid as a stimulant. China, at this time, wanted to alter the direction of its foreign trade and hoped to increase its trade with African countries. If this was a goal of Chinese aid, it was successful—one of the few cases where Chinese aid led to significant increases in trade. China found a market for its textiles, chemicals, machines, and hardware; in return, it bought cocoa, industrial diamonds, manganese, and timber.[24]

After 1962 several Chinese aid projects were started in Ghana. These included some freshwater fisheries, handicraft industries, rice paddies, and one or two industrial projects.[25] The government of Ghana confirmed that the projects were effective and helpful to its economic development. Thus in mid-1964 Peking extended another noninterest loan to Ghana in the amount of $22.5 million.[26] This was not the real value of this loan, however, because the unused portion of the earlier loan was included in this figure. It is uncertain how much of the earlier

loan remained outstanding. Peking also offered Ghana aid to help it finance more
guerrilla training camps. Documents found later suggest that by 1964 China had
military experts in Ghana and was conducting guerrilla training programs there.[27]
The new loan probably financed military assistance for revolutionary movements
in nearby countries or related to the second Afro-Asian Conference, which was
soon to be held in Algeria. Or, Mao may have wanted additional support for
China's nuclear test. In any case Ghana did support China's atomic test, and it
seemed to take a stance favoring China on the Conference.

In 1966 when President Nkrumah was in Peking talking with Chinese leaders, his government was overthrown. The Chinese Embassy was immediately informed by the new government to cut its diplomatic staff to eighteen and several
hundred Chinese technicians were asked to leave. Peking aggravated the situation
by openly criticizing the new regime, leading to a complete break in relations.
Subsequently, Nkrumah sought exile in Guinea and from there tried to organize
a movement to recapture power in Ghana. Peking offered $1 million to help
him.[28] But Nkrumah failed and the new government of Ghana established contacts with the West. It is uncertain how much aid China had delivered to Ghana
up to this time; but it is obvious that Chinese aid was being used—even at the
time Nkrumah was unexpectedly deposed. Thus, Peking's aid diplomacy suffered
an unexpected setback.

In February 1972 China restored its diplomatic ties with Ghana. In September an economic and technical agreement was signed, and in December it was
reported that Chinese agricultural teams were in Ghana and that Peking might
respond to a request for assistance on a dam project. Peking thus started to rebuild its relations with Ghana, and aid played a part. It is doubtful, however, that
Peking will be able to influence the government of Ghana the way it once did.
The present government is not as radical as Nkrumah's regime was. Also the recent
drought in Africa hit Ghana hard, forcing the government to appeal to the United
States for food aid. Ghana remains highly dependent on Western aid and
trade.

Aid to Mali

In September 1961 China made a loan to the government of Mali for $19.4
million.[29] No details were released on the use of this loan, suggesting that some
of it may have been intended for the purchase of military equipment. The implementation of the loan was also postdated, which probably meant that China
wanted some response from the Mali government before the loan could be
drawn. However, during the next year Chinese technicians were seen in Mali and
government officials commented about the effectiveness of Chinese aid. Apparently Peking got the response it wanted. The first Chinese assistance went to
agriculture, which required Chinese technicians and gave Peking a presence in

the country. In early 1963 another aid pact was reached and China agreed to help the Mali National Film Board produce newsreels. A few months later, China promised a textile mill.[30]

Mao was motivated to extend economic assistance to Mali because it was a left-leaning country and was one of the first independent nations in black Africa. Also Mali was close to Ghana and Guinea, where Peking had also made aid commitments. In addition, like Guinea and Ghana the Soviet Union had given Mali extensive aid that had not been very successful. One of Moscow's first aid projects to Mali was a railroad to link Mali to the sea through Guinea. The project was postponed and eventually cancelled, but not before considerable money had been spent. Some other Soviet projects failed and had to be taken over by U.S. companies.[31] It is noteworthy that China's promise of aid came when it was apparent that Soviet projects were not working and just after Russian aid advisors were withdrawn from China.

Chinese aid projects were quite successful, even though they were undertaken rather slowly. And aid elicited the responses Peking wanted. The government of Mali became an outspoken supporter of China on a number of foreign policy issues. Mali backed Peking's position on Taiwan, on the Nuclear Nontesting Agreement, on China's own atomic test, on the desirability of an Afro-Asian Conference rather than a nonaligned nations' meeting, and even on China's suggestion that a new United Nations be built (coinciding with Indonesia's withdrawal from the world body). In 1964 when Chou En-lai visited several African countries, he received a special reception in Mali. In his welcome speech President Keita mentioned the reasonable cost of Chinese aid, the ease with which the Chinese adapted to life in Mali, and their noninterference in Mali's affairs. It was in this context that Chou En-lai made a statement of China's aid policies, which has since been frequently repeated. (See Appendix A for the text of Chou's eight points governing foreign aid.) This statement was incorporated into a joint communiqué by the two nations, issued upon Chou's departure.

During 1965 several Chinese-built projects were completed in Mali, including a textile mill and a cigarette factory. In June 1966 another agreement was signed, and Peking promised $3 million more in aid to help Mali through a financial crisis.[32] The Mali government had just experienced a serious foreign trade imbalance as a result of its Socialist policies. Peking's motives for extending this aid were generally the same as for its initial aid.

Up to 1968 Chinese aid continued to flow to Mali, and it helped support Socialist programs—including communes. But it was not sufficient to stave off economic crisis, and in that year President Keita's government fell. The new government criticized his economic programs and sought aid and trade with the West. The large Chinese Embassy in Mali was reduced in size, and Chinese influence in Mali declined.

However, the new government chose a policy of nonalignment and apparently felt that it would demonstrate this by asking the Chinese to remain. Some

Chinese aid teams did stay. In December 1970 another agreement was signed on economic cooperation, suggesting that Chinese aid would continue. Probably one reason why Peking decided to stay was that Mali's new government did not appeal to the Soviet Union for aid. Mali remained quite critical of Moscow. Thus, China maintains a presence in Mali, but is not as active as it once was. And the flow of aid is considerably less. In view of Mali's recent difficulties with food shortages and its appeals to the U.S., Australia, and the United Nations, China's aid will be less influential for a while. It is noteworthy, however, that Peking continues to give aid to Mali at all in view of Mali's closer relations with the West.

Aid to Somalia

Peking probably extended some unofficial aid to Somalia in 1961. There were reports at that time that China had sent a grant of $130,000 in medical supplies and had extended technical assistance in building a radio station.[33] The first official aid, however, was not granted until August 1963 and took the form of a $3 million grant to help Somalia balance its budget, plus an $18 million interest-free loan.[34] The loan was designated for building a national hall and buying Chinese products. However, it may have been intended for other things, including a road, technical assistance, and weapons.

Mao aided Somalia primarily because of tension there resulting from a territorial dispute with Kenya and Ethiopia. Both Washington and Moscow were involved with the latter two countries, giving them aid and weapons. Therefore, China had an opportunity to aid the other side. In addition, Mao may have felt that he could start a guerrilla campaign against French Somaliland, a neighboring colony with whom Somalia was on bad terms. Finally, Somalia was a very poor country. Economic development had to begin at the grass roots, and China was equipped to assist in such development. The Soviet Union had given aid to Somalia, but most of its projects were not very helpful. They were generally inappropriate to Somalia's level of development and economic situation.[35] Hence, Peking may have believed it could both supplant Soviet aid and at the same time demonstrate its deftness in aiding poor countries.

Moscow responded to Chinese overtures to Somalia by stepping up its aid—especially military assistance. In 1963 the Soviet Union offered the government of Somalia $30 million in military aid.[36] Shortly after this offer was made, it delivered a dozen MIG fighters and some T-34 tanks. The aid agreement stipulated that Somalia could not receive aid from any other country. However, it is uncertain if this referred to military assistance alone and for how long.

In any case, this probably explains why little Chinese aid was delivered. Chinese projects promised in 1963 were not visible even by 1967. Peking simply may have chosen to wait and see how Moscow would resolve the contradiction of aiding both Kenya and Somalia when they were locked in mutual conflict. As a consequence, in 1967 Somalia's Prime Minister complained that China had cut its aid, delivered goods late, and then demanded cash payment. He did not reject Chinese aid though, and perhaps he said this to induce China to deliver aid and create some aid competition.

In late 1967 Peking negotiated the development of some rice and tobacco farms with the Somalia government. Chinese technicians arrived in Somalia at this time, and in March 1968 a Chinese aid team completed a theater. Other teams were working on an electric station. Medical missions and laborers were also seen. Aid was being delivered to Somalia, unlike many other African countries, in spite of the Cultural Revolution. And aid to Somalia provided the opportunity for a long criticism of Soviet aid to Somalia in the official Chinese newspaper.[37] The article drew from local sources, accusing Moscow of allowing its aid personnel to live like capitalist exploiters, of building aid projects to produce goods for European consumption, and of using aid to gain economic control. This article followed a dispute between the Somalia government and the Soviet Union. It was the most direct criticism of the Soviet Union in the aid field up to that time, and reflected growing competition between the two Communist countries in aid-giving.

Chinese aid projects in Somalia continued to become more active, and in June 1971 Peking negotiated a new aid agreement with the government of Somalia. Aid was promised for the building of two roads, one 1,400 kilometers in length. The value of this loan was later put at $110 million.[38] This was one of China's largest aid donations up to this time, and it was Peking's biggest road-building enterprise. Chinese aid personnel had gained considerable experience in road construction elsewhere and were apparently confident that this project would present no difficulty. The road had strategic value in that it would give central Somalia better access to its major port city and thus closer contact with China. It also promised to link Somalia to Tanzania, where Chinese interests were growing.

Mao was evidently moved to make such a large commitment by Soviet failures in Somalia and the opportunity to render Moscow an aid defeat. At the time of this grant Soviet military aid was still visible in Somalia. Hence, China may have wanted to convince Somalian leaders that it could and would supplant Soviet aid. The loan also represented an effort by Peking to demonstrate that the Cultural Revolution did not disrupt China's economy and that China was determined to play a major role in world affairs by helping the developing countires. No doubt Mao was also influenced by China's investments in Tanzania and Zambia and by his growing interests in the Middle East and East Africa.

The Chinese aid promise prompted the Soviet Union to accept a previously rejected dam project and to reopen discussions on more arms shipments.[39] Up to the end of 1974 the Soviet Union had promised Somalia $90 million in economic aid and $50 million in arms. Its arms aid was crucial to Somalia's defense against

Kenya, who the Soviet Union was also arming. Thus, although Moscow gained considerable leverage over the Somalia armed forces, it was not able to win as much influence over the government as it might have otherwise. Also Moscow's aid was given in large part to finance its own naval expansion in the area; thus considerable money was spent on port facilities.[40]

Although the Soviet Union maintains about 400 advisors in Somalia and has aroused considerable apprehension in the West as a result of its facilities in Somalia, it has not erased Chinese influence. The government of Somalia finds it convenient to receive aid from both. And for the present, both Moscow and Peking are willing to aid Somalia despite the other. Whether this situation will remain is uncertain.

Aid to Tanzania

Before Tanganyika and Zanzibar united to form the nation of Tanzania, China had given aid to both. In February 1964, after a coup in Zanzibar, Peking promised the new government a free grant of $0.5 million.[41] This gift was intended to ingratiate the Chinese with the new regime, foster stability, and prevent another coup. Chinese engineers began work on a road in Zanzibar at that time, and it is possible that the aid funds went for that. In June Peking extended a loan to Zanzibar for $14 million designated for project aid.[42] But Chinese arms and equipment began to appear in Zanzibar at this time, probably accounting for most or all of the loan.

In May 1964 China made a small grant of $10,000 to Tanganyika.[43] It was labeled nonrepayable, but the use was not specified. Apparently it was intended to facilitate friendly relations with China in anticipation of the union of the two countries. Chou En-lai had just returned from a trip to Africa. He reported on the revolutionary situation in Eastern Africa and was apparently impressed with the possibility of a Chinese base of operations when Tanzania was formed. It is also noteworthy that this coincided with the failure of the revolutionary movement in the Congo and setbacks for China in Western Africa and Algeria. Peking sought a new protégé. Chinese leaders were also anticipating China's first atomic bomb test in 1964 and were working on a missile delivery system. This would eventually involve building an intercontinental ballistic missile which would be tested in the Indian Ocean. Tanzania was an ideal location for tracking facilities.

In mid-1964, when the union of the two countries took place, Peking announced aid promises to Tanzania in the form of a $2.8 million gift and a $42 million loan.[44] The loan was interest-free and repayable over a twenty-year period. Mentioned in the aid announcement were a textile mill, a farm-implements factory, an agricultural research station, a broadcasting station, a printing factory, and an irrigation system. Setting a precedent, the agreement also mentioned weapons and military training. In September Chinese arms and advisors were seen in Tanzania.[45] Some Chinese weapons were subsequently sent to the Congo, Tanzania being the transshipment point. In addition, Tanzanian troops made a foray into Mozambique in October—probably after some encouragement by Chinese advisors.[46] Chinese propaganda supported the raid.

In January 1965 further aid talks were held between the governments of China and Tanzania, and subsequently Peking dispatched several agricultural aid teams. A few months later, China delivered forty trucks for project assistance. President Nyerere responded by supporting China's position on a new "revolutionary" U.N., on the Afro-Asian Conference, and on other issues. He had already supported China's atomic test.

In June 1965 Chou En-lai visited Tanzania and initiated talks on the Tanzania-Zambia Railroad project. This marked a turning point in China's aid to Tanzania—an increase in Peking's commitments severalfold. It also showed a change in China's policy of building small projects that could be completed quickly and easily. (Due to the importance of this project, it is discussed separately later in this chapter.) Mao was apparently spurred to action by sizeable Soviet promises of military aid to Tanzania at this time, which meant that China's aid efforts might be nullified. This had happened in a number of countries after 1960. So Mao made the decision to commit his nation to bigger projects and more aid to countries where China had major interests. In the case of Tanzania, the reduction of American aid and the rejection of the railroad by Western companies were also incentives.

Although it committed a monumental sum to the railroad project, China also extended other aid to Tanzania. In June 1966 Peking sent four patrol boats.[47] A few months later Mao offered more aid in the form of a $2.8 million gift and a $5.6 million loan.[48] Almost at this same time, in July 1966, it was announced that the Sino-Tanzanian Maritime Transport Joint–Stock Company had been established. Peking provided $2.1 million in the form of a loan for Tanzania's share of the company.[49] In subsequent months more Chinese aid projects were finished and more begun. A textile mill was completed and a printing company started. In June 1967 the Tanzania government publicized the opening of the China-Tanzania Air Cargo Company. In early 1968 President Nyerere announced the building of a state farm project covering seven thousand acres, with an investment of over one million dollars provided by Chinese aid.[50]

During 1967-1968 projects of various kinds were started or continued: rural roads, two teachers' colleges, a police training academy, fisheries, poultry breeding stations, dams, a stadium, an art institute, etc. A state farm in Zanzibar managing 1,300 acres was opened. It was reported at this time that 3,000 Chinese technicians were in Tanzania in addition to those working on the railroad project.[51]

In 1969-1970 even more new projects were undertaken. These included a radio broadcasting station, a shoe factory, another textile mill, irrigation projects, medical assistance, etc.[52] There is no doubt that China had both a greater variety and a larger number of projects in Tanzania than in any other country it was aiding. In short, economic development in Tanzania was almost totally in the hands of the Chinese.

In 1970 military representatives from Tanzania visited Peking, and an agreement on military assistance was apparently signed. Shortly after, it was reported that China had started construction on a naval base in Tanzania.[53] In July a Chinese-built military hospital opened in Dar-es-Salaam. Chinese military aid at this juncture helped counter the threat, or perceived threat, of Portuguese troops in Mozambique on Tanzania's southern border, as well as intimidation from militarily superior Rhodesia and South Africa. In addition neighboring Somalia and Uganda were receiving Soviet military hardware and presented a possible threat to Tanzania.

In early 1971 Peking sent still more military aid to Tanzania: two 100-ton patrol boats (in addition to six gunboats delivered in late 1970), sixteen tanks, twenty-four field guns, one hundred military trucks, and large quantities of jeeps, mortars, and small arms. It was also reported that a Chinese military mission of 300 to 400 men was helping train the Tanzanian army.[54] In April 1972 the head of the Tanzanian Defense Forces announced that an air base was under construction eighty miles west of Dar-es-Salaam. This base, according to his statement, was being built with Chinese assistance and would be equipped with at least one squadron of Chinese-built MIG fighters in 1973.[55] Three hundred Tanzanian pilots were in China at this time receiving training; they were scheduled to return in 1973.[56] In addition, Peking reported building a powerful radar station in Tanzania, capable of tracking both missiles and planes.[57]

The value of Chinese military aid to Tanzania is uncertain, though it has been estimated at about one-half of China's total weapons assistance to African nations, which was put at $200 million during the period 1966–1970.[58] $100 million to $150 million may be reasonable or perhaps is too low. Including the squadron of fighter planes and the equipment and training required to keep it operating, Chinese aid may now be much more than this. Clearly, Tanzania at this time became one of the two major recipients of Chinese military aid outside the Communist bloc.

During 1972–1973 Chinese aid continued to pour into Tanzania—both economic development projects and military aid. Also work continued on the huge railroad project. In March 1974 China extended another interest-free loan to Tanzania worth $75 million, designated for the development of coal and iron mines in the south.[59] Tanzania at this time was hard hit by currency revaluations and by increases in the price of oil. Drought also hit; fifty thousand poeple were reported suffering from famine in April 1974. In addition, Tanzania's agricultural production declincd as a result of agricultural collectivization. China's aid was probably aimed at helping the Tanzania government resolve all of these problems.

Needless to say, Peking's largess has had a considerable impact. After 1964, trade between the two countries increased markedly. From 1964 to 1966 Chinese exports to Tanzania increased more than tenfold.[60] Tanzanian exports to China also increased rapidly. The influx of Chinese goods into Tanzania has been such that Western products are now seldom seen. Chinese aid has also influenced Tanzania's domestic policies. In 1967 the Tanzania government announced that English would no longer be the language of official business. At the same time, President Nyerere nationalized the banks and major industries in Tanzania, many of which were in the hands of Western companies. In 1968 he expelled Indian merchants. Later, other steps were taken to socialize the economy, and in January 1969 a "Cultural Revolution" was announced in Tanzania.

In foreign affairs the Tanzanian government followed the Chinese line on almost everything. Nyerere supported Peking's claim to Taiwan, its bid to lead the underdeveloped nations, etc. He also took China's side in the Sino-Soviet dispute. And, he allowed China to use Tanzanian territory to aid revolutionary movements elsewhere in Africa. In 1968 Chinese military aid was sent to Biafra from Tanzania.[61] Recently Tanzania has helped rebel groups in the white-ruled countries to the south with Chinese weapons. In short, Tanzania became China's spokesman and partner in Africa.

Tanzania is also a showcase of Chinese aid. China has demonstrated that it can support a large African country and keep it from depending on Western countries or the Soviet Union. Chinese aid personnel have likewise demonstrated their ability to build a major project—bigger than the Aswan Dam. They have also proved their abilities in a variety of other projects. Peking has in short shown that it is able to engineer economic development in a poor country on a broad front. In so doing China has won considerable publicity and acclaim for its aid program and its aid policies. And it has won credibility for its commitment to the poor nations and to Africa.

China's success has not, however, been purely a matter of the capabilities of its aid diplomacy. There are other important factors. During the period 1964–1969, Tanzania estimated that 78 percent of its development budget would be financed from external sources—mostly aid and investment from Western countries.[62] Only 34 percent materialized. U.S. aid to Africa declined markedly at this time. Soviet aid was promised in considerable quantities but was not delivered. Once Tanzania committed itself to Chinese aid, both the U.S. and the Soviet Union nearly shut off their aid. Tanzania's political behavior also had a negative effect on its search for trade and aid elsewhere. In 1965, for example, Dar-es-Salaam broke diplomatic relations with Britain over London's policy toward Rhodesia. This resulted in losing a $21 million loan. At almost the same time it lost West German military aid by recognizing East Germany. Canada also stopped its military assistance to Tanzania.

And Chinese aid has not been problem free. Although Peking's aid has generally been sufficient to supplant other aid and Chinese goods have replaced Western products, the transition has not been entirely smooth. The massive and not altogether well-planned influx of Chinese goods has suppressed the development of some industries in Tanzania. Also the Tanzania government has accumulated a large debt that will not be easy to repay. Further, it is questionable whether China can easily absorb enough of Tanzania's exports to repay its loans. Peking may have to resell many products on the world market. Finally, there is still a demand for Western goods in Tanzania. With the supply almost cut off, prices have increased rapidly, and black marketing has become much more profitable.

Nevertheless, there is no direct threat to aid relations between the two countries. China's aid to Tanzania will no doubt continue. Tanzania is commited to China and has little to gain by seeking Western or Soviet aid. To the Chinese, Tanzania is a better demonstration of China's abilities than other major recipients—North Vietnam, North Korea, and Pakistan. Tanzania is clearly China's most outstanding aid recipient.

Aid to Zambia

Peking first extended aid to Zambia in early 1964 in the form of a $0.5 million grant, probably to win recognition or to influence Zambia's position on the Afro-Asian Conference.[63] In 1967 the first official aid agreement was signed: China offered a $16.8 million loan that was interest free.[64] The use of this loan was unspecified. The date suggests that it was given to help Zambia through budgetary difficulties, following the crisis in Rhodesia which interrupted Zambia's export trade. Alternatively the loan might have been made to pay for Zambia's share in the surveying for the Tanzania-Zambia Railroad project, which was begun at this time. In any case, it was not immediately used. Then in February 1969 it was reported that China had agreed to build a 254-mile road in Zambia and that the funds were to come from the 1967 loan. Chinese technicians arrived in October, and work on the road started shortly thereafter.[65]

After construction began on the road in 1969, China began to provide other aid to Zambia, including technical assistance to build two radio transmitters. Simultaneously work began on the Tan-Zam Railroad. Although it started in Tanzania, survey and other preparatory work was being done in Zambia. China's major aim in providing aid for a road and for radio transmitters was probably to increase its influence as a prelude to starting the railroad project. Or Mao may have wanted to block other countries from building roads that might compete with the railroad. This, in fact, happened later.

Chinese leaders may also have perceived that the radicalization of Zambian politics, furthered by the Rhodesian crisis, gave them an opportunity to make significant inroads. Despite large doses of foreign aid, Zambia suffered economically from the crisis. And as the immediate effect of the crisis blew over, aid promises to Zambia diminished. In this connection Mao may have believed that

Zambia was destined to be a base for guerrilla operations against the white-ruled regimes to the south. He probably envisioned lasting conflict between the countries of black Africa and the white-ruled nations.

Peking may also have had some interest in Zambia's copper. Although it could not have hoped to buy a major portion of Zambia's copper exports, China was importing copper. Or, Peking may possibly have anticipated the development of sellers' cooperatives among the developing countries and hoped to gain some influence over them. Recent events following the oil crisis have, of course, made this more realistic. The possibility of a copper exporting cartel seemed good at that time. China also supported the trend toward Socialism in Zambia. In December 1969 "workers' councils" were established, and various other moves were made toward centralizing the economy and building Socialism. Legislation was passed limiting the profits that foreign companies could take out of the country, and many firms were nationalized. In other words, Zambia was following the Socialist model for economic development. Mao wanted it to be his model rather than the Kremlin's.

In 1970 Chinese aid diplomacy came under criticism by Zambians. It was said that Chinese medical help did not meet Zambia's standards. Also, the radio stations that were promised earlier and were to be finished by 1970 were not in operation, allegedly due to the fact that Peking did not provide the kind of technical equipment required.[66] This may have reflected some hesitation on the part of the Zambian government to become dependent on Chinese aid thus eliminating other donors; or it mirrored a desire for more extensive commitments on China's part.

Nevertheless work continued on the road, and in late 1972 it was reported that a 282-meter bridge was finished and that the major part of the road west from the capital was usable. When tension rose with Rhodesia again in late 1972, this road was used to carry Zambian copper ore to the Tanzanian border where it was loaded on freight cars of the Tan-Zam Railroad and shipped to the coast. This was a plus for China's foreign aid to Zambia.

In July 1973 it was reported that China extended a new loan worth $10 million to Zambia, but no further details were available on the loan.[67] In February 1974 Peking negotiated still another loan with the Zambia government and provided credits totalling $51 million.[68] The purpose of this aid was apparently to bolster Zambia's economy, in view of the failure of its tobacco crop that year and the drastic drop in copper prices during the same period.

China continues to give aid to Zambia, and its aid diplomacy there must be considered a success notwithstanding certain criticisms on the part of Zambians and despite the fact that it is not the outstanding success aid to Tanzania has been. If the unwillingness of the Soviet Union to offer aid is any measure of China's success, then it can be said that China has had little difficulty in Zambia. It remains questionable whether China will be able or willing to continue aid to Zambia in the amounts and kind that may be needed. China is not capable of using Zambia's copper exports, nor is it able to market them. Peking's success in Zambia may hinge on the utility of the Tan-Zam Railroad, which is discussed in following pages. The advantages and problems associated with the railroad apply to China's aid to Zambia in general.

The Tanzania-Zambia Railroad Project

The Tan-Zam Railroad is the biggest and most important foreign aid project China has undertaken. The project will cost at least $400 million. It is also one of the single most expensive aid projects undertaken by any nation, and it is by far the largest construction project in Tanzania or Zambia. In terms of cost, it outranks the Soviet's Aswan Dam project in Egypt. It is a major undertaking for China, and its magnitude indicates new directions in China's foreign aid program. It likewise suggests various salient changes in China's foreign policy. Thus China's motives for undertaking the project will be analyzed before looking at the actual work on the project attempting to assess its worth and implications.

First, the Tan-Zam Railroad project represents a change in China's aid guidelines. Up to this point, China has financed mostly small projects in terms of both the money committed and the time required to complete them. This project is an exception, demonstrating that Peking feels confident about its technological capabilities and financial resources. It may also reflect a greater commitment to foreign aid. Equally important, it is an attempt to insure that China's aid efforts will not be outdone by one of the superpowers. China has been literally pushed out of a number of countries through large aid offers by the United States or the Soviet Union, especially the latter. This project is so large that the two recipient countries cannot easily undertake other aid projects or consider competitive schemes.

Second, the Tan-Zam project insures China a base of operations in Africa and reflects China's geographical or geopolitical interest in Western Africa. Peking is already using Tanzania and Zambia as a center from which to expand its influence in the area. After the start of this project Peking expanded its aid commitments to include other nations in the region; thus it may be seen as part of an effort by Mao to establish a sphere of interest. And since Peking's support for wars of national liberation has diminished, it hints that in the future Peking's efforts to generate revolution may be sublimated into struggles for economic development. This mirrors a confidence by Chinese leaders in stable development of this part of Africa.

Third, the project may be seen as proof for China's commitment to the African continent. Since the project was refused by the West, its successful completion will attest to China's willingness to help African countries. Likewise it adheres to Peking's desire to help the poor countries. It will certainly attract the attention of developing countries and give Peking a reputation among Third

World nations like the Aswan Dam did for the Soviet Union. Mao clearly appears to be bidding for the role of spokesman and leader of the developing nations. Completion of the project will also support Peking's charges that the U.S., the Soviet Union, and Europe do not want to give genuine aid to the poor countries and help them develop economically.

The need for the project became evident in 1964 when Zambia became independent. Zambia needed an outlet to the sea and a route for the flow of its copper, without going through one of the white-ruled countries to the south. This was underscored in 1965 when Rhodesia declared its independence, and England called for an oil embargo. Rhodesia passed its problem along to Zambia who obtained its oil through Rhodesia. It also increased the tariff on Zambian copper going through Rhodesia to pay for more expensive sources of petroleum. Several Western countries responded by giving economic aid to Zambia and by starting construction of an oil pipeline into Zambia. But many other goods had to be airlifted to Zambia, and the need for a railroad became immediately evident.

In 1963 Zambia and Tanzania submitted a proposal to the World Bank for financial assistance to build a railroad. However, the project was rejected on the grounds that economic development in the two countries would be better served by other projects. In 1966 a survey was conducted by an Anglo-Canadian Consortium, which also ended in a rejection.[69] China was invited to take part in discussions on the problem, and in August 1965 sent a team that made a feasibility study. In November Rhodesia issued its declaration. For two years undisclosed negotiations were held between China and the two countries. Both Zambia and Tanzania continued to bargain with the West, and perhaps all along hoped for Western aid to build the project. However, this was not forthcoming. President Nyerere remarked later that Tanzania had no alternate proposals to choose from. Noting how the West and the Soviet Union had shunned Tanzania after China promised military aid, he probably assumed that there was no hope that Western companies would take the project.[70]

In September 1967 China signed an agreement with Tanzania and Zambia committing economic and technical aid for the project. Peking offered between $340 million and $400 million in aid for the railroad.[71] Surveying was supposed to start immediately and was to be finished in fifteen months. However, even after this agreement was signed, there was some question as to whether it would be carried out. Some observers felt that Tanzania and Zambia may have signed the pact to force the Western countries to change their attitude toward the project. Also there was doubt about whether China had sufficient foreign exchange to finance a project of such size. It was argued that generating finances locally would interfere with the domestic economies of both recipient countries. It was also questioned whether China could provide the engineers and technicians for the project as well as the equipment and supplies. And it was known that Tanzania and Zambia did not sympathize completely with Mao's efforts to instigate wars of national liberation on the continent. Thus, some observers wondered whether Peking had sufficient motive to go ahead with the project and whether Tanzania and Zambia would accept a Chinese offer. Mao had cause to be apprehensive of the stability of African countries in view of the frequency of coups there. And the two African countries had cause to question China's motives and its capabilities.

Nevertheless, in April 1968 three protocol agreements were signed: on the form of the loan, on the use of Chinese technical personnel, and on the working conditions of Chinese laborers.[72] Shortly afterwards a group of Chinese technicians arrived, and in November it was announced that surveying was going successfully and that the project was probably feasible. During 1969 Peking dispatched more technicians, and further talks were held on the actual building of the railroad. During the winter, equipment and supplies arrived from China.

In April 1970 all three parties announced that the surveying was done and that work on the project would begin. In October construction was inaugurated, and it was revealed that the cost of the project was $401 million and that China had provided an interest-free loan in that amount repayable over a thirty-year period beginning in 1983.[73] Both Presidents Nyerere and Kaunda made speeches praising China's generous aid and made reference to efforts by the imperialists to impede progress on the railroad.

In November 1971 it was announced that the first 313 miles of track had been laid and that trains were running on this part of the line carrying construction equipment and supplies.[74] In December, on the tenth anniversary of Tanzania's independence, President Nyerere entertained foreign guests by taking them for a twenty-minute ride on the train. At the end of the year there were 14,000 Chinese in Tanzania working on the project and construction was moving ahead rapidly.[75] Peking promised 102 locomotives, 100 passenger cars, and 2,000 freight cars for the railroad; and a few of these had arrived.[76]

In 1972 Rhodesia again closed its border with Zambia to cut off the infiltration of guerrilla troops operating from Zambia. Thus Zambia had to seek another route for the export of its copper. In January 1973 copper ore from Zambia was shipped on the part of the rail line that was finished to the east coast of Tanzania. In addition, 70,000 tons of materials were being imported into Zambia by the same route.[77] Thus the railroad was proving its worth; it was accomplishing its primary mission, that of giving Zambia an outlet to the sea, without going through one of the white-controlled countries to the south.

In September 1973 a ceremony was held on the Tanzania-Zambia border marking the completion of the railroad to that point. About half—or 556 miles— remained to be completed in Zambia.[78] In April 1974 the roadbed had been finished to the town of Mwenzo in northern Zambia, where it was carrying supplies for the final work on the line. It was 1,160 miles long and linked up with Zambia's existing railroad network. Final completion was set for 1976.[79]

Although the Tan-Zam Railroad project will no doubt be completed on time and will be of considerable benefit to both Tanzania and Zambia, the project has not been without problems. An examination of the nature and seriousness of these problems and the efforts made to resolve them will provide the basis for some conclusions concerning the ultimate success of the undertaking.

The most obvious problem for both sides is the cost. China is not a rich country and does not have large reserves of foreign currencies. In addition, what resources China has to devote to economic development it can use itself. Thus the project has caused a drain on China's resources and has used up precious foreign exchange. Peking has minimized the use of foreign currency by using its own materials for construction of the project. Also, expenditures for the project have been spread out over a period of several years. During the period 1965-1967 China spent very little on the project. During 1968-1969 it spent less than $7 million. Under $70 million was estimated as the annual expenditure from 1970 until the project is completed.[80] Since the loan is without interest, the cost to China is considerable. Peking has compensated for this by raising the cost of surveying, equipment, materials, etc. The estimate made by the World Bank in 1963 for the project, not including interest, was $163 million. A later estimate by another Western group was higher but still considerably lower than the Chinese estimate.[81] Peking gave the loan without interest for propaganda reasons but made up for this by pricing the goods it provided higher. It has done this on loans it has made to other countries. Another way that China has kept its costs low is by supplying its own technicians and workers. Of the Chinese aid personnel working on the project, two-thirds are laborers.[82] China has an oversupply of labor and seems to have a sufficient number of technicians of the kind used for railroad building.

Tanzania and Zambia have generated the funds for their part of the project by importing Chinese goods, which are sold in the two countries. Sixty percent of the project is to be financed this way, which means that each country will have to purchase more than $120 million in Chinese goods.[83] Since both Tanzania and Zambia traditionally traded with Western countries, the changeover to Chinese goods presents some problems to local consumers. Some consumer products will not be available or will be obtainable only at high prices. This has already engendered the smuggling of Western consumer products. Furthermore, the importation of goods such as textiles, which are also produced locally in both Tanzania and Zambia, has had the effect of stifling native industry. Since the list of things that the two countries can import from China is quite limited, this is an unavoidable problem. In 1970 the Minister of Commerce in Tanzania remarked that China had flooded the market with certain goods.[84] Zambian businessmen have complained that Chinese textiles threaten local industry in Zambia. Yet, since Chinese products will probably not amount to more than 5 and 10 percent of Zambia's and Tanzania's imports respectively, both can probably adjust.[85] Repayment of the loan over a long period of time will also lessen this impact.

Tanzania and Zambia will suffer from a related problem in exporting local products to China to repay the loan. China needs such things as cotton, sisal, copra, tobacco, and copper. Since these exports have traditionally gone to the West, Zambia and Tanzania will no doubt experience further shortages of foreign exchange if they export large quantities of these goods to China. China imports considerable amounts of copper, but at the same time that it started the Tan-Zam project it began to grant aid to Chile and bought Chilean copper. In 1971 Peking had a considerable stockpile of copper. It is ironic that the overthrow of the leftist government in Chile may be a blessing in disguise for China. As the stockpile is used up, China will be able to import more Zambian copper. However, China will not be able to use more than a small part of Zambia's total export of copper.

Another problem that has arisen is China's obligation to supply all of the construction materials and equipment for the project. In 1969 the Chinese government purchased a number of large bulldozers from Japan. Later ninety-seven of these were sent to Tanzania for use on this project.[86] China manufactures tracks, locomotives, and rolling stock sufficient for local needs and has so far been able to meet the needs of this project as well. But the Cultural Revolution and increased aid to North Vietnam probably lessened Peking's capabilities. It remains uncertain if China will be able to deliver all of the cars and other equipment for full utilization of the railroad.

Still another problem is the large number of Chinese aid personnel in Tanzania and Zambia. The number of Chinese there has reached nearly 20,000, and certainly some are experiencing difficulties living in a different climate, eating different food, etc. Rigid discipline has been imposed on them and they live in seclusion. Thus far no serious problems are known. However, because of their unwillingness to mingle with the local population, the charge has been made that they are no different than the white imperialists of the past. Also there have been rumors that, like the Indian workers who came to work on a railroad in East Africa under British auspices, they may not go home. In 1970 a newspaper in Nairobi published a picture showing a recruiter in China promising volunteers free land in Tanzania if they would go there to work on the railroad project.[87] Although the picture was denounced by President Nyerere as an imperialist plot, it no doubt reflects such a fear among local residents in Tanzania and Zambia. Mao has tried to counteract this problem by sending medical teams and sponsoring cultural interchange programs with the people in the area of the project. Whoever built this project would encounter apprehension and fear by the local people. And it is difficult to say whether the self-imposed isolationism by the Chinese is a wise policy or not; it does avoid problems, yet it causes charges of aloofness and racial superiority.

Finally, an American-financed road is under construction in Tanzania. So far, work on the road has not been smooth and is behind schedule. It has been a source of inspiration to the Chinese finish the railroad ahead of schedule. And it has made good propaganda material for Peking. Nevertheless, the road will compete with the railroad. And when it is finished, it will be easier to use, since Tanzania already has trucks and can easily buy more. The Tan-Zam Railroad was not intended to be profitable when it was started; it was undertaken largely for political reasons. Thus China may thus have to continue to support the project after it is finished.

So far, however, the railroad has been a success for China's aid diplomacy. The project has demonstrated Peking's technological capabilities and its determination to help Zambia and Tanzania struggle against the white governments of Africa. Peking has likewise made considerable propaganda mileage on the project. It is a symbol of China's commitment to the black African countries and the underdeveloped countries at large. It bolsters Mao's bid for leadership of the underdeveloped nations. It is hardly coincidence that China frequently mentions the project in this connection and has asked Tanzania and Zambia to publicize the project and support Peking's leadership of the "have not" countries.

China has also won a struggle with the Soviet Union. It has built a bigger project than Moscow in Africa, and Soviet aid cannot outdo Chinese aid in Tanzania and Zambia. Their commitment has already been made. Mao has also gained a foothold in a vital area in Africa, one that may be crucial if the Soviet navy challenges China's presence in Africa or tries to interfere with its international trade.

But the project is still a gamble. It is certainly questionable whether it will be profitable, and in the long run this may ultimately determine whether it is worthwhile or not. The American-built road will compete. Rhodesia may open up its border again. With the independence of Portugal's colonies, tension may decline in Africa. The international market prices of Zambia's exports, especially copper, will be a factor. Recently the international market price of copper has declined. There are certainly many unknown variables that will influence the ultimate success or failure of this project.

Aid to Kenya

In May 1964 China and Kenya signed a cultural and economic agreement, which contained a provision whereby China would extend aid to Kenya in the form of a $2.8 million cash gift and a $15 million interest-free loan.[88] The loan was to be used over a five-year period and would pay for the use of Chinese technicians. China's aid may have been given to express appreciation for diplomatic recognition. Kenya recognized Peking immediately upon independence—in spite of the fact that it had received some flood relief aid from Taipei. Mao also sought a greater presence in western Africa particularily a base of operations to aid the revolution in the Congo. This probably explains why the aid agreement contained a provision for the use of Chinese technicians. Chinese arms and supplies were subsequently seen in Nairobi, presumably enroute to the Congo.[89] Or Peking may have planned to use its official connections with the Kenya government to aid revolutionaries in Kenya. At the same time that diplomatic relations were exchanged, the Kenya police intercepted a convoy of 75 tons of Chinese weapons whose destination was not known.[90]

Alternatively, Chinese aid may have been given to allay Kenyan concern over Chinese military aid to Somalia in view of their territorial dispute. Aid to Kenya may have been intended to show that China supported Somalia's territorial claims against Ethiopia and French Somalialand but not Kenya. Or Mao may have intended to buy Kenya's support at the upcoming Afro-Asian Conference. Chinese aid money was used to bribe several public officials in Kenya, including Home Minister Odinga. A branch chairman of the Kenya African Union and some important trade union officers also received Chinese monetary "gifts."[91]

Nevertheless little Chinese aid was drawn. Kenya was receiving large quantities of economic aid from Western countries; Britain alone had contributed $300 million by the time China presented its first offer. Also, the U.S., West Germany, and Japan were major donors. In addition, in the very same month that China made its aid promise, Moscow made an offer of $44 million.[92] For these reasons, Peking used aid funds to help revolutionary groups overthrow the government. In 1966 it was reported that Peking was providing military training to rebel groups without the official consent of the Kenya government. Later Kenya officials said that Mao was trying to overthrow their government and had spent up to $1 million to accomplish this.[93] At this same time, Kenyan newspapers said that Chinese aid only allowed for the purchase of goods so low in quality as to be unsalable, or goods that Kenya was producing in ample quantity.[94] In 1967 it was reported that none of the Chinese loan had been drawn.[95]

In June 1967 Kenya declared the Chinese Charge d'Affaires persona non grata—the fourth Chinese official expelled in two years. Subsequently Peking was accused of distributing "seditious pamphlets." In 1969 and 1970 bomb explosions were reported by Chinese officials in or at the Chinese Embassy.[96] In this context, no further aid was promised and the aid already granted was not used.

In summary, China used its aid funds for other than the stated purposes, i.e., to aid rebels in Kenya and elsewhere. Very little aid was actually given to the Kenyan government. Thus Chinese aid was more promise than reality. Peking took a gamble in Kenya, but lost. In financial terms, however, its losses were very small. Since 1973 Peking has made some moves to restore official contacts with the Kenya government. In 1974 the Chinese Red Cross made a donation to Kenya of nearly $0.5 million.[97] But this did not lead to an improvement in relations and thus was not followed by the reinstatement of earlier aid promises or the establishment of new ones. In view of Kenya's other aid sources and a legacy of suspicion on Kenya's part a meaningful aid relationship probably won't be established and China's aid diplomacy to Kenya must be considered a failure.

Aid to the Congo Republic (Brazzaville)

In July 1964 Peking offered the government of the Republic of the Congo (Brazzaville) an interest-free loan in the amount of $5.6 million.[98] This loan was called a development loan but was apparently used by the Brazzaville government to balance its budget. The next month Peking gave a $25,000 grant for refugee relief.[99] In October the Brazzaville government announced it had received an interest-free loan for approximately $20 million.[100] Whether this was another loan or an increase of the first one is uncertain.

China's major concern was a "war of national liberation" that was in progress in the other Congo. At this time the rebels controlled roughly one-fifth of the country and had broad international support for their cause. Peking's $20 million grant thus can be seen as a response to U.S. and Belgian intervention, which was followed by a storm of protest throughout Africa. The Soviet Union opposed U.S. intervention but did not take any aggressive actions. Mao hoped to goad Khrushchev into taking positive action or to debunk his "nonrevolutionary" position. Peking's efforts may also have been aimed at the United Nations, under whose auspices the U.S. and Belgium acted. Or Mao may have sought support from the Brazzaville government for his position on the coming Afro-Asian Conference. Leaders in the Congo Republic were revolutionaries and might have been expected to take China's side on many international issues. They were disappointed with Moscow and angry at the West.

In late 1964 the Soviet Union also offered aid to Brazzaville, though it did not match Chinese aid. This may have induced Peking to give more aid or promptly deliver what is had promised. During 1965 talks were held in Peking with Congo leaders on three occasions, and each time aid was discussed.[101] Nothing was published on these talks except at the last meeting in September, when a document was signed on the construction of a textile mill. Probably these talks centered on military aid and the revolutionary movement in the nearby Belgium Congo. At this time a large Chinese arms shipment was seized in Kenya, apparently heading for Brazzaville. Chinese arms were also being transshipped through Algeria and other African countries for eventual use in the Congo. Brazzaville, however, provided the best point of dissemination or final transshipment.[102] In addition, the Brazzaville government was directly involved in the conflict and French military aid was halted for this reason. Peking's military assistance made up for this.

Although the revolt in the neighboring Congo began to fizzle out at this time, Peking wanted to keep it going. And Chinese leaders sought to start revolution elsewhere. Brazzaville served as a revolutionary base. In 1967 a radio station constructed with Chinese aid funds was completed and provided coverage for a radius of 6,000 miles. It identified itself as the "Voice of the Congolese Revolution."[103] It was also reported that Chinese advisors were providing guerrilla training to revolutionaries from five nearby countries: Congo (Kinshasa), the

Central African Republic, Chad, Cameroon, and Gabon. And in September 1968 Peking delivered a sizeable shipment of arms to Angolan revolutionaries based in the Congo Republic.[104]

During 1969 a Chinese-built textile mill was finished near Brazzaville and an agreement was concluded whereby Chinese aid would be used to build a shipyard.[105] Apparently this facility would repair both civilian and military vessels. In 1970 Peking promised to send medical missions to Brazzaville and agreed on a ship-building project to be financed by Chinese aid. A military agreement was also signed whereby China would provide heavy equipment to the Congo's armed forces.[106]

In early 1972 China signed an agreement on military aid to Brazzaville but no details were released. In October an agreement was signed on economic and technical cooperation and aid was mentioned.[107] Shortly thereafter Brazzaville announced that it had received another loan for $391,000.[108] In December a protocol was signed on the construction of a dam using Chinese aid. In July 1973 Peking promised another loan estimated at worth $20 million to $40 million.[109] In February 1975 Congolese President Lopez visited Peking, and another economic agreement was signed. This may have concerned earlier aid, or could have included fresh aid. In any event, China's aid to the Congo is still being delivered.

Chinese aid to Brazzaville was vital to building good relations between the two countries. And it has sustained close ties. Brazzaville has been one of the most adamant supporters of China's foreign policy aims in general and Mao's efforts to spread revolution in Africa. In terms of per capita aid and military assistance delivered, Brazzaville is among China's major recipients in Africa. This plus the little aid that Brazzaville has received from the West or the Soviet Union goes far to explain the continuing close relations between Brazzaville and Peking.

Aid to the Central African Republic

In September 1964 Mao extended a credit to the government of the Central African Republic for $4 million.[110] In view of the timing, it seems that this loan bought diplomatic recognition or was a reward for such. Also, the Central African Republic sought aid and endeavored to adopt a more clearly nonaligned foreign policy. Peking may have seen this as an opportunity to advance its policies in the area. Mao may have felt that he could win support from the Central African Republic for China's position at the scheduled Afro-Asian Conference. In fact, Chinese diplomats tried to persuade the government of the Central African Republic to oppose the participation of the Soviet Union, but this they refused to do.

Very little of this small promise of aid was drawn during 1964–1965. Then in January 1966 the Central African Republic government was overthrown, and the new leadership accused China of supporting armed revolt in the country. The new president provided the press with documents and showed them Chinese arms to prove these allegations. Whether these charges were true or not, relations deteriorated between the two countries, and shortly after, diplomatic ties were broken. Needless to say, no aid was delivered after that. To date, this situation has not changed, and Peking must consider the Central African Republic a failure for its aid diplomacy, even though little aid was actually delivered.

Aid to Uganda

In April 1965, when Ugandan President Obote visited Peking, Mao offered him $15 million in aid in the form of a $3 million grant and a $12 million interest-free loan.[111] Half the loan was given in convertible currency, the other half in goods and services from China. The timing of the grant suggests that it was intended to influence Uganda's position at the Afro-Asian Conference. The Soviet Union had just extended a loan to Uganda in exactly the same amount as China's. Mao may have felt he had the edge since Ugandan leaders were dissatisfied with Moscow's performance during the Congo crisis. There was also a strong wave of anti-Americanism in Uganda, as well as intense racial sentiment. Likewise, there was concern about growing Japanese imports, which had cornered the market in several areas, and about India's reduced purchases of Ugandan cotton. In short, Uganda was at odds with all of China's competitors.

Since the use of China's initial aid promise to Uganda was not specified, it may have covered military assistance China had already delivered. Uganda received large quantities of Chinese weapons during the height of the Congo crisis, though most of the weapons were for use in the Congo.[112] Or this aid was intended to arm, train, and supply Watusi refugees in Uganda, who were sent to Rwanda and Burundi to start guerrilla movements.[113] Peking had aided the Watusis elsewhere with weapons and supplies. Alternatively this aid may have been given with the intent of strengthening the position of the government vis-à-vis the army. In 1964 there had been an insurrection in Uganda, which had to be put down by the army with the assistance of British troops. Mao's assistance may have been intended to strengthen President Obote's position.

In 1967 another crisis occurred and the army strengthened its position considerably. Shortly after, army leaders complained of Chinese activities in Uganda and expelled a Chinese mission. Large shipments of Russian military aid arrived, and a Soviet loan to build some textile factories and other projects was drawn. In 1971 President Obote was overthrown by the army, and the new leadership complained of his leftist policies and his attitude toward businessmen. Later that year the Uganda government accused Chinese workers on the Tan-Zam Railroad of helping Tanzania in a border skirmish with Uganda. Peking denied the charges, but relations with Uganda continued to deteriorate.

Very little of China's aid was officially drawn. And there was no evidence of work on any projects after 1967. Probably China gave Uganda substantial quantities of weapons, but mostly for use in the Congo or for the Watusis. Other aid was modicum. In 1973 the political situation in Uganda changed, and Peking began to implement its aid promises and started several projects.[114] Relations have improved somewhat, though no new aid promises have been made.

Aid to Mauritania

In February 1967 China signed an agreement on trade and cultural and technical cooperation with the government of Mauritania, and at the same time promised economic aid. Later it was reported that Peking had given Mauritania a $4 million loan.[115] This loan was probably given in reward for diplomatic recognition, and it was intended to encourage other African countries to do likewise. Mao may also have perceived a revolutionary situation in Mauritania. And at this time he was less concerned about relations with Morocco or Mali, with whom Mauritania had experienced conflict. Finally neither the West nor the Soviet Union had given extensive aid to Mauritania.

All indications are that most of this loan was used. In 1967 Chinese exports to Mauritania doubled.[116] In April 1969 China sent food aid in the form of 3,000 tons of grain. And in November an agreement was signed to drill wells using Chinese aid.[117] This aid was given despite the fact that Mauritania began receiving aid from a number of other sources at this time, especially the World Bank and several Western European countries. However, it received little from the U.S. or the Soviet Union, which probably encouraged Peking to deliver its aid.

In April 1971 Mao invited a delegation from Mauritania to Peking, and it was announced that China had promised an interest-free loan worth $20 million.[118] Subsequently, it was reported that China had agreed to finance the building of a deepwater port in Mauritania, presumably with these funds. Chinese influence subsequently increased. In 1972 Mauritania cosponsored the Albania resolution in the U.N. that proposed seating Peking and expelling Taipei. The Mauritania government also supported China on other issues.

In 1973, however, Mauritania suffered a drought and had to request Western governments to grant a moratorium on loan repayments. At this time the U.S. promised further aid to Mauritania. Subsequently, Mauritania became the benefactor of U.S. food aid. In this context, the influence of Chinese aid diminished. But Peking has not withdrawn; Mao seems to have accepted competition with the West in Mauritania. Nevertheless, China's future aid relationship with Mauritania is uncertain.

Aid to Ethiopia

In October 1971 Emperor Haile Selassie traveled to Peking and visited Mao and other Chinese leaders. His purpose seemed to be to ask for aid, and he was not disappointed. Mao extended an $84 million interest-free loan designated for the development of agriculture.[119] This was one of China's largest single loans and marked a turnabout in Chinese policy toward Ethiopia. The loan may have been even larger than the announced figure; some reports suggested that it was as high as $150 million.[120] Shortly after, China signed an agreement promising to purchase $2 million worth of Ethiopian coffee to adjust their trade balance.[121] Peking also promised to send engineers and technicians to assist Ethiopian development. It is likely that this was part of the original agreement and was intended to give China a presence in Ethiopia.

Mao was ostensibly motivated to aid Ethiopia because of growing anti-Americanism there, which was followed by the expelling of the Peace Corps and the cutback of American aid. There were also rumors that the large U.S. intelligence base in Ethiopia might close. The Soviet Union could not exploit this situation, since it was giving large quantities of military aid to Somalia. Somalia and Ethiopia were at odds concerning a territorial dispute. In addition, Peking had changed its attitude toward the Eritrean rebels in northern Ethiopia that it had earlier supported. They began to stress religious values more than socialist goals, and due to floods in areas under their control, they became less effective. Meanwhile, the Ethiopian army dealt them several severe setbacks.

Mao at this time sought admission into the United Nations, and Haile Selassie could influence a number of other African nations. Selassie also had considerable following among several regional organizations and could support China's bid for leadership of the underdeveloped countries. In addition to aiding agriculture and financing road and other projects China's loan may have been intended to develop commercial air routes. All of this promised to increase China's influence in Ethiopia and Eastern Africa which was high on Peking's list of foreign policy priorities.

During 1972 protocols were signed on several Chinese aid projects: a highway, wells, a veterinary station, and a diesel power station.[122] A number of Chinese study groups and teams of technicians arrived to do survey work. This gave China a clear presence in the country. During 1973 Chinese aid flowed to Ethiopia. It did not, however, alleviate the food shortage, and late in the year it was reported that 1,000 people were dying each week. Some food aid was granted by the United Nations, but this was not sufficient. Amid the crisis Haile Selassie's power began to wane, and in September 1974 he was deposed by the army. At that time Chinese aid was put in cold storage. It is uncertain at this time whether or not China will continue to deliver aid to Ethiopia.

6

Summary and Conclusions

This assessment of twenty years of China's aid diplomacy makes possible conclusions in two general areas. First, foreign aid reflects China's foreign policy objectives both in the short run, i.e., the more specific goals, and in the long run, i.e., future goals related to Peking's view of the world. Foreign aid reflects both strategy and tactics. Second, China's foreign aid program can be appraised from the point of view of its effect upon development. This latter perspective involves examining its unique characteristics, its limitations, and how it compares to the foreign aid programs of other countries. Here the focus of concern is on China's aid program itself and China's ability to aid the economic development of other countries.

In drawing conclusions about China's foreign aid program, a special effort will be made to point out the positive and negative sides of China's aid diplomacy both as an instrument of foreign policy and as an economic assistance program per se. Certainly there is much to say on both sides. Peking has experienced some brilliant successes with its foreign aid in terms of accomplishing foreign policy aims. Likewise, China's aid program at times has succeeded in fostering economic development to the extent that it can be seen as a model. Yet Peking has also met some disastrous and embarrassing failures in both realms.

Economic Aid and China's Foreign Policy

An assessment of China's foreign aid program affords evidence for generalizations about China's foreign policy in at least four specific realms: (1) Sino-Soviet realtions, (2) changing geopolitical views and locational areas of concern over two decades, (3) the nature of China's world view, i.e., international interests or concerns, including periods of introversion and extroversion, and (4) the influence of domestic problems and economic growth upon external policies and endeavors. Below China's foreign aid program will be taken as a reflector of aspects of China's foreign policy. The reader should bear in mind that these subheadings represent major constraints or concerns to Chinese policy makers. As well it is worthy of note that Chinese foreign aid diplomacy offers proof of an empirical nature for the conclusions offered here and generally substantiate evidence from other sources.

Sino-Soviet Relations

When Peking first extended economic aid to North Korea on an unofficial basis in 1950, it was merely an extension of Soviet aid. Mao had just allied with the Soviet Union and signed a treaty of friendship and mutual assistance, which he no doubt envisioned would be the basis for massive Soviet assistance to China. When the Korean War broke out a "fraternal" Communist state was threatened, and both Moscow and Peking came to its aid. China gave assistance while at the same time receiving aid from the Soviet Union. Peking viewed its assistance to North Korea, and later its aid to North Vietnam and Mongolia, as simply a facet of bloc solidarity and economic ties between Communist countries. At this time Mao probably expected more assistance and better terms from the Soviet Union than he got. Nevertheless, Peking was not in a good bargaining position due to the new regime's ideological commitments and alienation of the West.

This explains why China set forth no aid policies: its aid was merely an extension of Soviet aid. Peking's purpose was to cement economic and other ties between members of the bloc and to provide China with allies against the West. China's aid relationship with the Soviet Union and with North Korea, North Vietnam, and Outer Mongolia did indeed build bonds between the Asian Communist countries, and it was no doubt beneficial to all of the countries involved. On the other hand, it made the Soviet Union suspicious of China's intentions. As early as 1950 China's economic ties with bloc nations may have been seen in the Kremlin as a challenge to the Soviet Union's leadership of the Communist world. If this was not true then, it was in 1953 when Stalin died. The new leadership had to make concessions to Mao, and one of these may have been a sphere of influence in Asia—an economic one. It was probably no accident that it was at this time that Peking embarked on an official aid program.

It was also at this time that Mao began to express disappointment in Moscow's aid to China. He became apprehensive about Soviet efforts to gain a hold over China's economy and to interfere in China's internal problems; and he took actions to preserve China's independence. Thus, differences over money matters, one of the most sensitive barometers of relations between all countries (but especially among Communist countries because of their economic view of the world and concern about imperialism), can be perceived.

In 1956 Khrushchev openly criticized Stalin, demonstrating that he had won out in the struggle for power in the Kremlin. He then demanded that he be recognized as the unquestioned leader of the Communist world. Khrushchev intended to establish a new direction in the Communist movement and asked that members of the bloc follow his lead. Mao reacted by giving aid to Hungary after the revolt there to show that China also had a voice in Communist affairs. Further, he began to aid non-Communist Asian countries, thus showing that he also was a leader of the Communist world and not just another satellite of the Soviet Union. Moscow reacted by giving aid to some of the same countries that Peking aided, intimating that China should not go on its own and, perhaps even more, that the Kremlin did not sanction China's effort to win an independent sphere of influence.

In 1958 when further strains developed in the relationship between Moscow and Peking over the Offshore Islands (Quemoy and Matsu), peaceful coexistence with the West, and other important matters, Peking increased its aid promises to non-Communist countries. Doubtless this was an expression of its independence and of its disagreement with policies emanating from Moscow. Moscow reacted in kind: it gave more aid and again made promises to countries China aided.

These events were repeated in 1960, in even more serious form. Peking openly expressed opposition to Moscow's leadership and to the policies the Kremlin set forth for the Communist world. Moscow retaliated by discontinuing its aid to China, by terminating aid projects already underway there, and by calling its technicians home. Mao responded by criticizing Soviet aid and escalating the ideological dispute. He also enlarged China's foreign aid program to prove that China did not need Soviet assistance—which he alleged was an attempt to control China's economy and encroach on its sovereignty.

Peking granted aid to Cuba and more aid to North Korea, Outer Mongolia, North Vietnam, and Albania in order to keep them from siding with Moscow or falling into the Soviet orbit. However, only in the case of Albania did China manage to win over a Communist country. And to accomplish this China had to match dollar-for-dollar the Kremlin's financial support to Albania. With the exception of North Vietnam, which generally remained neutral in the Sino-Soviet feud, Chinese influence in the other Communist countries was overshadowed; and it was Soviet economic aid that was used to accomplish this.

After 1960, because of its defeats at the hands of the Soviets in bloc affairs, the thrust of China's aid diplomacy turned toward non-Communist Asia, the Middle East, and Africa. In these areas Peking favored the more revolutionary nations. Here Mao employed aid as a means to support wars of national liberation. Subsequently, efforts to fan the flames of revolution or even to create revolution where it hardly existed were at least partly a result of Mao's intense desire to prove that the Soviet Union was not a revolutionary country. It was part of his effort to create an alternative kind of Communism—a revolutionary one. And it was a way to gain international recognition for his regime, which in his view both Washington and Moscow sought to deny him.

Even though Mao promised support for "People's Wars," he gave very little in monetary terms. China's niggardliness, when examined next to its boastful claims, suggests that Mao knew that he could not go very far in starting revolutions and that he feared U.S. or the Soviet Union intervention. This was especially true of China's military aid to dissident groups. It is also surprising that, though "People's Wars" were aimed at Western neocolonialism and imperialism, the effects of Mao's efforts were just as upsetting to Moscow as to Washington and engendered Soviet reaction as much as U.S. counterefforts. The fact that

Mao did not spend very much on support for revolutionary wars notwithstanding, the money he did spend was often effective in causing problems for Western countries and the Soviet Union.

In some senses Mao's efforts to aid revolutionary movements were purposefully secondary to winning diplomatic recognition. Mao knew that relations with his regime was a way for many African and Middle Eastern countries to demonstrate their dissatisfaction with the West and show their own revolutionary character. He was also aware that the Soviet Union desired to keep China isolated so it could run the international Communist movement alone. Thus China had a second reason for seeking diplomatic ties. Peking also coupled its aid to revolutionary movements and to Asian and African countries with the concept of an Afro-Asian bloc. Both were reactions to Moscow's efforts to win over the underdeveloped countries.

In 1964–1965 aid competition between Moscow and Peking escalated and centered on the Afro-Asian countries. Both countries provided loans and gifts to Afro-Asian countries to win their support at the second Afro-Asian Conference, scheduled to open in Algeria in 1965. Peking sought to have Moscow excluded from the Conference on the grounds that the Soviet Union is not an Asian country, though Peking really intended to categorize Moscow with the imperialist countries. Mao also sought support for his world revolutionary aims. Moscow wanted to be seated at the Conference and criticized Mao's unorthodox views and efforts to split the Communist movement.

The range and depth of China's aid program increased during those two years. Peking made promises of economic assistance to nearly twenty Asian and African countries at that time; many of them had not received China's assistance before. In total, Mao spent more than $500 million to win over adherents to his views and get promises of support for the Conference, which was never held. Moscow spent more than twice this much. (See Table 4-2.) This was a high point in Sino-Soviet competition in the Third World—reflected very accurately by their competitive aid promises.

In 1970 when China again significantly increased its foreign aid program, Sino-Soviet differences seem to have been a major motivating factor. Fighting on their common border had become serious, and Moscow turned the conflict into a worldwide effort to isolate and contain China—or at least this is the way Chinese leaders perceived the situation. Mao used aid to buy diplomatic recognition and made a concerted effort to get votes to support Peking's bid for U.N. membership. With membership in the United Nations, especially with a seat on the Security Council, Mao could make the Sino-Soviet conflict a matter of international concern and perhaps stave off demands by the Soviet military for a "surgical" strike on China. Peking, in short, needed support from the world community, and Mao was quite successful in using aid to get it.

At this time, Moscow initiated a détente policy vis-à-vis the United States.

In response, Mao sought to win a position of leadership of the less-developed, have-not countries and turn them against the superpowers, especially the Soviet Union, since Peking also pursued closer relations with America. This elucidates Mao's intentions in broadening China's foreign aid program in 1970 and after— both in giving greater amounts of aid and by adding more countries to China's list of recipients. Mao wanted support from the international community to help balance Soviet threats. And he wanted to appease Third World countries that perceived that warming Sino-American relations would mean that China would sacrifice its anti-imperialist stance and its support for the poor and revolutionary countries.

Noting the close relationship between the Sino-Soviet dispute and China's foreign aid diplomacy, it is not surprising that of the twenty some major non-Communist recipients of Chinese aid up to 1970 the Soviet Union had also aided all but one.[1] Likewise, it is not unusual that most of the new recipients of Chinese aid during or after 1970 had received, or were receiving, Soviet economic assistance.[2] Sino-Soviet differences started over economic matters; therefore economic means were used to carry on the feud. In addition, when their differences came to a head, Moscow withdrew its aid in an attempt to force China to accept the Kremlin's leadership and then used the aid it had formerly given to China to aid countries that Peking aided. It is natural that Mao was angry about this and sought to outdo Soviet aid where and in any way he could.

Thus, China's foreign aid program can be seen as a barometer of Sino-Soviet relations. It suggests that the Sino-Soviet Alliance was never as meaningful as most Western observers thought and that significant differences may have existed as early as 1953–1954. Increases in China's aid in 1956, 1958, 1960, 1964–1965, and 1970 parallel the widening of the rift and attest to the fact that irreconcilable differences developed much earlier than can be gleaned from other evidence. The current level and direction of Chinese aid indicates that the split will continued.

Whether economic aid as a Chinese foreign policy tool has been employed successfully against the Soviet Union is more difficult to say. Certainly it was an effective way to escalate Sino-Soviet differences. Mao caused the Kremlin considerable embarrassment by criticizing its economic policies and pointing out how they were exploitive and ungenerous. And this is still true. This probably explains why Chinese loans are generally without interest: because Moscow's loans are with interest. Peking also found aid useful where there was a danger of antagonisms leading directly to open military confrontation, which Peking no doubt wanted to avoid. Finally aid competition could be carried on in an area where the Soviet Union was at a disadvantage—the Third World.

Yet in most cases where there was direct competition Moscow won. This was especially true of Communist bloc countries. Moscow's greater ability to give aid proved to be an advantage. This displayed Peking's failures in economic growth and in some senses debunked the Chinese model for development. In more recent years it has compelled China to limit its aid to specific geographical areas and to bigger projects.

The Geographical Focus

The second area where China's foreign aid program mirrors foreign policy goals is in indicating a geographical focus or interest area. China's foreign policy strategies have changed frequently since 1949; in fact, its foreign policy in some respects may be seen as a trial-and-error strategy. Thus shifts of area concern are clearly evident in Chinese foreign policy-making. There seems to be frequent controversy in Peking concerning foreign policy goals including which regions are better prospects for success in winning friends and increasing China's global influence not evident to the outside observer. The direction of Peking's aid funds, which is easily observable, will thus help to identify China's primary geographical areas of concerns or its geopolitical outlook at any specific time.

Initially all of China's foreign aid went to Communist countries on China's borders: North Korea, North Vietnam, and Outer Mongolia. The thrust of China's economic aid efforts was first directed toward Korea. Mao perceived a threat from the West and committed his nation to repelling that threat. This was repeated shortly after in the case of North Vietnam. However, in this case China's efforts were somewhat more offensive. Nevertheless, in both cases aid was used to support military action against Western imperialism. During this period Peking also extended aid to Outer Mongolia. This aid reflected an effort by Mao to improve bloc relations and ties with the Soviet Union, but also aimed to help resolve a territorial problem. Nationalist China claimed that Outer Mongolia was a part of China, and Mao espoused, at least discreetly, a similar view. Mao also then sought to improve economic relations with Mongolia and perhaps tie its economy to China's.

Hence, during the initial phase of China's foreign aid program (1953–1955), aid was spent to protect China from a perceived threat from the West and to solidify bloc relations. The limited nature of China's foreign aid reflects the generally narrow focus of China's foreign policy goals. Peking's paramount concern during this period was with consolidating internal control and repairing damage caused by more than a decade of war. China's aid diplomacy during this period was also corollary to the fact that Mao viewed foreign policy strategy in a narrow framework, i.e., in the context of objectives of the Communist bloc, which were set forth by Moscow. Political and economic relations were closely connected and Mao saw China's future in both areas in relation to the bloc in general. On the other hand China's commitment to this limited sphere was intense and Peking was willing to make considerable sacrifices where its security was threatened—which it obviously perceived was the case during conflicts in Korea and Vietnam.

China's foreign aid during this period also suggests that Peking saw itself as a land-based power. This is confirmed by the fact that China maintained a huge army but made little or no effort to build a navy or merchant marine. Apparently Mao perceived that in the immediate future China's influence would be limited to Asia and countries close to China. This may have reflected a geopolitical outlook founded upon Sino-Soviet control of the world's major land mass in opposition to the Western imperialist nations that controlled the sea lanes and world trade.

In 1956 a new phase was inaugurated in China's aid diplomacy, when Peking extended aid to non-Communist countries. This reflected a disappointment in Sino-Soviet relations and a newly developed interest in South and Southeast Asia. Mao saw that there was very little room for maneuver in Northeast Asia and that Moscow did not support his efforts to turn Asia into a Chinese sphere of influence. Thus he looked to Southeast Asia, which had been a traditional area of Chinese control and an area where Moscow had little influence. Mao also directed aid to nations in South Asia, apparently seeing India as a competitor for control of Asia, at least Southeast Asia.

The new direction of China's aid manifests a broader concern for security and an enlarged view of China's sphere of influence. It also suggests a broader view of the world among Chinese leaders. Mao had by this time consolidated power internally and sought to define China's borders. These borders were in most cases not marked and had generally been drawn by the European powers to China's disadvantage. As differences with the Soviet Union and India became more acute during the period 1956–1960, Mao sought to reach agreements with the other countries on China's periphery so that he could deal with the two big problems. Aid made border agreements easier and projected the image that China was reasonable and, even more than this, generous. Likewise road building, which became a central theme of China's aid program at this time, facilitated trade ties with neighboring countries. And it enhanced China's military presence in nearby countries since the Chinese army could use the roads.

However, Mao was only moderately successful in these efforts—leading to further changes in his geographical interests in 1958. At this time Mao gave aid to Egypt and Algeria, perhaps perceiving that the prospects for revolution were better in the Middle East and Africa than in Asia. Then in 1960 Peking offered aid to a number of Middle Eastern and African countries confirming a new emphasis for Chinese foreign policy makers. Thus during the period 1958–1964, China's geographical foci in South and Southeast Asia were supplemented by efforts to establish beachheads in the Middle East and Africa. Mao sought to cope with Soviet and U.S. efforts to contain Chinese expansion in Asia by aiding revolution in the Middle East and Africa. Cairo was a base from which Mao could make useful contacts with national leaders in the area; and Nasser helped China win diplomatic recognition from other countries in the region. Peking also sought to use Algeria as a base from which it could support revolutionary wars. And, no less important, Mao found several countries in West Africa receptive to his theories, and enlisted their support for a revolution in the Congo.

During this period China continued to emphasize its relations with Asia and sought to win a sphere of interest there, either with North Vietnam as a protégé or otherwise. But at the same time Mao began to look to other areas of the world. Initially, Egypt and Algeria in the Middle East and several countries in Western Africa were the best prospects. For several years China's foreign policy seemed to vacillate. New donations of foreign aid went to countries in various regions.

By 1964 Peking had cultivated a new geographical sphere of concern in Eastern Africa and the southern part of the Middle East. From here Mao could support guerrilla warfare aimed at the white-controlled regimes to the south and could exert some control over naval traffic at the southern entrance to the Red Sea. With the failure of the Chinese-inspired Communist movement in Indonesia in 1965 and the U.S. escalation of the war in Vietnam China's interests in this area became even more important. Countries in this area for the first time began to receive more Chinese aid than non-Communist Asian countries.

At present China's foreign aid has three general areas of focus: Southeast Asia, South Asia, and East Africa-Southern Middle East. In each region Peking's goals are different. In Southeast Asia, China intends to preserve its position of influence and probably continues to see prospects for a sphere of interest. Likewise Chinese leaders perceive that Southeast Asia is now a power vacuum, and that the Soviet Union, Japan, and India will try to fill the void. Aid is an effective tool whereby China can preserve its hold over North Vietnam. And it may make Cambodia a Chinese satellite. It also gives Peking a foot in the door of other Southeast Asian countries and a vantage position in guiding the course of the economic development in the era of peace that may follow.

In South Asia Peking's assistance has weaned several countries away from India and has helped maintain a balance of power in the region for a number of years. Chinese aid continues to keep some of the smaller South Asian nations from succumbing to Indian pressure. More aid has been required to support Pakistan, however, in the wake of the December 1971 War and the independence of Bangladesh. So far, China has managed to give Pakistan important bargaining cards and has inhibited Indian expansion. Aid to countries in this area has also helped slow the Soviet Union's naval expansion. Several countries, most important of which is Sri Lanka, have given strong support to China's proposal that the Indian Ocean be a "zone of peace" where the arms race should be halted.

In East Africa and Southern Middle East China has managed to demonstrate its ability to handle a big aid project and establish a sphere of interest far from its borders. Here China has supported revolution and garnered for itself a reputation as a leader of the anti-status-quo powers and Third World nations. Peking has manifested a confidence in countries in this area that the West and the Soviet Union have not. Finally, Peking may be able to exert some authority over commercial and military sea traffic in this area, and in this way counter Moscow's efforts to contain China with naval power.

In addition to these geographical areas of focus, Peking has also attempted to gain footholds in Cuba and Chile, though unsuccessfully. And Peking maintains a base of operations in Albania. In 1960 China supplanted Soviet aid there and has since used Albania as a base to disseminate propaganda and spread its influence in the area in other ways. Currently Peking seems to seek further influence in Eastern Europe in order to strike back at Soviet efforts to undermine Chinese influence in Asia and elsewhere. Thus Mao has continued to support Albania economically and has also given aid to Rumania.

Aid, therefore is an accurate measure of China's changing geopolitical perspectives. In some cases the figures clearly indicate a switch in focus, such as in 1956 when China first gave aid to non-Communist countries. In 1960 aid figures suggest that China sought broader interests abroad; and in 1964 when China began giving more aid to African countries than to non-Communist Asian nations, this was even more clear. The year 1970 marked another expansion of Chinese aid, reflecting more global interests. It is not yet clear, however, if China has developed any new area interests to parallel the expansion of its aid program.

Even though aid donations reflect quite accurately Peking's geopolitical thinking, a measure of caution must be exercised when assessing the significance of new donations or when using aid to predict the future direction of China's foreign policy. Although the overall aid figures are suggestive, single donations are not necessarily indicative of changing interests. Only after China has made extensive promises and has carried these out is a geographical change of focus confirmed with any degree of certainty.

China's World View

A third area where foreign aid is a useful measure of China's foreign policy is in confirming China's periods of introversion and extroversion in external relations and in predicting the beginning or end of such cycles. Since 1949 Mao has guided China's foreign policy through periods of hostile and aggressive attitudes toward foreign countries alternating with conciliatory and soft-line periods. Although there is some regularity in the cycles, it is difficult to predict them, based on past periods of change. These cycles seem to be in part a product of the rise and fall of internationalist or universal outlooks on the part of Chinese decision-makers and successes and failures of China's exploits abroad. They are also, however, related to China's current view of the world situation and domestic problems. Since data sources on the decision-making process are inadequate, external behavior must be utilized to predict such cycles. Economic aid is a useful test. (See Table 6-1.)

Before 1956 China's external concerns were limited, and so was its aid. Peking was concerned primarily with bloc relations, and all of its aid went to bloc countries. Antiforeignism and nationalism in China reached a high pitch, and China saw foreign countries as either friends or enemies. Mao felt antagonistic toward the West and toward countries that had relations with the West, noting that there was no such thing as nonalignment. Thus, up to 1956 China was generally isolated and considered foreign relations unimportant, except those with bloc countries.

During the mid-1950s Mao came to see that this policy was not realistic; China had to deal with neighboring countries and could not regard all non-Communist countries as enemies. Peking likewise perceived that it could deal with other Asian countries from a position of strength. Mao had successfully consolidated power on the mainland of China and had made successful repairs to the economy. In 1956 Mao was ready to deal with the outside world, or at least make a start. Hence, although there were certainly other indicators, the fact that Peking sent foreign aid to non-Communist countries at this time presents empirical proof of a switch to soft-line policies.

The fact that aid was given first to neutral countries in Asia that were former tribute nations suggests that China was not as ambitious as Chou En-lai's pronouncements at the Bandung Conference that year suggested. It also reflected a compromise: Peking could deal with neighboring states on a pattern similar to the past. And the fact that little aid was given to non-Communist countries in 1957 further suggests that this policy was only experimental, or that Mao foresaw returning soon to a more aggressive stance.

In any case it was soon evident that liberal policies at home had not been successful. And Moscow had just demonstrated what Peking perceived to be a superiority over the West in weaponry by launching Sputnik. Thus, the "East wind would blow back the West." So Peking returned to a hard-line policy and more hostile attitudes toward non-Communist countries. However, Peking's regression to a hard-line stance was not supported by Moscow and produced negative reactions abroad. Thus it too was only short-lived.

In 1958 China once again increased its foreign aid commitments, denoting the synthesis of its soft- and hard-line policies. China continued an aggressive stance toward the West but adopted more moderate policies toward the non-aligned and neutral countries. This mirrored an inhibited or cautious approach toward the outside world—a transition phase in Chinese foreign policy.

In 1960–1961 Mao once again increased the scope of China's aid program. This signified clearly the beginning of an internationalist policy. Mao became more concerned about the West's and Moscow's efforts to isolate China diplomatically. He therefore used aid to buy recognition. At the same time he gave aid to support liberation struggles. This was an effort to force the world to concede that China was a world power that had to be dealt with, and that China of-

Table 6–1
China's Official Aid Promises by Year
(In Millions of U.S. Dollars)

Year	Amount	Number of Recipients
Before 1953	75	1
1953	394.9	2
1954	12.5	1
1955	378	2
1956	112.7	6
1957	15.8	1
1958	125.6	8
1959	135.25	6
1960	298.2	7
1961	447.2	8
1962	0	0
1963	87	3
1964	344.9	14
1965	124.7	5
1966	10.5	2
1967	437.8[a]	6
1968	56.5	3
1969	10	1
1970	1124.3[b]	8
1971	421.7	14
1972	922.5	15
1973	430	13
1974	282	7
1975	110	5

[a]This includes $400 million promised for the Tan-Zam Railroad.

[b]This includes $300 million in aid to Rumania which was officially promised, but the amount was not disclosed. The $300 million figure is an estimate.

fered an alternative road to Communism. As in 1956, China's foreign policy became more extrovert; but still with limits. In 1956 Mao appealed to the neutral Asian countries that had been former tribute bearers; in 1960 he appealed to the revolutionary forces of the world.

The following year China's aid promises declined to about 10 percent of the previous year, reflecting disappointment in efforts to win over the revolutionary forces and some important foreign policy failures. Specifically, China engaged in a border feud with India and was probably unhappy with the reaction of many nonaligned nations. Even some of the countries China had aided sided with India or at least failed to support China's claims. This came at a time when China also experienced economic hardships that sullied its image abroad and made it difficult to grant more aid. Thus Peking again turned inward.

In 1964 China again came out of its shell—probably as a result of sanguine views of the situation in Indonesia, Vietnam, and Africa. In Indonesia the Communist Party leaned toward Peking and was a growing force in Indonesian politics. In Indochina the government of South Vietnam was experiencing serious problems and appeared about to fall. In Africa revolution seemed to be in the offing. Simultaneously, the Sino-Soviet dispute escalated, and Moscow was again trying to isolate Peking, especially in the Afro-Asian world. Finally, China had joined the nuclear club, and Mao probably felt this gave him an advantage in foreign policy: China could become a major power.

China's foreign aid promises increased by severalfold in 1964, and a high level of aid continued through 1965. But China experienced serious failures abroad that year: a coup in Indonesia destroyed the Communist Party there; the U.S. joined directly in the fighting in Vietnam; Pakistan and India again went to war without China being able to control the course of events. These events and the Cultural Revolution, which began shortly thereafter, caused China to enter once again a period of isolationism and introversion. This lasted through 1969. During this period China's foreign aid donations decreased markedly.

In 1970 China returned to a period of extroversion and global interests. Aid donations registered a new high; in fact Peking's promises to non-Communist countries totalled more than its offers in all previous years. More nations were added to Peking's list of recipients, and most were distant from China. Mao seemed to have adopted a true global foreign policy. Peking won diplomatic recognition from many new countries through the use of aid and then sought admission to the United Nations. Nearly all of the nations that China aided, including both new and old recipients, voted for Peking's right to membership in the world body.

Since 1970 China has continued its soft-line, internationalist policies and has sustained a high level of aid-giving. There was a moderate decline in aid promises in 1973 and 1974, but this probably suggests little more than an inability to sustain the 1970 level of aid donations. Continued aid donations of a much higher level than in the past suggest that China will not in the immediate future return to a closed, isolationist attitude.

In summary, the level of China's foreign aid promises—especially to non-Communist countries—relates directly to Peking's perceptions about the external world, to China's cycles of introversion and extroversion, or isolationism and internationalism. These cycles are pronounced because of the experimental, nature of Chinese foreign policy. Since the cycles are of varying length, it is not possible to anticipate a period of isolationism or internationalism from the time lapse since the last cycle. However, aid is an accurate measure of Chinese foreign policy maker's views and thus can be used to discuss or anticipate such cycles in China's foreign policy.

Domestic Variables

The fourth area where Chinese foreign aid illuminates its general policy goals is in the relationship between domestic problems, particularly economic growth, and foreign policy. Since foreign aid requires economic support and since domestic problems can be tied to developmental problems, aid provides a reading of the effect of these domestic variables on China's foreign policy.

Before 1953 Peking was preoccupied with consolidating its control over the mainland and repairing vast economic damage resulting from years of war. Mao and his followers were uncertain about how successful they would be in coping with economic dislocation, controlling inflation, etc. By 1953, however, the economy was being managed with skill, and economic problems did not appear to be serious. Thus Mao was able to embark upon an official foreign aid program. In 1956 when Peking first granted aid to non-Communist countries, it also had special cause for optimism. Economic growth had been sustained at a high level, and industrialization was showing astounding results.

Yet it was also a time of reckoning: bottlenecks had developed in the economy, and though the growth rate had been substantial, there were signs that it could not be sustained and was slowing down. Also there was domestic opposition to Communist rule manifested openly when Mao initiated the Hundred Flowers Campaign. This may account for a decline in aid promises in 1957. Nevertheless, in 1958 aid commitments were increased amid further cause for concern and at the onset of new economic development plans. Perhaps increases in foreign aid in this context can be seen as a demonstration of confidence and a positive approach. On the other hand, it may suggest that China's reasons for giving aid do not relate that closely to economic conditions in China or to prospects for development.

In 1960 this was certainly the case. Peking once again expanded the scope of its aid-giving, even though there was economic dislocation caused by the failure of the Great Leap Forward launched in 1958, the cancellation of Soviet aid, and the closing of Soviet projects in China. China had no new funds to draw on from the Soviet Union and was faced with the repayment of past loans. Thus, increased foreign aid at that time was inversely related to economic growth and optimism in Peking. Mao used aid to disguise the serious nature of economic setbacks. It was also a way of proving that Soviet aid had not been vital to China's economic growth. Further, Mao wanted to show that China could develop on its own. Aid donations may also have been an attempt to distract attention from a leadership crisis, which transpired in China at this time. Mao's authority was challenged because of his primary role in the Great Leap, and his position of leadership was weaker after this.

Nevertheless, in 1962 China's aid ledgers reflect a sharp cut in foreign economic assistance. And this remained until 1964. Foreign policy decision-making during this period was clearly influenced by domestic problems, most particularly the economy. Near-starvation conditions created serious problems for the regime: Peking had to use large amounts of foreign exchange to buy grain and machines and technology to increase food production. The fact that China's foreign aid program was not cancelled or temporarily held in abeyance probably indicates that Mao wanted to give the impression that conditions in China were not so bad or that China would be back on its feet again soon.

In 1964–1965 aid donations were again increased. The climate was one of cautious optimism; the economic crisis was over, and China experienced a moderate level of growth. Again, however, there was debate over economic development plans. Aid seemed to generally reflect positive attitudes about domestic problems and greater unity among Chinese decision-makers on all policy questions.

From late 1965 to 1969 Chinese decision-makers were preoccupied with the Cultural Revolution, which wrought both political chaos and economic dislocation. The former was more serious than the latter, suggesting that the decline in aid during this period was more a result of lack of decision-making or a preoccupation with internal events rather than a lack of the economic wherewithall to support an aid program. Events of this period also fostered isolationism and introversion which, as was indicated previously, typically parallels a decline in foreign aid.

In 1970 when stability returned, but without any significant rise in production or economic growth, China increased its aid-giving severalfold. Since 1970 a high level of aid promises has been sustained. In 1973, which was a good year for China in economic terms, its foreign aid commitments showed a slight decline. Thus, again there is evidence for the lack of a positive correlation between economic growth and China's foreign aid giving.

Hence, the relationship between aid and domestic problems and economic growth is a complicated one. Only very optimistic views concerning economic growth, or, in contrast, extremely serious economic problems seem to be directly related to China's aid diplomacy. Other domestic problems have a close bearing on aid-giving, but again the relationship is not clearcut. In some cases Chinese leaders have seemingly increased aid to project a positive image abroad and disguise domestic problems. It may be that decisions concerning specific aid grants have been subject to considerable debate and infighting, and this has affected the level of promises. There is no way for us to know, however, if this accounts for several instances where there was an inverse relationship between economic growth or domestic problems and aid-giving.

The fact that the Chinese economy is large and not seriously drained by foreign aid except during times of extreme hardship may be the best explanation possible. Also, of course, the fact that public opinion has little effect on decision-making in China is another factor. Finally, China has given aid for political reasons and, as has already been noted, it has only in a few instances paved the way for important trade contacts. Consequently, decisions to give aid are more often political rather than economic and therefore would be based upon external goals more than on the economic situation or domestic problems.

Conclusions Regarding China's Aid and
Foreign Policy

China's foreign aid diplomacy is an important tool of China's foreign policy and thus inextricably related to important foreign policy goals in a number of ways. Furthermore, since aid reflects China's historical system of diplomacy as well as its current nationalism, anti-imperialism, and other ideological tenets, it is a sensitive and accurate reflector of trends in China's external aims and behavior. In short, it seems to mirror the essence of Chinese foreign policy and has considerable predictive value. And, crucial to studying Chinese foreign policy, unlike other tools of Peking's diplomacy it is easily observable and quantifiable.

As a reflection of the Sino-Soviet dispute, China increased its aid program as differences with Moscow became more actue. This was a manifestation of China's determination to play a greater role in both bloc and world affairs. Later it became a means of directly competing with the Soviet Union abroad and embarrassing Kremlin leaders. Peking's efforts to win diplomatic recognition and spark wars of national liberation, especially since 1960, can be seen to relate as much to Sino-Soviet differences as to China's antagonisms with the West. This explains why Peking has given aid to only a few countries that were receiving U.S. aid at the time and has given aid to most of the countries that the Soviet Union has aided. Washington's greater capacity to give aid seems not to be crucial. The present status of China's foreign aid diplomacy suggests that this situation will continue and that Sino-Soviet differences have not been resolved.

China's economic aid figures also give evidence of shifts of geographical emphasis in Chinese foreign policy and attest to the importance of geopolitical thinking in Peking. In the case of important changes of geographical focus, aid either anticipated or paralleled these changes very closely. In retrospect, it confirmed changes in outlook in Peking and probably will continue to do so in the future. In specific terms, Peking's aid diplomacy gives cause to believe that China saw India as a competitor earlier than other signals indicated and that this was more important than has been generally realized. It now suggests a marked concern for the Soviet Union's naval buildup. Mao's interests in the southern part of the Middle East and East Africa are indicative of such apprehension. Finally, in spite of setbacks in South and Southeast Asia, the direction of Chinese aid suggests these areas are still important to Peking.

Aid is also an accurate measure of China's external commitment or international perspectives over a two-decade period. Larger and more numerous aid promises clearly indicate global interests and perhaps a predominance of internationalists among Chinese decision-makers. It certainly suggests changing perspectives on the part of Chinese leaders. The aid ledger likewise confirms cycles of introversion and extroversion, or increases and decreases, in China's expectations in its relations with other countries. Since these cycles are not consistent in terms of months or years, aid figures can be a useful means of charting them and predicting future trends.

Finally, China's foreign aid program can be related to internal developments and the Chinese economy. In both cases, however, aid may relate inversely as well as directly. Since China is a closed nation and foreign policy decision-making not subject to mass approval, aid can be used to disguise or cover up internal political crises or disagreements about policy as well as economic problems. Thus a general rule can be stated: foreign aid is affected in a direct way by extreme crisis or economic dislocation; otherwise, it may relate inversely—that is, more aid is given when problems arise in order to deceive outside observers.

Any effort to measure the success of China's foreign aid in fulfilling its foreign policy goals is much more difficult. In certain areas, such as undermining the Western alliance system in Southeast Asia, supporting a costly war for the U.S. in Vietnam, gaining diplomatic recognition, and embarrassing the Soviet Union, it has been quite successful. In other areas it has been less successful: supporting the Arabs in the Middle East conflicts, establishing a base of operations in Northern or Western Africa, and supporting wars of national liberation. However the unavoidable conclusion is that China's aid is primarily politically motivated. This will become even more evident in the following examination of the special aspects of China's aid diplomacy and its success in fostering economic development.

Special Aspects of China's Aid Diplomacy

Throughout this study it has been pointed out that China's foreign aid program is unique. Distinct differences can be observed between China's aid and foreign aid given by other countries. Here generalizations and conclusions will be made concerning the character and nature of Chinese aid in comparison with assistance given by other aid-giving nations. Some of these differences are explainable in terms of China's history and its status as an underdeveloped, anti-status-quo nation. Some are the result of ideological views, China's experience with imperialism, and the Sino-Soviet rift. Others are Chinese innovations.

For the purpose of simplification and because China's decision-making cannot be observed, several rather simple categories of comparisons will be made to assess China's aid program. They are: (1) the scope of China's aid program, (2) bilateral versus multilateral aid, (3) military aid versus nonmilitary aid, (4) the ratio of grants to loans, (5) conditions tied to aid, and (6) long-term projects versus short-term projects. Some other interesting or special features of Chinese aid will also be discussed.

The Scope of China's Aid Program

Looking simply at the number of nations to which China has given economic assistance and the broad five-continent scope of this aid, it would appear that Peking's aid diplomacy is truly global. In addition Peking has been in the aid business for more than two decades and China's foreign aid has been competitive with the external aid given by both superpowers. Moreover, Peking has not restricted its aid to nations that are poorer than itself, nor necessarily always to friendly, pro-Communist or socialist regimes.

But this portrayal is not totally objective. To date the United States has given approximately one-half of all aid given by the aid-giving nations of the world. Up to 1965 official U.S. assistance totalled more than $80 billion in economic aid and $33 billion in military aid—in addition to a considerable amount of disguised aid.[3] The entire Communist bloc during the same time frame granted only $8 billion in economic aid and $3.5 billion in military aid.[4] The Chinese portion of this was less than $1 billion (officially promised), about half of which was delivered. Up to 1965 China had offered less foreign aid than the following nations: Belgium, Canada, France, West Germany, Italy, Japan, and the United Kingdom. The Netherlands, with a population of only eleven million, had extended aid in amounts equal to China. Although Peking granted more aid than it officially announced, these comparisons are still meaningful.

Between 1965 and 1970 China's foreign aid promises declined. During that period the scope of China's aid program was very limited. Only since 1970 has the list of recipients of Chinese aid been large, and only in one year—1970—did China's aid promises equal those of the Soviet Union. Never has China's aid program come close to matching U.S. aid in either amounts or the number of recipient nations.

China's aid program has had the impact it has because Peking has been selective. With the exception of Indonesia and Pakistan (and the former is not now receiving any aid from China), Peking has aided only small countries. Much of its aid was given during times of need or crisis, and in most cases it has been singularly politically motivated. In addition, recipient nations have almost always publicly expressed gratitude and amazement that China would give them economic assistance. Frequently Chinese aid is praised by the recipient country in order to induce the U.S. or the Soviet Union to give them more aid. And in most cases Chinese aid is followed by a Western or Soviet reaction. Thus, Chinese aid invariably receives considerable news coverage and publicity in the recipient countries as well as in Western capitals and Moscow—not to mention Peking's propaganda efforts. In the U.S. the importance of Chinese aid has been at times exaggerated in order to influence Congress to vote for more U.S. aid, which is consistently unpopular with the public.

Another reason that China's foreign aid program appears to be large in scope is that in 1970 Peking increased its aid promises significantly. In that year Chinese official aid promises to non-Communist countries exceeded its total commitments up to that time, and the number of new recipients was almost double any previous year. And since 1970 a high level of aid promises has been sustained. This can be juxtaposed with the declining U.S. and Soviet bilateral aid programs.

Still another reason that China's aid diplomacy gives the impression of a global nature is that both the United States and the Soviet Union have regarded China as an enemy and have taken considerable effort to counteract its foreign aid. Fresh in the minds of many is the Vietnam War, which was supported by Chinese economic aid and weapons. China's economic and military aid to other revolutionary movements as well as rebel groups is likewise important in this respect.

Hence, although China's foreign aid program has not been large and for that reason should not be considered international in scope when compared to the aid programs of the U.S. or the Soviet Union, it has increased in size recently and has had an impact which in many ways can be seen as global. And one can speculate about the trends: China seems more committed to bilateral aid than other countries. This situation will probably remain true in the immediate future.

Bilateral Versus Multilateral Aid

The second basis of comparing Chinese aid to that of other aid donors is by examining how much is given bilaterally, and how much multilaterally or through regional or international agencies. In recent years the United States and most other Western nations, and even the Soviet Union, have channeled an increasingly larger portion of their aid through various regional and international organizations for distribution. In 1965, 20 percent of Western aid was dispensed through international agencies.[5] Since that time, multilateral aid as a portion of Western aid has more than doubled.[6]

The reason for this trend is that a large number of organizations in Western nations are in the aid business, and this causes confusion in nations that are recipients of aid from a large number of donors—sometimes as many as fifty. Aid programs compete with each other for skills and materials in recipient countries, and there is little or no coordination of projects. In addition, a number of Western countries, especially the United States, find that there is less cause for bickering and competition among recipients if they turn over decision-making authority to an international organization. Frequently, allies complain that Washington gives more aid to neutrals than to friends. The Soviet Union has also supported international aid-giving organizations for similar reasons, although considerably less so than the U.S. and other Western countries.

Until 1970 China did not participate in a meaningful way in any important international organizations, especially any giving aid. In fact, up to that time Peking expressed hostility and disdain for the United Nations and its related agencies. Therefore, it is understandable that Peking did not grant any of its aid through these organizations, and China's aid was exclusively bilateral. Now, although Peking is represented in the U.N. and has joined or expressed an interest in participating in organizations affiliated with the U.N., it is unlikely that China's foreign aid policies will change in this regard. There are several reasons for this.

First, any aid that China would give to an international organization would be overshadowed by aid from other nations, especially Western capitalist countries. China would not be able to exercise much influence on the use of aid by these agencies, since decision-making is generally based on the size of contributions. Furthermore, most international aid-giving organizations favor capitalist-type projects, and Peking does not want to see its aid funds used for this way.

Second, Peking negotiates aid projects directly with recipient governments and does not usually consult with, or even meet, local businessmen. There is no business community in China that plays any role in aid-giving or aid projects. Therefore, China is not faced with the problem of a multitude of donors. Chinese leaders could also argue (though they have not made this case) that regional and international aid-giving agencies are notorious for their inefficiency and bureaucratic problems, and this would only be to the disadvantage of the recipient country should China change its aid policies.

Third, since Chinese aid is primarily politically motivated, Peking would not be able to realize its foreign policy objectives if it turned over its funds to an aid-giving agency where decisions are generally made on the basis of economic goals. Because China's foreign policy and its global views are anti-status-quo while most aid-giving agencies endeavor to preserve stability and advocate slower change, their positions are at odds. In short, giving aid to an international organization would contradict the purposes of Chinese aid.

Finally, it is highly possible that Peking will seek to borrow money from some international institutions in the future. There has already been considerable speculation to this effect. Certainly China would qualify as an underdeveloped country and no doubt could present projects that would be worthy of support by such organizations as the World Bank and the Asian Development Bank. Recently Peking has departed from its traditional policy of not borrowing money and not relying on foreign trade to enhance economic development. If these policies can change, so can Peking's attitude toward borrowing from international agencies. In the event that China should borrow funds from some aid-giving agencies, it would certainly be contradictory to grant or loan money to these institutions or other related institutions at the same time. Thus it can be expected that China's aid policies in this respect will not change, and Chinese aid will remain wholly bilateral.

Military Aid versus Nonmilitary Aid

Another mode of comparison for assessing China's foreign aid program is military aid versus nonmilitary aid. This dichotomy is not always a clear one, since nonmilitary aid can be used to support military operations or military goals, and military aid is frequently used in development projects. Nevertheless, some broad or general analysis of Chinese aid and some comparisons with other aid-giving nations is enlightening.

According to official statements, United States aid in 1952 and several subsequent years was more than 50 percent military aid.[7] This percentage dropped in the mid-1950s and by 1965 constituted only about one-third of U.S. aid abroad.[8] After 1965 the percent of military aid increased because of the Vietnam War to somewhat over 50 percent and since 1971 has dropped again. Comparable figures—between one-third and one-half—apply to other Western countries (with the exceptions of West Germany and Japan). Soviet military aid as a percent of its total aid fluctuates more than U.S. aid; for example, in 1969 military aid constituted about one-third of Moscow's aid program, but in 1970 military aid was four times as much as nonmilitary assistance.[9] Nevertheless, the average is around the 50 percent mark.[10]

Although there are no published figures on China's military aid, it is certain that China has given a much smaller percent of its aid as military aid than either of the superpowers or most other aid-giving nations. Peking has given military assistance to at least eighteen non-Communist countries and has aided a number of liberation groups; but only in the case of Pakistan and Tanzania can this be called substantial. In other cases Chinese aid in weapons and military supplies has either been small or temporary. In total, Chinese military aid to non-Communist countries has been just over $500 million or about 15 percent of its official aid to these nations.[11] And although its military aid has increased considerably in the last five years, it has not increased as rapidly as its foreign aid generally.

On the other hand, a considerable portion of China's aid to Communist countries has been military, especially to North Korea and North Vietnam. Since Peking supported these two countries during periods of military conflict, this is understandable. Hence, much of China's aid in supplies and equipment to North Korea and North Vietnam can be categorized as military assistance. Peking has also given considerable military aid to Albania to compensate for the withdrawal of Soviet aid. If it is assumed that one-half of China's aid to North Vietnam and North Korea constitutes military aid—which is probably an overestimate in view of the way U.S. and Soviet military aid is categorized—and official figures are used, then China's military aid is more than 25 percent of its total aid. If high estimates are used, the figure rises to about 35 percent. No matter how the figures are read, China has given much less of its aid in the form of weapons than either of the superpowers. There are a number of reasons for this.

First, the two superpowers and several Western European countries support allies or former colonies with advanced weapons. In the case of the superpowers this is a product of the confrontation between the two blocs. Several European countries have committed themselves to guarantee stability in their former colonies or to preserve the regime that they put in power. Thus their military aid programs are extensive. Also, some are protecting foreign investments. And in many cases, allies ask for military aid so that they can divert their own resources into economic development and obviate charges of foreign economic imperialism.

Second, weapons usually represent advanced technology and thus are expensive; or they are obsolete and are dumped through military aid programs. In almost all cases they are overpriced: in the first case because the technology has to be developed anyway, and in the second because they are no longer of any use to the donor country. Therefore, Western and Soviet military aid tends to be overvalued. China does not generally have the technology to develop military equipment that would be competitive with the U.S. or the U.S.S.R., and when it does develop such weapons or weapon systems, it needs them at home. Furthermore, Chinese military assistance usually provokes a response from Washington or Moscow, so Peking, realizing that it cannot compete, does not try. Furthermore, many Third World countries are reluctant to ask for military aid from China, knowing that the U.S. or the Soviet Union might give more and better weapons to its enemies.

Finally, Peking claims to eschew giving military aid. Mao asserts that U.S. and Soviet military aid is used to practice imperialism and support reactionary military regimes. Military aid, as the Chinese experienced during the 1950s with Soviet assistance, provides for foreign influence over the recipient country's army. Then Mao generally advances the notion of civilian control of government (in the case of China, Party control) and applies this to other countries—except in the case of some liberation struggles. Anyway, the military in most countries, including the underdeveloped nations, is a conservative force in national politics, usually anti-socialist or antileftist. Peking also wants to give the impression of being a peace loving country and argues that the superpowers are responsible for unrest in the world due to their practice of selling or giving away weapons. Related to this, China might have to extend credits on less generous terms if it got into the business of military aid on a larger scale; and certainly it would become more status quo oriented, since it would expect repayment for its weapons.

The Ratio of Grants to Loans

A fourth means of analyzing China's foreign aid program is to examine the ratio of grants to loans and compare this to other aid-giving countries. In assessing aid in this way, there are special difficulties that need to be realized: much aid is in credits and thus tied to purchasing in the donor country; the availability of goods and the price are usually set by the donor and are not constant; the means of repayment affect the generosity of any loan; low-interest loans, where the interest rate is less than the rate of inflation, carry an element of gift; long-term loans are more generous than short-term loans, since they provide for building economic infrastructures; and loans are sometimes cancelled. In spite of these problems, looking at the ratio of grants and loans in China's aid is useful.

Because of its bad experience trying to collect loans made before and during World War I, the United States was ill-disposed to make more loans after World War II. Hence, most American aid in the immediate postwar period took the form of nonrepayable grants. This was no doubt also influenced by the ability of recipient nations to repay. As late as 1960 only 12 percent of U.S. bilateral aid was repayable in U.S. dollars.[12] However, during the early 1960s Washington changed its aid policies and by 1965, 45 percent of new commitments anticipated repayment in dollars.[13] Recently almost all official aid, except aid to Vietnam, some military assistance elsewhere, and food aid, has taken the form of loans.[14]

Other Western countries and the Soviet Union, when they set up aid programs, did not follow the U.S. example and from the beginning provided more loans than grants. A greater percent of loans has also been a growing trend in these countries in recent years. There are various reasons why most aid-giving nations now favor loans. They are more business-like and thus not so degrading to the recipient country. Many recipient countries ask for loans for this reason. Loans are easier to make for Western countries since aid requires the approval of an elected body. Loans provide for revolving pools of credit and a certain amount of self-perpetuating funds. Finally, loans are regarded as more effective in promoting economic development, since they will be made only when projects can be demonstrated economically feasible. This tends to reduce the amount of money that will be expended on luxury items and makes the recipient more responsible.

However, much more Western aid is nonrepayable (and thus should be categorized as grant aid) than is generally realized. Low-interest, long-term loans are as much as 50 percent or more grant since they are repayable after the value of the currency has dropped due to inflation. Some loans given by the U.S. are repayable in local currency on which the rate of inflation is much faster—sometimes making them 80 to 90 percent grant the first year.[15] Repayment funds in local currency cannot usually be taken out of the country, and this tends to have a beneficial effect on a growing economy, since it stimulates business. In this regard it can be pointed out that most international agencies that are in the aid business give loans, and these loans carry a higher rate of interest and more strict repayment policies than bilateral aid given by most Western nations. The same is true of private loans that are made to underdeveloped countries.

When China initiated its aid program, Mao espoused the attitude that loans were characteristic of imperialism and provided a means of control of one country over another. Therefore, in the early years most of China's foreign aid took the form of nonrepayable grants. In addition, China gave most of its early aid to North Korea and North Vietnam—nations that were at war or repairing war damage. They could not be expected to repay loans.

When Peking extended aid to non-Communist countries in 1956, it still emphasized grants. Mao wanted to use aid for propaganda purposes and thus sought to emphasize differences between Chinese aid and Western aid. During the period 1956–1960 China made some loans, but most of them were noninterest-bearing loans. When loans with interest were given, the interest was low, usually from less than 1 percent to 2.5 percent.

Beginning in 1960 more Chinese aid took the form of loans, though grants still predominated. Peking found that it could expand the scope of its aid program by giving more loans and fewer outright grants. During the period 1963–1965 Peking extended aid to a number of Afro-Asian nations, largely to win their support on issues to be presented at the second Afro-Asian Conference and to exclude the Soviet Union from the Conference. By substituting loans for grants, Peking could extend more aid to more countries. Also, Chinese leaders discovered that loans committed recipients to support Chinese foreign policy goals as much or more than gifts. However in order to preserve its reputation as a generous aid donor, Peking made almost all of its loans without interest.

Yet the generosity of Chinese aid can be questioned when compared with the aid programs of other nations. Aid given by most Western countries, especially the U.S. takes the form of long-term loans and they are low-interest—considerably less than the rate of inflation. The longer repayment period of U.S. loans and those given by most other Western countries and the faster rate of inflation on U.S. dollars or the local currency of the recipient country makes up for the fact that Chinese loans bear no interest. Since most Chinese aid is repayable in commodities, this eliminates the influence of inflation completely and thus reduces the grant factor. Hence the grant percentage in U.S. loans and other Western loans is generally higher than in Chinese loans.[16]

Furthermore, when considering the fact that Peking ties its aid to its own products, the prices of which are set arbitrarily or to match international market prices, it is relevant to point out that Chinese goods are generally inferior in quality and the range of products available restricted. This makes Chinese aid more expensive. To this must be added the fact that Mao has frequently dumped goods given in repayment of Chinese loans on the world market, thus driving down the price of that commodity, to the disadvantage of the recipient country. Thus the notion that Chinese loans are generous because they are noninterest-bearing is deceptive. The reason that Peking makes nearly all of its loans noninterest-bearing is for propaganda reasons—to set China's aid program apart from others, especially the U.S. and the Soviet Union. Recipient countries cooperate in publicizing this image in order to enlist more aid at better terms from the West and the Soviet Union.

On the other hand, Chinese loans have generally been higher-risk loans, going to countries that international organizations and even Western countries and the Soviet Union do not want to aid. Also much Chinese aid has been given during times of political instability, bringing to question the capacity or willingness of the nation to repay. Peking has likewise undertaken projects which are regarded as economically not feasible; the Tan-Zam Railroad, China's biggest aid project, is a good example. Hence a higher charge for goods supplied by Chinese loans may be justified. Another factor to consider is that some of Peking's recipients are offered goods at less than the world market price, and sometimes the goods are of high quality. Finally, Chinese engineers and labor are generally provided at bargain prices, and support for Chinese aid personnel is kept to a minimum.

The Conditions of Aid

A fifth way of comparing China's economic assistance to other aid programs is by examining the conditions of aid. Since all aid is intended to influence the recipient country in some way, there must be some controls put on the aid by the donor. At a minimum, aid donations are overseen so that they go to the persons or organizations intended and are used for the designated purposes. Almost all aid is managed by the donor to the extent that it does not fall into the hands of dishonest politicians or end up in foreign bank accounts.

The foreign aid programs of most Western countries are under the purview of an elected body and, to a lesser extent, public opinion. Thus, if the recipient country does not use aid for legitimate goals or behaves in an unfriendly way to the donor, aid probably will be discontinued the next year. In a sense, then, recipient countries are under the pressure of the Western donor's congress or parliament, or public opinion. In addition, there are many other ways a donor country may control its aid. It may supply aid in the form of goods rather than credit or currency, transport the goods directly to the recipient country, and oversee their dispensing. The donor country may also stipulate that its aid go for certain projects or, as in the case of Western aid, assist the business or capitalist sector. The donor may even request that the recipient make public statements favorable to the donor country, alter its ideological position, take a different stance on certain global political problems, remove or appoint certain officials, or even change its system of government.

Controls of any kind give the donor country some influence over the recipient. The latter kinds mentioned above act to reduce the independence and sovereignty of the recipient country and are subject to justifiable criticism. Controls that are used as a lever by businessmen in the donor country so that they can dump excess or poor quality goods or sell at inflated prices are also condemned. The same is true of loans that carry a high rate of interest and force the recipient country into debt.

Because of Mao's aversion of colonialism and his experience with aid relations with the Soviet Union, he is an advocate of aid without strings.[17] Mao equates strings on aid with imperialism and criticizes Western and Soviet aid for being contingent upon specified uses, etc. Peking, however, cannot simply hand out aid without conditions. In fact, because of the political motivations behind most of China's aid promises, its aid must be controlled as strictly or even more so than aid given by Western countries or the Soviet Union. This also results because China has less aid to give and because it can supply few, if any, products that are not available elsewhere. Its aid is less "habit forming" than aid from the developed countries. Thus, Peking must control its aid but in a manner that evidences few or no conditions. At minimum, Chinese aid must appear more altruistic than Western or Soviet aid. Peking has a variety of ways of controlling or overseeing its aid donations while avoiding so-called strings.

Aid talks are usually held simultaneously with official meetings or negotiations on other matters, during the visit of a high official of the recipient country to Peking or during the visit of a Chinese official to the recipient country. Thus the resolution of various political problems can be subtly tied to aid. Treaties are frequently signed at the same time as aid agreements, as has been shown to be the case of nonaggression pacts and border treaties. Subsequent meetings or protocols are usually required before the aid project is started, and consequently there is a delay from the time the aid project is promised to the time it is actually implemented. During this time Peking can hint that it expects a change of view on certain issues; and if this is not forthcoming, the project can be delayed or changed, if necessary, to the point where it is unacceptable to the recipient. Almost all Chinese aid promises have entailed a considerable time lapse between the original promise and the follow-up negotiations. This has been especially true of first donations. There have also been other kinds of delays, and it is not infrequent that Chinese aid promises have gone unused for three to five years or more. Peking can justify delays on the basis that China is a poor country and suffers shortages of goods, foreign exchange, transport facilities, etc. This same excuse is used for changing the conditions or scope of an aid project. Seldom is this questioned, and needless to say, it is effective in enlisting concessions from the recipient, or non-use of the aid.

Also, China grants much of its aid in goods or credits that are used to purchase Chinese goods or services. Since Peking sets (in fact publishes a list) the goods that can be used for foreign aid and the prices, Chinese decision-makers have a handle over aid that has already been promised and is being drawn. Certain goods can simply be declared unavailable or not for export, the prices raised considerably above the world market price, or the quality lowered. This accounts for the fact that a sizeable amount of Chinese aid has not been used, even when protocols and secondary agreements have been signed.

Finally, a great deal of China's aid is given in the form of projects that are designed by Chinese aid officials. The project is then offered to the recipient to accept or reject. Most specify who will be hired to work on them, the site, the relation of the project to the economy as a whole, marketing of the produce resulting from the project, etc. Many of them specify that China will furnish engineers and labor. If the recipient does not approve of the nature of the project or the controls Chinese aid personnel have over its construction, it can simply reject the project or renegotiate at a later date. This probably accounts for the fact that Peking frequently announces aid agreements, but provides no details at the time about the nature or purpose of the aid.

Thus Chinese foreign aid does not have fewer strings and is not less controlled or managed than Western or Soviet aid. In fact, it is controlled more rigorously. The difference lies in the kinds of controls that Peking employs. They are more subtle and better concealed. Also Chinese decision-makers are able to offer credible excuses when they do not want to make aid deliveries. Western nations and the Soviet Union can hardly say that they are experiencing economic hardship themselves or cannot provide certain materials or kinds of aid. And, as in the case of the generosity of Chinese aid, many recipient nations cooperate to project the image that Chinese aid is not controlled so as to win better conditions on aid from other donors.

Long-term Projects versus Short-term Projects

The final method of comparative analysis of China's foreign aid program is the percent of long-term aid and short-term aid. This dichotomy may be related to aid intended for infrastructure, or over-all, economic development as opposed to short-term, or show projects. The former is aid which is influenced by efforts to help the recipient nation develop economically and is generally designed by economists rather than political decision-makers or propagandists. Often this aid is given to assist development in the recipient country so as to stimulate trade with the donor country or provide raw materials that the donor country needs. Nevertheless the criterion used here is whether or not the aid facilitates the economic development of the recipient in the long run.

The foreign aid program of the United States (this is also true of other Western countries' aid programs, though to a somewhat lesser extent) was originally based on the security motive of defending the free world against Communism. The U.S. directed most of its aid toward the reconstruction of Europe in the early years and has since given more aid to countries bordering on Communist countries or where the threat of Communism seemed imminent. Nevertheless, from the onset economists played a major role in America's foreign aid program, in designing allocations, use, etc. Helping economic development was seen as a way of preventing the recipient nation from going Communist. During the 1950s and 1960s U.S. scholars produced scores of studies on development, and their influence upon aid decisions became considerable. Long-term aid became more common and concern for such things as balanced development, inducing local savings and investment, the spread effect, etc., became popular. American aid was described as "not for the benefit of the present host government, but for that of its successor."[18] U.S. foreign aid policies became the model for other Western donors, and promoting development became an overriding concern to aid officials in the West.

More recently the United States and other Western countries have employed other methods besides aid, such as reduced tariffs to underdeveloped countries on a nonreciprocal basis, guaranteeing business investment, etc., to promote economic development in the poor countries. The Vietnam War and inflation in the U.S. and other Western countries have also been a boon to the developing countries, since their goods are now more competitive in Western markets. And Western governments have generally tried to preserve the advantages these countries have gained. Where aid at one time simply produced a "revolution in rising expectations" and provided some needed goods for the poorer countries while tending to suppress local industrial development, trade preferences have truly stimulated growth in underdeveloped countries.

Thus much Western "aid" is given through trade preferences and indirectly. Most direct aid given by the U.S. and other Western nations still takes the form of long-term loans for infrastructure, or general development, projects. Well in excess of half of Western aid can be so categorized if the common practice of renegotiating loans and lengthening the repayment period is considered. This is also true of most Western aid that is funnelled through regional or international organizations.

In contrast, most of China's aid projects have been short-term projects: projects that could be completed quickly and easily with immediate results. Nor have China's aid donations generally taken into consideration local economic problems. They are generally unrelated to long-term planning or long-range economic growth. The primary reason for this is that China has few economists and little knowledge of the mechanisms which produce economic development. China's own development has been primarily improvisation and has proceeded on an almost trial-and-error basis. Certainly China's development has been uneven. Another problem is that China has tried to promote the development of the public sector of the recipient countries. But even in the case of small countries this usually requires considerable outlay of money and supplies and generally a bigger commitment than China wants to make to any specific country.

This is the reason that Chinese leaders emphasize the reciprocal nature of China's aid. And it suggests why Peking criticizes Western aid and advice that aims at stabilizing the local currency and generating export earnings. Western aid that is highly planned does not always take into consideration the recipient's feelings or special conditions in the recipient country, especially in rural areas.

China tries much harder to tailor its aid to local conditions, since its understanding of balanced growth is minimal and its capabilities to foster long-range growth in foreign countries are insufficient.

On the other hand, about one-half of China's foreign aid has gone for project assistance, and most of the rest—excluding military aid and some food aid—has gone for budget relief. Most of the projects have aimed at socialist and thus infrastructure development: for example, China's road and railroad building efforts. Many others have been fairly effective in using local labor. Likewise, China's projects have been unselfish in the sense that China has built factories that produce goods that compete with its own exports and frequently tend to reduce the level of trade between China and the recipient. This has been particularly true of China's aid for the construction of textile mills.

Recently, Peking has embarked on some bigger projects, which might suggest that in the future a greater emphasis will be placed on long-term loans and thus on over-all economic development in the recipient country. China's biggest project, the Tan-Zam Railroad, may be crucial to the future economic development of Tanzania and Zambia. China may also direct more of its aid to long-term investment in the future, but it is unlikely that it will be able to compete with Western countries in this respect. And although many of China's loans are long-term in the sense that repayment is not demanded soon, they are fixed to projects that facilitate development in the short run.

Conclusions Regardin the Unique Aspects of China's Foreign Aid

China's foreign aid program is global if one considers the number of nations that have received Chinese aid and the wide geographical distribution of these recipients. Furthermore, China's economic assistance is even larger than official figures suggest—probably severalfold. Most of Peking's aid to North Vietnam, North Korea, and perhaps several other countries has not been announced, and aid to these countries, particularly North Vietnam, has been considerable. Nevertheless, in terms of amounts of aid given, China's aid program is quite small when compared to the foreign assistance given by the United States, several other Western countries, and the Soviet Union.

China's foreign aid is overwhelmingly bilateral. Peking can see no benefit in giving aid through regional or international institutions where Chinese funds would be lost amid greater amounts of Western or Soviet aid. Since China's aid will probably remain politically motivated and short-termed, it is unlikely this situation will change.

China's foreign aid program has contained little military aid, though it has been costly to counter as in the case of revolutionary movements, it has given

Peking aclaim, and in a few cases it has been important to the course of events in the world—namely in Korea, Indochina, and to a lesser extent in South Asia. And it is doubtful that China's military aid will increase appreciably particularly as a percentage of its foreign aid. China cannot compete with the superpowers in military aid and does not want to try. Notwithstanding, China's military assistance will probably remain vital to several countries that are now major recipients of Peking's military hardware. And it is certainly not inconceivable that other nations will be added to this list.

China initially gave much of its aid in grants because aid to North Korea and North Vietnam could not be repaid. China continued this policy for a while even after granting aid to non-Communist countries, but free aid was eventually sacrificed as China expanded its aid program. Noninterest-bearing loans are now the rule; but due to the prices of Chinese goods and the fact that most loans are tied to repayment in goods, inflation does not affect Chinese loans to the extent it influences Western loans. This, among other reasons, makes the grant element smaller than on most Western loans.

Chinese aid is said to have no strings attached, but Chinese decision-makers are able to control their aid by various means. In fact, it is less free of conditions and ties in a political sense than Western aid.

Finally, many Chinese loans are repayable over an extended period of time with liberal grace periods before repayment begins, but they are not on the average as long-term as Western loans. In fact, smaller easier to complete projects are more common to China's foreign aid program. Chinese loans are not designed to produce long-range economic development at least when compared to Western loans. China does not have the ability to plan long-term development, and its political motives for giving aid predominate. Peking's policies in this regard may be changing; China has recently undertaken some big projects. But its primary motivation appears to remain political.

One of the principle reasons China's aid program has seemed bigger, more generous, freer of complications and ties, and more beneficial to recipient nations is the fact that there has been a major reaction to Chinese aid in the West and in the Soviet Union. Both have justified their own aid policies on the basis of competing with Chinese aid. The U.S. government has frequently mentioned Chinese aid when its administration lobbies in Congress for bigger appropriations. Much U.S. military aid is justified by pointing out that China aided the other side. Soviet decision-makers have done this too and have directed their aid to countries that China aids. They want to be sure that they can control the Communist movements throughout the world.

The fact that most Third World countries, especially the nonaligned countries, realize that both Washington and the Kremlin are sensitive to China's aid efforts prompts them to want Chinese aid, so that they can get more from the U.S. and the Soviet Union. It is no wonder that they frequently publicize Peking's aid efforts in their country and sometimes direct their publicity efforts toward Washington and Moscow. Chinese aid has been very effective in stimulating aid competition, from which the poorer countries benefit. In fact, China for this reason may be credited with helping the underdeveloped countries way beyond the scope of its own foreign aid program. Both the amounts and the conditions of Western and Soviet foreign aid are more beneficial to the poor countries because of China's aid program and its propaganda associated with aid.

That China is an underdeveloped country also wins much attention for its foreign aid program. China is the only poor country that has an extensive foreign aid program, one that could in any sense be termed global. This makes excellent grist for Peking's propaganda mill. And it makes Peking appear generous and committed to the underdeveloped countries. Certainly it bolsters China's bid for leadership of the less-developed countries.

Future Trends

It seems clear that China's foreign aid will remain politically motivated and will in the future, as now, be an accurate reflection of policy and policy objectives. Peking will no doubt be less concerned with winning diplomatic ties in years to come, since Mao has already attained considerable success in winning global recognition for his regime. However, aid will no doubt be used to realize other specific foreign policy objectives. Probably winning support from the underdeveloped countries for leadership of the poor nations will be one of the most important. Peking wants to foster unity among the have-not countries and endeavor to use its leadership of this bloc of nations against the superpowers and the rich countries.

Peking will likely continue to use much of its aid to counter efforts by the Soviet Union, and secondarily India, to contain China and to halt the spread of their influence. Moscow will no doubt remain China's main aid competitor in the future. Competition with the U.S. will probably continue to decline. Contention with Japan which has been minimal up to now may be expected to increase. Tokyo's aid giving has increased markedly in recent years and its most important recipients are Southeast Asian nations. Some rivalry will inevitably occur.

The thrust of China's aid program in geographical terms cannot be expected to change markedly. African nations will doubtless remain important. The Middle East as a region will probably not increase in importance due to the oil money there and the potential of several Arab nations to give large quantities of aid. China's aid to Middle Eastern countries may even decline. Peking can be logically predicted to maintain its aid giving to South and Southeast Asian countries, and it will certainly continue to give aid to selected Communist bloc countries—

adding to its list any bloc country that wants to alter its economic ties with Moscow.

China will likely continue to give greater quantities of aid to countries in areas where it perceives special geographical or geopolitical interests. These areas may change but the policy of concentrating aid will probably not. It has been successful in countering Soviet aid efforts and has prevented the aid defeats at the hands of the Soviets that once plagued China's aid diplomacy.

More consistent aid giving may also be expected from China. Its aid diplomacy has matured over the last two decades. Probably this will lead to less wide swings in the yearly amount of money allocated to aid and the number of recipients. Also, less aid will be given to revolutionary groups since China's success in this realm, except in the sense of costing the U.S. and the Soviet Union much to counteract, is not impressive.

Aid will continue to be given on a government-to-government basis and will probably be negotiated in the same way it has in the past. Peking will no doubt continue to tie its aid. Its aid will probably remain short-term, and Mao will likely continue to emphasize projects that are quick to build. Publicity will doubtless be as important to China's aid diplomacy in the future as is now the case. Larger projects will probably be undertaken, assuming that the Tan-Zam Railroad is a success. But these will be few in number. Peking may use them to guarantee spheres of interest as its foreign policy dictates.

Peking will probably continue to emphasize technical assistance; it has amplified this aspect of its foreign aid program in recent years. In 1972 China sent over 22,000 technicians abroad—more than the Soviet Union and the Eastern European countries combined.[19] China wants a presence in the underdeveloped countries, and Chinese leaders apparently feel that their aid personnel and technicians help Peking's reputation. This is especially true in South Asia, Africa, and the Middle East. In Southeast Asia there is considerable sensitivity to the Chinese presence and Peking has avoided sending more technicians and aid personnel. This will probably remain true unless China can legitimize its presence there.

Peking will probably endeavor to emphasize technical aid in lieu of further commitments of money and credits. If successful, China will likely be able to retain and perhaps increase its influence among the less-developed countries. China cannot afford to increase its aid program by much, but it can be a model for foreign aid thus enabling China to speak for the Third World countries.

Peking can also be expected to increase its emergency and disaster assistance. This kind of aid is generally not expensive and carries much publicity value. It also substantiates Peking's bid for favor with the poorer countries. Peking has given an increasing portion of its aid in this form and this will no doubt continue to be true. China's Red Cross is more active than in the past and will probably remain so. Mao gave emergency budget assistance in the past, and aid of this kind may be more common in years to come.

China has not given much food aid to date because of a lack of food at home and the fact that Peking has to use its foreign exchange, which is in short supply, to purchase grain from Western countries. This is a weakness of China's economic aid program, and it is one the Chinese cannot rectify. Peking may continue to give some emergency food aid in small quantities but cannot be expected to do more than this.

China may also find that its aid facilitates development in many nations to the point that they no longer need Chinese aid. Some recipients of Chinese aid themselves give aid, such as North Korea, North Vietnam, and Rumania. The development of some nations may require more sophisticated aid that only Western countries or the Soviet Union can offer. This is one of the basic contradictions in Chinese aid-giving. Peking will likewise meet increasing competition from other new aid-giving nations. The same is true of international aid-giving agencies. China will no doubt have to alter its aid policies to compete with these new aid donors.

Thus, while Peking's foreign aid program will probably continue to grow and become a more important tool of diplomacy in the future, in monetary terms it will grow slowly. And China will face more competitors in the future than in the past. But as the nature of international politics continues to be characterized by multipolarity, China will have more maneuvering room. Diplomacy will be even more important. Hence, China's foreign aid program will probably continue to serve China's foreign policy decision-makers, and it will remain a valuable instrument of China's foreign policy. The importance of China's aid diplomacy in the future seems assured.

Addendum

After 1970, when Peking expanded its foreign aid program, it extended aid to a number of new recipients. In some cases donations were small, and in others they were only promises. In some instances the grant seemed to bear little relevance to Peking's foreign policy, or it was a donation that was not followed up by more aid and thus of questionable significance. In most cases it is too early to assess the meaning of the aid. These promises and commitments are discussed below.

In mid-1971 the Chinese government granted $2 million to the government of Chile to aid victims of storms there.[1] This was the first aid to a Latin American country. In November Peking promised the government of Guyana assistance to develop local industry; no amount of aid was mentioned at this time.[2] In December Peking promised the government of Peru a $42 million interest-free loan.[3] Thus it appeared that Peking had developed interests in Latin America. The emergency assistance to Chile was obviously given to help the new Marxist government there. Subsequent aid donations to Chile will be discussed below.

In April 1972 a protocol was signed to implement aid to Guyana, and Chinese experts were sent.[4] Seven projects were started shortly thereafter. It was then revealed that China had extended a loan worth $26 million to Guyana.[5] In the fall of 1972 the Chinese government announced it would assist the government of Peru in solving its irrigation problems. Initially there was speculation that China might give military aid to Peru, since the delegation which went to Peking was a military one.[6] However, no protocols were signed to work out the details, and there is no evidence of any deliveries of military equipment or weapons. China's aid program to Latin America appeared to be meaningful in the early 1970s; recently, however, it has been dormant.

Also, in June 1971 China signed an agreement with the government of Iraq for an interest-free loan worth $40 million.[7] It was announced that repayment would be scheduled for the ten-year period beginning in 1984 and that the loan would be used for factories, equipment, and technical assistance.[8] Negotiations for this loan had gone quite far, but the loan was not drawn in coming months and a protocol agreement was signed only in December of 1972.[9] Currently, there is no evidence of the loan being used. In view of the Soviet Union's donations of large quantities of military equipment to the Iraq government in 1973, it appears that Peking will probably not deliver its aid.

In 1971 China also made aid commitments to Equatorial Guinea and Sierra Leone for the first time. In the case of the former, Chinese sources report that a protocol on the aid was signed and that Chinese specialists were sent to Equatorial Guinea.[10] No details were made known about the amount or use of this aid. No protocol was signed with the government of Sierra Leone, and no aid was seen there in subsequent months. Since then, however, China has implemented its aid promises to these two countries; this will be discussed in following pages.

In April 1972 Peking added another European nation, the first non-Communist European country, to its list of recipients when it granted aid to Malta. Malta's Prime Minister visited Peking at that time and returned with a promise of $42 million in the form of a loan.[11] The agreement provided that Chinese technicians would work on projects in Malta, thus giving Peking a presence on the strategically located island. In August Chinese technical personnel arrived in Malta and started work on several aid projects.[12] The major project was a dock.[13]

Also, in 1972 Peking promised aid to another Middle Eastern country—Tunisia. In August an agreement was signed whereby China would provide credits worth $40 million.[14] In 1973 there were Chinese medical workers in Tunisia but no other evidence of aid money being used.[15]

Several African countries also became first recipients of China's aid in 1972: Burundi, Mauritius, Rwanda, Cameroon, Togo, Nigeria, Malagasy Republic, and Dahomey. In the case of Burundi, no official announcement of aid was made; however, in February 1973 the Cabinet in Burundi discussed the use of a "Chinese loan given in 1972."[16] It was later reported that this loan was for $20 million. Aid to Mauritius was apparently promised when the Prime Minister visited Peking in April. A loan worth $31.6 million was announced shortly after that.[17] Initial evidence supports the report that this aid was given for building an airport. There has been some speculation that China lacks the technology for this project, and there has been some adverse reaction to the Chinese demand that its goods be sold locally to pay for part of the project.[18]

In May Peking reached an economic and technical agreement, including aid, with the government of Rwanda, and a protocol to this agreement was signed in October.[19] It was later reported that an interest-free loan worth $22 million was given, and that Chinese credits were to be used for the construction of a road linking Rwanda and Tanzania and for a cement factory.[20]

In August it was reported that Peking had signed an aid agreement with the government of Cameroon.[21] It was subsequently revealed that this was an interest-free loan for $73 million, repayable over a ten-year period with a grace period of ten years.[22] No mention was made of the use of this loan, however; and no Chinese aid activity has yet been observed in Cameroon. This aid may have been given for building a dam, which the Chinese had talked about before. This would explain the size of the loan.

In September Peking signed an economic and technical accord with the government of Togo. Later it was disclosed that China had promised an interest-free loan worth $45 million to Togo as part of this agreement.[23] No further details have been forthcoming regarding this aid, and there is no evidence to date of Chinese aid delivered to Togo. The loan was apparently related to diplomatic ties, which were established at this time.

In November Mao penned an agreement on economic and technical cooperation and a trade pact with the government of Nigeria. Three months later the Chinese press mentioned sending agricultural specialists to Nigeria.[24] Later Nigerian sources reported that there were development projects in Nigeria being built jointly by China and Nigeria; Chinese technicians were also mentioned.[25] This suggests that the earlier economic agreement contained a provision for aid, but no official announcement has been made to confirm this.

In December Peking signed an agreement on economic and technical cooperation with the government of Dahomey. Later it was reported in Dahomey that China had offered a loan worth $45.1 million.[26] No further details have been published. This loan was made simultaneously with the reestablishment of diplomatic ties. A Chinese loan of $9 million to the Malagasy Republic was also reported to have been made in 1972.[27] But no date was cited, and there was no official agreement or pronouncment coming from either government. The reporting source noted only that the loan was for a tourist complex and rice and supplies. Later it was revealed that China agreed to finish a hotel started by South Africa but discontinued when relations were severed.

In 1972 Peking signed a protocol agreement with Equatorial Guinea suggesting that its aid promised in 1971 might be drawn.[28] Subsequently, Chinese were seen in Equatorial Guinea working on agricultural projects, and Chinese equipment of various kinds was observed on display in the capital of Equatorial Guinea.[29] Also, Chinese medical personnel were sent.[30] Additional agreements were also signed with the government of Sierra Leone, including a protocol on the construction of a sports stadium and two bridges.[31] Chinese medical teams were observed in Sierra Leone, and an agreement was reached whereby Peking would build eleven rice stations.[32] It was reported at this time that the Chinese loan to Sierra Leone was worth $30 million.[33]

Also, beginning in 1972 Peking extended more aid to Chile: $70 million for small- and medium-sized industries.[34] It was reported that this loan was in foreign currencies to be used over a four-year period and was to be repaid over a term of ten years.[35] In December another loan was announced for $12 million, interest-free and for foodstuffs.[36] In early 1973 it was reported that Chinese aid to Chile had reached $100 million.[37] Peking's share of total Communist aid to Chile was about one-fourth.[38] Mao wanted a voice in the Communist Party there and perhaps hoped to influence leftist movements throughout the rest of Latin America. However, the overthrow of Allende destroyed these prospects and brought an end to Chinese aid to Chile. Probably the main portion of this aid had not been used.

In January 1973 Peking made a promise of aid to the government of Zaire in the form of an interest-free loan reportedly worth $100 million for the development of agriculture.[39] This promise was made during President Mobuto's visit to Peking, and Mao allegedly said at the time: "I have lost much money and arms trying to overthrow you." This aid was apparently an effort to put relations between the two countries on a friendly basis and mark the end of China's support for forces seeking liberation of the country. It probably reflected as well a greater concern for events in Angola.[40] In June 1974 it was reported that Chinese advisors in Zaire were helping train troops for use in Angola.[41]

In July diplomatic relations were established between China and Niger. It was later reported that China gave Niger a loan or grant worth $1 million.[42] The two were probably related. In September Peking signed an agreement with the government of Upper Volta and promised a loan.[43] This loan was later estimated at $50 million.[44] Also, in September China negotiated a loan with the Chad.[45] This loan was also said to be worth $50 million.[46] However, since these aid promises are recent and no details were published on the agreements, it is unknown at this time what they will be used for. And there is no way to know that they will actually be drawn. Chinese aid may also have been given to Gabon, but neither side has provided any confirmation.

During 1974 no new countries were added to China's list of recipients. In addition to China's already established aid recipients, most new donations went to African countries. Tanzania, Zambia, and Mauritania received major donations, which have already been discussed. Niger received a second small grant worth $5 million and Upper Volta $2 million, suggesting that China's initial promises to these countries in 1973 were sincere. Somalia and Guinea also received small sums.

In 1975 Peking continued to make aid donations and included more new recipients. In March Guyana's prime minister traveled to Peking and was granted credits to buy Chinese goods worth $10 million.[47] It is uncertain whether this was part of the grant promised in 1972 or if this was a new donation. It is also possible that none of the 1972 aid was actually given, and this announcement merely reflected a renegotiation of that aid. In that same month Peking negotiated a long-term trade agreement with Morroco, which included two aid agreements.[48] No other details were made available. In March it was reported that China had granted aid to Mozambique.[49] Again no details were available. This aid was probably given to help friendly forces there during the independence movement. In June the official Chinese News Agency reported that China has the "responsibility of supporting our brothers' struggle for liberation."[50]

In April 1975 it was reported that China turned over telecommunications equipment as a gift to the government of the Maldives.[51] This was probably a follow-up to an earlier promise of aid and reflects China's strategic interests in the Indian Ocean. No details were made known about the cost or conditions, if any, of this aid. It was also reported during 1975 that China gave aid to Angola, but this doubtless was in the form of military arms and supplies and cannot be confirmed as to amount or conditions.

These recent donations, if they are fulfilled, represent a much greater Chi-

nese interest in Africa and a continued desire to win diplomatic recognition—
perhaps to completely isolate Taipei in order to force the Nationalist Chinese to
negotiate a reversion of Taiwan. Alternatively Peking may seek leverage in dealing
with the Soviet Union in the U.N. and other international organizations. Most of
the new countries China has aided in the past three or four years have received
little or no aid from the Soviet Union. China's new aid also expresses a reorienta-
tion concerning national liberation, which appears to be redefined to be aimed
at the white regimes in Africa. Also, China seems to be more concerned with
trade relations and attaining certain vital raw materials. Zaire for example has
large quantities of uranium. Peking's aims also include winning commitments
from more Third World nations in an effort to lead the underdeveloped world.

In September 1975 it was reported that Peking made a loan without interest to the government of Cambodia for $1 billion and was presenting $20 million
as a gift.[51] This was to pay for economic and military assistance over a period of
five or six years. If this donation is confirmed it marks the largest single donation
in the history of China's aid-giving and it boosts China's total aid commitments
considerably, as well as changing the focus of China's aid program. This promise
probably represents an attempt by Peking to insure the new Cambodian government the economic support it needs in view of competing Vietnamese and Soviet
influence. It may also suggest that Peking is resigned to the fact of greater Soviet
influence in Vietnam and may be cutting its aid to Hanoi. Likewise it hints that
Chinese decision makers foresee considerable rivalry for influence with the Soviet
Union and feel that they must try to make Cambodia a Chinese satellite after the
Albanian model and write off Vietnam and possibly Laos. Alternatively China
may see Cambodia as a beachhead for expanding its influence into Laos. Certainly the implications of this promise are far reaching.

Appendixes

Appendix A

Speech by Chou En-lai, January 15, 1964,
Setting Forth the Eight Principles of
China's Foreign Aid[a]

In providing economic and technical aid to other countries, the Chinese Government strictly observes the following eight principles:

First, the Chinese Government always bases itself on the principle of equality and mutual benefit in providing aid to other countries. It never regards such aid as a kind of unilateral alms but as something mutual. Through such aid the friendly new emerging countries gradually develop their own national economy, free themselves from colonial control, and strengthen the anti-imperialist forces in the world. This is in itself a tremendous support to China.

Second, in providing aid to other countries, the Chinese Government strictly respects the sovereignty of the recipient countries, and never asks for any privileges or attaches any conditions.

Third, the Chinese Government provides economic aid in the form of interest-free or low-interest loans and extends the time limit for the repayment so as to lighten the burden of the recipient countries as far as possible.

Fourth, in providing aid to other countries, the purpose of the Chinese Government is not to make the recipient countries dependent on China but to help them embark on the road of self-reliance step by step.

Fifth, the Chinese Government tries its best to help the recipient countries build projects which require less investment while yielding quicker results, so that the recipient governments may increase their income and accumulate capital.

Sixth, the Chinese Government provides the best-quality equipment and material of its own manufacture at international market prices. If the equipment and material provided by the Chinese Government are not up to the agreed specifications and quality, the Chinese Government undertakes to replace them.

Seventh, in giving any particular technical assistance, the Chinese Government will see to it that the personnel of the recipient country fully master such techniques.

Eighth, the experts dispatched by the Chinese Government to help in construction in the recipient countries will have the same standard of living as the experts of the recipient country. The Chinese experts are not allowed to make any special demands or enjoy any special amenities.

[a]From *Afro-Asian Solidarity Against Imperialism* (Peking: Languages Press, 1964).

Appendix B

**China's Economic and Technical Aid
to Other Countries[a]**

Equality and mutual benefit, mutual support, respect for the recipient countries' sovereignty and absence of any attached conditions—these are the basic principles guiding China's economic and technical aid to foreign countries.

In the dark years of old China, the Chinese people were subjected to untold enslavement and plunder by the imperialist powers. Their heroic and unyielding struggles have earned them the right to live equally and independently among the world's nations. From the day of its founding the People's Republic of China, as a Socialist country, has stood firmly for equality among countries and has opposed the imperialist policy of aggression, especially the rabid plans for world domination by U.S. imperialism. The Chinese people will never bully others, nor will they allow others to ride roughshod over them and order them about.

At the same time, the people of China hold that the struggles waged by the proletariat and other working people of different countries are indivisibly linked together. The imperialists' domineering acts have stirred up an angry wave of resistance among the oppressed peoples and nations everywhere. Struggles of the peoples, no matter how far apart they are from each other geographically, are closely co-ordinated and mutually supporting. In the united front of the peoples against imperialism, those countries where revolution has triumphed, including the Socialist and anit-imperialist nationalist countries, also assist and support each other in their national construction.

China's Economic Relations with Fraternal and Friendly Countries

The Chinese people are guided by these conceptions in handling their economic relations with fraternal and friendly countries.

Proletarian internationalism is the principle guiding China in her economic relations with the fraternal countries in the Socialist camp. The common aim of the proletariat of the world and of the people of the Socialist countries is to realize the great ideal of Communism and build a new world without imperialism,

[a]Ai Ching-chu, in *Peking Review,* August 21, 1964.

without Capitalism, and without exploitation of man by man. In the light of this common aim, the Socialist countries should assist and support each other; each country should exchange what it has for what it hasn't and what it abounds for what it lacks. On the basis of self-reliance, they should promote the common upsurge of their respective economies and continuously increase the strength of the Socialist camp; at the same time, they should treat each other as equals and respect each other's independence and sovereignty. In this spirit, the Chinese people have consistently worked for strengthening economic cooperation with fraternal countries.

The Chinese people greatly appreciate and are eternally grateful for the support given by the fraternal countries to China's Socialist construction. At the same time, they regard it as their bounden duty to support their fraternal countries in national construction.

Economic and technical cooperation between China and friendly nationalist countries is built on the five principles: mutual respect for sovereignty and territorial integrity, mutual nonaggression, noninterference in each other's internal affairs, equality and mutual benefit and peaceful coexistence. It is also carried out in the spirit of mutual support. Despite the fact that China and these friendly countries have different social and political systems, they are bound closely together by their common experiences under imperialist and colonialist aggression and oppression, their common struggle to oppose imperialism, safeguard national independence, and defend world peace and their common task of national construction. This has opened up great practical possibilities for their economic and technical cooperation.

When China offers economic and technical aid to these friendly countries, she regards them as close friends who can sincerely cooperate in a common task. By persisting in their struggle against imperialism and continuously increasing their anti-imperialist strength, the new emerging independent countries are rendering great support to China as well as to the people of the rest of the world who cherish peace and justice. In providing them with aid, China has done nothing more than her share of international duty. How can it be conceived that such mutual support would have any conditions or privileges attached?

The Nature of Imperialist "Aid"

To anyone who respects facts, it is clear that the "aid" given by the imperialist countries which are pursuing a "jungle law" policy is characterized by severe conditions and demands for a variety of privileges. A most typical example is the "aid" by U.S. imperialism. While exporting large sums of government capital in the form of foreign "aid," the U.S. Government uses its "aid" to interfere crudely in the internal affairs of the recipient countries, seize various privileges to make investments, dump commodities, and plunder raw and strategic materials in these countries, and force them to follow its dictates. It even resorts to sub-version to turn them into its satellites.

Today when the revolutionary storm is sweeping Asia, Africa, and Latin America, U.S. imperialism, of course, sometimes has to adopt certain hypocriti-cal measures, using small favours as bait to trap recipient countries. But no nominal changes, however numerous, can conceal the true nature of U.S. "aid."

In the 1960s anyone is bound sooner or later to be rolling in the dust if, defying justice, he tries to fish in troubled waters behind a smokescreen of "aid," and indulges in subversion, in the new emerging independent countries. He will be sneered at if he poses as a "benefactor" because he has provided others with something, and throws his weight around, demanding privileges.

In the field of international economics, as in others, all the intrigues of imperialism and the reactionary forces in its service will eventually go bankrupt. The principles of equality and mutual benefit and mutual support and respect will break through every barrier put up by all reactionary forces and play their role with overwhelming efficiency.

Aim of China's Foreign Aid

The aim of China's economic and technical aid for foreign countries is to help them gradually build and develop their independent national economies by relying on their own efforts.

The success of a revolution in any country depends first of all on the strug-gle of its people; no outsiders can do the job for them. Similarly, a country which has taken an independent path must rely in the main on the spirit of its people for hard work, the display of their wisdom, and the full utilization of its own resources to build its own economic system in the light of its specific condi-tions.

The Chinese people have consistently carried out the policy of relying main-ly on their own efforts in their revolutionary struggle and economic construction. Their experiences and those of many fraternal countries have fully confirmed that this policy is practical and effective.

Some might ask: Is this not in conflict with the principle of mutual support among the people of different countries? No, not in the least. Only on the basis of self-reliance is it possible to render mutual support. Only on this basis, too, can foreign aid play its proper role through internal factors.

Under the savage rule of imperialism and colonialism in the past, the rich natural resources of the new emerging independent countries were unscrupulous-ly plundered and the wisdom of their working people was inhibited. This has resulted in the lop-sided development of their economies and the impoverish-ment of their people. After winning their political independence, the people of these countries demand that, while continuing to persist in their struggle against imperialism and old and neo- colonialism, they should built up their independent national economies as quickly as possible and catch up with the world's advanced level of economic development. Thus, by consolidating their political independence with their national economies free of foreign control, they can eliminate the internal economic sources of comeback attempts by imperialism and old and nèo- colonialism and forestall all the reactionaries' schemes of subversion. It is necessary for these countries to rely steadfastly on the strength of their people, energetically develop their domestic resources, and bring into full play all the potentialities at home, while receiving aid from friendly countries on the basis of equality and mutual benefit. So long as they do this it is certain that they will be able to build up and develop their independent national economies according to their specific domestic conditions. This will enable them to support the struggles of the people of other countries.

Objective conditions vary from country to country. For instance, among the countries with vast land and rich natural resources some may have large populations, while others may be sparsely populated. There are also countries with a relatively small area and a big population but rich in special products. In short, each country has its own favorable conditions for developing its economy. If every country implements a correct policy of economic development in accordance with its specific conditions and practices economic cooperation with other countries on the basis of equality and mutual benefit, international economic cooperation will become two-way traffic. Each country will exchange what it has for what it hasn't and what it abounds for what it lacks.

Helping Recipients Build Independent Economies

Proceeding from the principle of equality and mutual benefit and mutual support, China's foreign aid aims at helping the recipient countries to regenerate by their own efforts; she never has any national egoism in mind. Based entirely on the practical needs of and possibilities existing in the recipient countries, China helps them build and develop their independent national economies. She never starts from her own economic interests and tries to serve its own economy by placing the economies of the recipient countries in a dependent position.

First, in the light of the natural conditions of the countries concerned, China helps them to make use of all favourable factors to develop a diversified agriculture suited to domestic needs. No attempt is made to turn them into mere bases for supplying her with certain agricultural products.

Appendix C

China's Economic and Technical
Cooperation with Friendly
Countries[a]

Guided by Chairman Mao's revolutionary line on foreign affairs, China's relations with foreign countries have steadily developed over the twenty-five years since the founding of the People's Republic. "We have friends all over the world," as Chairman Mao has said. Socialist revolution and construction in China have all along enjoyed the sympathy and support of friendly countries of the Third World and of the people elsewhere. The Chinese people, on their part, regard it as their internationalist duty to support the just struggles of the oppressed nations and people of the world and help friendly countries develop their national economies independently and self-reliantly. China has established economic and technical cooperation relations with more than fifty countries, providing them with aid to the best of her ability. The magnitude of her foreign aid has registered a marked increase since the Great Proletarian Cultural Revolution. Supporting each other politically and economically, China and the friendly countries of the Third World have thus promoted their respective independent development and constantly enhanced their friendship.

Internationalism—the Guiding Principle

Proletarian internationalism is the guiding principle of China's foreign policy and also of her foreign aid.

In providing economic and technical aid to other countries, China abides by the eight principles made known by Premier Chou En-lai in late 1963 and early 1964 during his visit to Africa; these principles epitomize the basic policies of China's foreign aid in the spirit of internationalism.

Chairman Mao has said: "The just struggles of the people of all countries support each other." China is a developing Socialist country belonging to the Third World. She and the friendly countries of the Third World have experienced similar sufferings in the past and are today facing common militant tasks. The struggle against imperialism, old and new colonialism, and hegemonism has linked

[a]Chin Yi-wu, in *Peking Review,* October 25, 1974.

161

them together; national construction also calls for their mutual help and support. Therein lies the solid foundation of economic and technical cooperation between China and other Third World countries. Today China is still comparatively backward economically and technically. While working hard to build their country industriously and frugally, the Chinese people manage to save what they can to help friendly countries of the Third World develop their national economies through active economic and technical cooperation. Cooperation like this means mutual aid between developing countries. The victories of the friendly Third World countries in their struggles against imperialism, colonialism, and hegemonism are a support and inspiration to the people of China and the rest of the world. The steady development of the national economies of the Third World countries has added strength to the joint struggle of the people of the world against imperialism and hegemonism—this, too, is a support to China.

The carrying out of internationalist duty makes it imperative to strictly respect the sovereignty of the recipient countries and their status as equals. Countries, big or small, poor or rich, receiving or providing aid, should treat each other on an equal footing. China only has the duty of helping her friends wholeheartedly but no right whatsoever to order others about. Whether in discussing economic and technical agreements or in the course of honouring such agreements, China strictly respects the sovereignty of the other country concerned in full and friendly consultations; in no way will China ever impose any condition on the recipient countries or interfere in their internal affairs. This is a principle a Socialist country should abide by in foreign aid. On the contrary, if a country asks for various privileges in the name of "foreign aid" and rides roughshod over others, controlling and plundering them, it is out-and-out hegemonism and neo-colonialism, anything but internationalism.

Aim of China's Economic and Technical Aid to Foreign Countries

In providing economic and technical aid, China aims at helping friendly countries develop their national economies independently and self-reliantly. This is also a concrete manifestation of the principle of internationalism.

In national construction, the Third World countries depend mainly on their own people. Foreign aid is only supplementary. The reliable way for these countries to develop their national economies and win economic liberation is to rely on their own efforts, supplemented by foreign aid given on the basis of equality and mutual assistance. In her aid to friendly countries, China helps them proceed from their actual conditions, rely on the strength and wisdom of their people, make use of their own resources, step by step build up agriculture, light industry, and heavy industry that suit the needs of their own people, and gradually free themselves from economic dependence on other countries.

To help friendly countries set out on the road of self-reliance, it is necessary
to arrange the aid projects in order of importance and urgency according to the
recipient countries' needs. Prolonged colonialist and imperialist rule has resulted
in a lop-sided, single-product economy in some developing countries. In the light
of actual conditions, China first of all helps them develop agriculture and light
industry to solve the problem of food, clothing, and other daily necessities. On
this basis some heavy industrial projects will be built up step by step. Results
show that this practice conforms to the actual needs of the developing countries
and the interests of their people and serves to help them gradually end their economic dependence on others by establishing and developing their national economies.

In helping friendly countries develop their national economies self-reliantly,
the scope of aid projects is decided by both their needs and China's own ability.
At present, medium-sized and small projects form the bulk of the items China
offers to build in cooperation with the friendly countries. These projects which
require less investment but produce faster results, yielding fairly quick returns
for the accumulation of funds. To meet the actual needs for economic development of friendly countries, China also has started helping them build certain big
projects such as metallurgical complexes, oil refineries, heavy machinery plants,
power stations, railways, and highways. In all this aid, be it big projects of heavy
industry and communications, or medium-sized and small projects of agriculture
and light industry, the aim is always the same, i.e., to help friendly countries
develop independently and through self-reliance. In helping friendly countries
develop a complete industrial branch covering everything from raw materials to
finished products, China aims at helping them make full use of their own resources and gradually free themselves from being exploited through the exchange
of unequal values in which they export raw materials cheap and import finished
products at high prices. In the case of countries lacking raw materials for a certain branch of industry, China first of all helps them solve the raw material
problem. For instance, she helps some countries plant sugarcane before she pro-
ceeds to help them construct sugar refineries.

In helping friendly countries develop their national economies self-reliantly,
China also helps their people master technical know-how. Chinese technicians
helping build aid projects in friendly countries pass on their skills in real earnest
to local people. They withdraw as soon as the local people have mastered the
techniques involved. Passing on techniques and learning to master them are also
a form of mutual help for common progress. The technical force in some friendly countries grows in the construction of the aid projects; at the same time, Chinese technicians are tempered in the process since they too have much to learn
from the local people.

To help Third World countries develop independently and self-reliantly or
to make use of "aid" to try to make the recipient country become dependent
economically so as to control and plunder it—this is the test for distinguishing

genuine from sham aid. Under the signboard of "helping" developing countries, Soviet revisionist social-imperialism tries its utmost to control the vital branches of the economy of some developing countries and rob them of strategic raw materials and other important products. Soviet revisionism wildly attacks China's foreign aid policy of helping the friendly Third World countries stand on their own feet. Its attempt is to sow discord between China and the countries friendly to her and undermine the united struggle of the people of the Third World. This is futile. If people compare the demagogic propaganda by the Soviet revisionist clique with its ugly performance, they will see clearly that like U.S. imperialism, it is the biggest international exploiter and oppressor of our time and is even more sinister in the way it exploits and overreaches.

Sincere Cooperation

China's aid to foreign countries is either gratis or loans on favorable terms, a form of cooperation between friends. In consultations to decide the use and repayment of the loans, China fully respects the sovereignty of the recipient countries and takes into consideration their actual needs. As a Socialist country, China neither exports capital nor practices usury. Before 1964 most of her loans to foreign countries were interest-free, with the rest of them at low interest. All her loans to foreign countries extended after that year have been interest-free. The time limit for repayment is long. If the recipient country cannot repay when a loan is due, repayment can be deferred time and again. China does not give loans to friendly nations in order to derive economic gains by an early recovery of the capital or sharing the specified products of the recipient countries. She never exerts pressure on them or tries to control them through extending loans or pressing for repayment of loans.

Bearing in mind Chairman Mao's teaching "In our international relations, we Chinese people should get rid of great-power chauvinism resolutely, thoroughly, wholly, and completely," Chinese personnel working on aid programs abroad treat the people of the recipient countries as equals, strictly abide by the laws and ordinances of the governments of these countries, and respect the customs and habits of the local people. They modestly learn from the strong points of the people in the host countries. Chinese technicians have been shown kind concern by the governments and people of the friendly nations. They have forged a profound friendship with the local people in the course of caring for each other, learning from and helping each other, and working together . . . .

China's economic development is still at a rather low level and her material strength is limited. In providing aid to foreign countries, her strength is not equal to her will. Friends in various countries have praised China for the way she provides aid to foreign countries. This is a great encouragement to China. It also helps Chinese personnel working on aid programs to pay attention to examining and overcoming the shortcomings in their work. It helps them to work harder so that China's economic and technical aid can be more effective and beneficial to the people of the recipient countries and contribute more to the development of the national economies of the friendly nations and to the common cause of the Third World against imperialism and hegemonism.

Notes

Notes

Chapter 1
The Roots of China's Foreign Aid Diplomacy

1. *World Bank Atlas* (Washington, D.C.: International Bank for Reconstruction and Development, 1969).
2. *Ta Kung Pao* (Tienstin), October 13, 1959.
3. *The China Quarterly,* Quarterly Chronicle and Documentation, November-December 1962.
4. Arthur G. Ashbrook, Jr., "China: Economic Policy and Economic Results, 1949-71," in *People's Republic of China: An Economic Assessment* (Washington, D.C.: U.S. Government Printing Office, 1972).
5. See C.P. Fitzgerald, *The Chinese View of Their Place in the World* (London: Oxford University Press, 1964) and John K. Fairbank (ed.), *The Chinese World Order: Traditional China's Foreign Relations* (Cambridge: Harvard University Press, 1968).
6. Immanuel C.Y. Hsu, *China's Entrance into the Family of Nations: The Diplomatic Phase, 1858-1920* (Cambridge: Harvard University Press, 1968), chapter 1.
7. John K. Fairbank, "On the Ch'ing Tributary System," *Harvard Journal of Asiatic Studies,* June 1941.
8. John K. Fairbank, *The United States and China* (New York: Viking Press, 1958), p. 108. Cf. Mark Mancall, "The Persistence of Tradition in Chinese Foreign Policy," in *Annals of the Academy of Political and Social Science,* September 1963.
9. Immanuel C.Y. Hsu, *The Rise of Modern China* (New York: Oxford University Press, 1970), p. 177.
10. Albert Feuerwerker, "Relating to the International Community," in *China's Development Experience* Michael Oksenberg (ed.) (New York: Praeger Publishers, 1973), p. 44.
11. Mary C. Wright, *The Last Stand of Chinese Conservatism* (New York: New York University Press, 1970), pp. 222-250.
12. See Ping-ti Ho and Tang Tsou (eds.), *China in Crisis: China's Heritage and the Communist Political System* (Chicago: University of Chicago Press, 1968). Various aspects of this problem are discussed in this two-volume book by a number of China scholars.
13. See John Gittings, *The World and China, 1922-1972* (New York: Harper and Row Publishers, 1974).
14. Harold C. Hinton, *China's Turbulent Quest: An Analysis of China's Foreign*

Relations since 1945 (New York: The Macmillan Company, 1970), chapter 5.

15. See Peter VanNess, *Revolution and Chinese Foreign Policy* (Berkeley: University of California Press, 1971).

16. Arthur Huck, *The Security of China* (New York: Columbia University Press, 1970), chapter 1.

17. Harold C. Hinton, *Communist China in World Politics* (Boston: Houghton Mifflin Company, 1966), chapters 11 and 12.

18. *Ibid.* chapter 15.

19. See Vidya Prakash Dutt, *China's Foreign Policy, 1958–62* (Bombay: Asia Publishing House, 1964).

20. Alexander Eckstein, *Communist China's Economic Growth and Foreign Trade: Implications for U.S. Policy* (New York: McGraw-Hill Book Company, 1966), chapter 2.

21. A Doak Barnett, *Communist China and Asia: A Challenge to American Policy* (New York: Vintage Press, 1960), Chapter 9.

22. See Jerome Alan Cohen (ed.), *The Dynamics of China's Foreign Relations* (Cambridge: Harvard University Press, 1970). This is the theme of most of the articles in this book.

23. See J.D. Simmonds, *China's World: The Foreign Policy of a Developing State* (New York: Columbia University Press, 1970).

24. See Cheng Chu-yuan, *Economic Relations Between Peking and Moscow, 1949–1963* (New York: Praeger Publishers, 1964).

25. See Alice Langley Hsieh, *Communist China's Strategy in the Nuclear Era* (Englewood Cliffs, N.J.: Prentice-Hall, Inc., 1962), chapter 2 in connection with China's military policies vis-à-vis dealing with U.S. atomic power.

26. R.G. Boyd, *Communist China's Foreign Policy* (New York: Praeger Publishers, 1962), chapter 3. The author notes a major change in China's foreign policy at this time.

27. See Herbert Passin, *China's Cultural Diplomacy* (New York: Praeger Publishers, 1963).

28. Barnett, *Communist China and Asia,* chapter 7.

Chapter 2
Aid to Communist Bloc Nations

1. See Peter S.H. Tang, *Communist China Today: Domestic and Foreign Policies* (New York: Praeger Publishers, 1957), p. 483 for a list of the reasons for Mao's alliance with the Communist bloc. Also see James C. Hsiung, *Ideology and Practice: The Evolution of Chinese Communism* (New York: Praeger, 1970), p. 189.

2. Arthur G. Ashbrook, Jr., "Main Lines of Chinese Communist Economic Policy," in *An Economic Profile of Mainland China, I* (Washington, D.C.: U.S. Government Printing Office, 1967), p. 22.

3. See Barnett, *Communist China and Asia,* pp. 373–374.

4. See Donald S. Zagoria, *The Sino-Soviet Conflict, 1956–1961* (Princeton: Princeton University Press, 1962), p. 68 and p. 87; Barnett, *Communist China and Asia,* p. 275; and David Floyd, *Mao Against Khrushchev* (New York: Praeger Publishers, 1963), p. 10. These authors are in agreement that Soviet aid was not a lot measured in terms of what China needed, and it was not given on generous conditions.

5. This point deserves special emphasis if one accepts the argument presented by a number of scholars that Stalin started the war without consulting the Chinese, and Mao was dragged into a war he didn't want. See Allen Whiting, *China Crosses the Yalu: The Decision to Enter the Korean War* (New York: Macmillan, 1960), p. 90.

6. Zagoria, *The Sino-Soviet Conflict,* p. 21.

7. *North Korea: A Case Study in the Techniques of Takeover* (Washington, D.C.: U.S. Department of State, 1961), pp. 116–117.

8. Werner Levi, *Modern China's Foreign Policy* (Minneapolis: University of Minnesota Press, 1953), p. 294.

9. Eckstein, *Communist China's Growth and Foreign Trade,* p. 161.

10. New China News Agency, November 23, 1953.

11. *People's Daily,* September 28, 1958.

12. *Peking Review,* October 7, 1958.

13. *People's Daily,* October 14, 1960.

14. Marshall I. Goldman, *Soviet Foreign Aid* (New York: Praeger Publishers, 1967), pp. 24–25.

15. *Ibid.,* pp. 24–25.

16. Joseph C. Kun, "North Korea: Between Moscow and Peking," *The China Quarterly,* July–September 1967.

17. *The New York Times,* February 1, 1968.

18. *People's Daily,* March 3, 1970.

19. *Ibid.,* October 18, 1970.

20. New China News Agency, September 9, 1971.

21. *The Japan Times,* June 20, 1975.

22. Wu Chih-ying (ed.), *Hu Chih-ming Ch'uan (Biography of Ho Chi-minh)* (Shanghai: Pacific Press, 1951), p. 49.

23. Bernard B. Fall, *Street Without Joy* (New York: Schocken, 1972), p. 29.

24. Joseph A. Buttinger, *Vietnam: A Dragon Embattled* (New York: Praeger Publishers, 1967), p. 767.

25. *The New York Times,* June 29, 1951.

26. Melvin Gurtov, *The First Vietnam Crisis: Chinese Communist Strategy and United States Involvement* (New York: Columbia Univ. Press, 1968), p. 15.

27. New China News Agency, December 29, 1954.

28. *Ibid.,* July 8, 1955.

29. William Kaye, "A Bowl of Rice Divided: The Economy of North Vietnam," in *North Vietnam Today: Profile of a Communist Satellite,* P.J. Honey (ed.) (New York: Praeger Publishers, 1962), p. 115.

30. *People's Daily,* February 19, 1959.

31. P.J. Honey, *Communism in North Vietnam* (Westport, Conn.: Greenwood Press, 1973), p. 40.

32. *People's Daily,* February 1, 1961.

33. Charles B. McLane, "U.S.S.R. Policy in Asia," *Current History,* October 1965.

34. Letter from the Central Committee of the Communist Party of the U.S.S.R. quoted in *The New York Times,* March 24, 1966.

35. *People's Daily,* December 6, 1965.

36. *The New York Times,* July 28, 1968.

37. *U.S. News and World Reports,* April 3, 1967.

38. *The New York Times,* January 9, 1968.

39. Sreedhar, "China's Economic Aid Program in 1972," *China Report,* March-April 1973.

40. *The New York Times,* April 7, 1973.

41. *Ibid.,* May 1, 1975.

42. *People's Daily,* April 10, 1954.

43. *Ibid.,* August 30, 1956.

44. Goldman, *Soviet Foreign Aid,* p. 37.

45. *People's Daily,* December 30, 1958.

46. *Ibid.,* June 1, 1960.

47. Harrison Salisbury, *War Between Russia and China* (New York: Norton, 1969), p. 16.

48. Goldman, *Soviet Foreign Aid,* p. 37.

49. Salisbury, *War Between Russia and China,* p. 16.

50. Goldman, *Soviet Foreign Aid,* p. 37.

51. Dennis Warner, *Hurricane from China* (New York: Macmillan and Co., 1961), p. 101.

52. *People's Daily,* December 1, 1960.

53. *Ibid.,* February 23, 1963.

54. Goldman, *Soviet Foreign Aid,* p. 160.

55. *Ibid.,* p. 165.

56. Samuel B. Griffith, *Albania and the Sino-Soviet Rift* (Cambridge: M.I.T. Press, 1963), p. 22.

57. *People's Daily,* December 8, 1954.

58. *Asian Recorder,* No. 3912.

59. Goldman, *Soviet Foreign Aid,* p. 35 and Griffith, *Albania and the Sino-Soviet Rift,* p. 27.

60. *Peking Review,* January 20, 1959.

61. Goldman, *Soviet Foreign Aid,* p. 35.

62. *People's Daily,* April 26, 1961.

63. *Ibid.,* June 26, 1965.

64. *Ibid.,* October 20, 1966.

65. *1968 Yearbook on Communist China* (Taipei: Ministry of Defense, 1968), p. 174.

66. New China News Agency, November 21, 1968.

67. David Bligh, "Red China in Europe," *America,* March 8, 1969.

68. Sreedhar and S.K. Ghosh, "China's Foreign Aid Program," *The Institute for Defense Analysis Journal* (New Delhi), July 1972.

69. *People's Daily,* January 21, 1970.

70. Fan Wei-yuan, "Communist China's Economic and Technical Assistance to Albania," *Chinese Communist Affairs Monthly* (Taipei), September 10, 1972. The author cites as his source a Bonn newsreporter.

71. *Peking Review,* July 11, 1975

72. *People's Daily,* November 7, 1956.

73. Eckstein, *Communist China's Economic Growth and Foreign Trade,* p. 140.

74. *Peking Review,* May 29, 1970.

75. *People's Daily,* November 26, 1970.

76. *Far Eastern Economic Review,* November 27, 1971. This source cites the value of the loan at $300 million. Cf. Kang Hua, "An Analysis of Communist China's Economic Aid to the Third World," *Studies on Chinese Communism* (Taipei), October 1972. The author puts the amount at $240 million.

Chapter 3
Aid to Non-Communist Asian Nations

1. See Barnett, *Communist China and Asia,* p. 291; and Hinton, *China's Turbulent Quest,* p. 231.

2. Morton Halperin, "China's Strategic Outlook," in *China and the Peace of Asia,* Alastair Buchan (ed.) (New York: Praeger Publishers, 1965), p. 96.

3. Barnett, *Communist China and Asia,* p. 41.

4. *Ibid.,* pp. 291–292.

5. Huck, *The Security of China,* p. 44.

6. For further details, see Shigeham Matsumoto, "Japan and China," in *Policies Toward China's Views from Six Continents,* A.M. Halpern (ed.) (New York: McGraw-Hill Book Company, 1965), p. 134.

7. See Vidya P. Dutt, *China and the World: An Analysis of Communist China's Foreign Policy* (New York: Praeger Publishers, 1966), chapter 3.

8. New China News Agency, June 22, 1956.

9. Thomas Fitzsimmons, *Cambodia: Its People, Its Society, Its Culture* (New Haven: HRAF Press, 1959), p. 235.

10. New China News Agency, August 24, 1958.

11. R. Smith, "Cambodia," in *Governments and Politics of Southeast Asia,* George McKahin (ed.) (Ithaca: Cornell University Press, 1964), p. 235.

12. Dennis Warner, *Hurricane From China,* p. 87.

13. P.H.M. Jones, "Cambodia's New Factories," *Far Eastern Economic Review,* May 9, 1963.

14. "Communist China's Economic Aid to Other Countries," U.S. State Department, Intelligence Information Brief #375, February 20, 1961.

15. Alain-Gerard Marsot, "China's Aid to Cambodia," *Pacific Affairs,* Summer 1969.

16. Eckstein, *Communist China's Economic Growth and Foreign Trade,* p. 215.

17. *Peking Review,* May 6, 1966. The amount was not announced by the Chinese government and was determined from other sources. See Leo Tansky, "China's Foreign Aid: The Record," *Current Scene,* September 1972 and

Kang Hua, "An Analysis of Communist China's Economic Assistance to the Third World," *Studies on Chinese Communism,* October 1972.

18. *The New York Times,* January 5, 1968.
19. *People's Daily,* August 10, 1970
20. Laura Summers, "Consolidating the Cambodian Revolution," *Current History,* December 1975.
21. *People's Daily,* November 4, 1956.
22. *Ibid.,* March 22, 1960.
23. E. Mikaly, *Foreign Aid Politics in Nepal* (London: Oxford University Press, 1965), p. 92.
24. *People's Daily,* September 9, 1961. Details of this agreement are found in *People's Daily,* October 29, 1961.
25. "Chinese Communist Road Projects," *China Topics,* August 18, 1964.
26. Goldman, *Soviet Foreign Aid,* p. 139.
27. Leo E. Rose, "Nepal in 1965: Focus on Land Reform," *Asian Survey,* February 1966.
28. Eckstein, *Communist China's Economic Growth and Foreign Trade,* p. 214 and Goldman, *Soviet Foreign Aid,* p. 137. The latter suggests that only $3 million of the $12.7 million Chinese grant made in 1956 had been used in 1964.
29. *People's Daily,* September 8, 1965.
30. *Ibid.,* October 20, 1966.
31. *Far Eastern Economic Review 1968 Yearbook,* p. 241.
32. *Far Eastern Economic Review 1969 Yearbook,* p. 236.
33. New China News Agency, November 4 and November 27, 1972.
34. *Hong Kong Standard,* November 30, 1972.
35. *The Japan Times,* December 29, 1975.
36. *Survey of China Mainland Press,* 1406:52.
37. *Peking Review,* April 22, 1958.
38. Colin Garrett, "China as a Foreign Aid Donor," *Far Eastern Economic Review,* January 19, 1961.
39. Goldman, *Soviet Foreign Aid,* pp. 125–127.
40. *Asian Recorder,* 3949.
41. *People's Daily,* January 28, 1965.
42. New China News Agency, January 3, 1953.
43. *People's Daily,* October 4, 1957.
44. *Peking Review,* September 30, 1958.
45. See Goldman, *Soviet Foreign Aid,* p. 46. The author suggests that the deal was made in October 1960. Another source confirms the figures. See "The Communist Economic Offensive through 1964," U.S. Department of State, Research Memorandum, August 4, 1965.
46. *People's Daily,* June 16, 1964 and October 27, 1964.
47. "The Communist Economic Offensive through 1964," U.S. Department of State, Research Memorandum, August 4, 1965.
48. *People's Daily,* February 12, 1970.
49. *1971 Yearbook on Communist China,* part 12, p. 48.

50. A Jayaratnam Wilson, "Ceylon: A Time of Trouble," *Asian Survey,* February 1972.
51. *Ceylon Daily News,* May 11, 1972.
52. *The Nation,* (Sri Lanka), July 21, 1972.
53. *Far Eastern Economic Review,* May 6, 1972.
54. *The Nation,* February 25, 1972.
55. *Far Eastern Economic Review,* October 15, 1973.
56. *Ibid.,* October 3, 1975.
57. New China News Agency, December 2, 1954.
58. Hinton, *Communist China in World Politics,* p. 415.
59. New China News Agency, January 9, 1958.
60. *Peking Review,* January 13, 1961.
61. Eckstein, *Communist China's Economic Growth and Foreign Trade,* p. 214.
62. Robert A. Holmes, "Burma's Domestic Policy: The Politics of Burmanization," *Asian Survey,* March 1967.
63. F.S.V. Donnison, *Burma* (New York: Praeger Publishers, 1970), p. 234.
64. Goldman, *Soviet Foreign Aid,* p. 143.
65. Frank N. Trager, "Burma: 1967—A Better Ending than Beginning," *Asian Survey,* November 1967.
66. *Far Eastern Economic Review,* October 9, 1971.
67. *Peking Review,* April 28, 1961.
68. New China News Agency, December 2, 1962.
69. *The New York Times,* May 24 and 27, 1964.
70. *Far Eastern Economic Review 1970 Yearbook,* p. 180.
71. *1969 Yearbook on Communist China,* part 3, p. 12.
72. *Far Eastern Economic Review,* September 11, 1971.
73. *The New York Times,* January 14, 1973.
74. *Far Eastern Economic Review,* June 13, 1975.
75. *The China Quarterly,* Chronicle and Documentation, June 1975.
76. *The New York Times,* May 30 and 31, 1975.
77. *Ibid.,* June 27, 1975.
78. *Time,* October 20, 1975.
79. *The New York Times,* August 1, 1964.
80. *Ibid.,* March 24 and 27, 1966.
81. S.K. Ghosh, "China's Military Assistance Programme," *Institute for Defense Study and Analysis* (New Delhi), February 1969.
82. *People's Daily,* June 23, 1966.
83. "Communist Governments and Developing Nations: Trade and Aid in 1968," U.S. Department of State, Research Memorandum, September 5, 1969.
84. *The New York Times,* July 10 and 25, 1968.
85. *Ibid.,* January 20 and 27, March 20 and 28, 1969.
86. *Peking Review,* January 10, 1969.
87. *The New York Times,* November 15, 1970.
88. *The Military-Balance, 1970–71,* Institute of Strategic Studies (London), 1971.

89. T.J.S. George, "Peking's Pre-War Message to Pakistan," *Far Eastern Economic Review*, February 5, 1972.
90. *Facts on File 1971.*
91. New China News Agency, February 2, 1972.
92. *The New York Times*, June 3, 1972.
93. *The China Quarterly*, Chronicle and Documentation, June 1975.
94. *People's Daily*, March 26, 1965.
95. *Ibid.*, July 29, 1966.
96. *The China Quarterly*, Chronicle and Documentation, January-March 1971.
97. Radio Pakistan, May 23, 1972.
98. *The New York Times*, June 7, 1973.

Chapter 4
Aid to Middle Eastern Nations

1. Joseph Khalili, *Communist China's Interaction with the Arab Nationalists Since the Bandung Conference* (Jericho, N.Y.: Exposition Press, Inc., 1970), p. 29.
2. *Ibid.*, p. 79.
3. Manfred Halpern, *The Politics of Social Change in the Middle East and North Africa* (Princeton: Princeton University Press, 1963), p. vii.
4. Walter Z. Laqueur, *The Soviet Union and the Middle East* (New York: Praeger Publishers, 1959), p. 349.
5. Hinton, *Communist China in World Politics*, p. 179.
6. New China News Agency, November 10 and 12, 1956.
7. Malcom H. Kerr, "The Middle East and China," in *Policies Toward China*, Halpern (ed.), p. 445.
8. *Peking Review*, December 24, 1964.
9. Goldman, *Soviet Foreign Aid*, p. 73.
10. *The New York Times*, June 12, 1967.
11. *Ibid.*, December 1, 1958.
12. Hinton, *Communist China in World Politics*, p. 185; Goldman, *Soviet Foreign Aid*, p. 46; and Richard Lowenthal, "China," in *Africa and the Communist World*, Z. Brzezenski (ed.) (Stanford: Stanford University Press, 1963), p. 13. Lowenthal says the grant was to be repaid after the revolution and was for $12 million.
13. *Newsweek*, January 13, 1964.
14. *Statistical Yearbook* (New York: The United Nations, 1968), pp. 692–695.
15. Goldman, *Soviet Foreign Aid*, p. 147.
16. *Peking Review*, October 18, 1963.
17. *The New York Times*, February 4, 1965.
18. *Ibid.*, February 12, 1965.
19. *People's Daily*, June 25, 1965.
20. Radio Algiers, July 20, 1971.
21. New China News Agency, July 27, 1971.

22. New China News Agency, November 6, 1972.
23. *People's Daily,* February 22, 1963.
24. "The Communist Economic Offensive through 1964," U.S. State Department, Research Memorandum, August 4, 1965.
25. New China News Agency, April 16, 1967.
26. *Al-Sayyed* (Lebanon), cited in *Facts on File,* January 10, 1969.
27. *New York Herald Tribune,* June 26, 1971.
28. *The New York Times,* February 1, 1972.
29. New China News Agency, January 13, 1958.
30. Eckstein, *Communist China's Economic Growth and Foreign Trade,* p. 235 and Khalili, *Communist China's Interaction with the Arab Nationalists,* p. 107.
31. Chiang Tao, "Economic Aid to Asian and African Countries by Communist China," *Studies on Chinese Communism,* February 28, 1967.
32. Goldman, *Soviet Foreign Aid,* p. 152.
33. *Ibid.*
34. *People's Daily,* June 9, 1964.
35. New China News Agency, September 21, 1967.
36. *China Topics,* September 1967.
37. *The New York Times,* February 11, 1969.
38. *Ibid.,* October 9, 1970.
39. Sreedhar, "China's Economic Aid Programme in 1972," *China Report,* March-April, 1973; UPI, August 7, 1972.
40. New China News Agency, September 18, 1968.
41. *The New York Times,* June 24, 1969.
42. Middle East News Agency, July 31, 1970.
43. *China Topics,* March 8, 1972.
44. *Facts on File 1971.*
45. *China Topics,* March 1973.
46. *The China Quarterly,* Chronicle and Documentation, July-September 1970.
47. *The New York Times,* October 17, 1971.
48. *Ibid.,* July 18, 1972.
49. *China Topics,* March 1973.

Chapter 5
Aid to African Nations

1. See Robert A. Scalapino, "Sino-Soviet Competition in Africa," *Foreign Affairs,* July 1964.
2. See Bruce Larkin, *China and Africa, 1949–1970: The Foreign Policy of the People's Republic of China* (Berkeley: University of California Press, 1971): and Zbigniew Brzezinski (ed.), *Africa and the Communist World* (Stanford: Stanford University Press, 1963).
3. Zbigniew Brzezinski, "The African Challenge," in *Africa and the Communist World,* Brzezinski (ed.), p. 206.

178 CHINA'S FOREIGN AID

4. Wilson, *Anatomy of China,* p. 214.
5. Simmonds, *China's World,* p. 24.
6. Hinton, *Communist China in World Politics,* chapter 7.
7. John K. Cooley, *East Wind Over Africa: Red China's African Offensive* (New York: Walker and Co., 1965), p. 24.
8. *World Knowledge Handbook* (Peking: World Knowledge Publishing Co., 1961), p. 408; and Peter Hann, "Africa: New Target for Peking," *China Factbook, 1962* (Hong Kong), p. 111.
9. *People's Daily,* September 14, 1960.
10. Larkin, *China and Africa, 1949–1970,* p. 94.
11. Goldman, *Soviet Foreign Aid,* p. 169.
12. Daniel Wolfstone, "Sino-African Economics," *Far Eastern Economic Review,* February 13, 1964; and Goldman, *Soviet Foreign Aid,* p. 173.
13. "China's Aid Failures," *Asian Analyst,* March 1966.
14. *African Report,* February 1967.
15. *People's Daily,* November 11, 1967.
16. *The China Quarterly,* Chronicle and Documentation, January-March 1970.
17. *People's Daily,* March 13, 1970.
18. *Time,* December 7, 1970.
19. *China Topics,* March 1973.
20. New China News Agency, June 25, 1973.
21. *Facts on File 1973.*
22. *People's Daily,* August 22, 1961.
23. Goldman, *Soviet Foreign Aid,* p. 173.
24. Eckstein, *Communist China's Economic Growth and Foreign Trade,* p. 232.
25. *Peking Review,* October 26, 1962.
26. *People's Daily,* July 15, 1964.
27. *Nkrumah's Subversion in Ghana* (Accra: State Publishing Corporation, 1966), p. 56.
28. *The New York Times,* October 26, 1966.
29. *People's Daily,* September 23, 1961.
30. *Ibid.,* May 18, 1963, December 30, 1963, and March 17, 1965.
31. Goldman, *Soviet Foreign Aid,* p. 126.
32. *People's Daily,* June 10, 1966.
33. Larkin, *China and Africa, 1949–1970,* p. 94.
34. *People's Daily,* August 10, 1963.
35. Goldman, *Soviet Foreign Aid,* p. 180.
36. Waldemar A. Nielsen, *The Great Powers and Africa* (New York: Praeger Publishers, 1969), p. 213.
37. *People's Daily,* November 15, 1967.
38. *China Topics,* March 8, 1972; *World Report* (Japan), August 24, 1972.
39. Helen Desfossess, "Naval Strategy and Aid Policy: A Study of Soviet-Somali Relations," in *Chinese and Soviet Aid to Africa,* Warren Weinstein (ed.) (New York: Praeger Publishers, 1975).
40. *Ibid.*
41. Helen Kitchen (ed.), *A Handbook for Africa* (New York: Praeger Publishers, 1963), p. 182.

42. Larkin, *China and Africa, 1949–1970*, p. 94.
43. *Ibid.*
44. *People's Daily*, June 17, 1964.
45. Cooley, *East Wind Over Africa*, p. 52.
46. *Ibid.*, p. 20.
47. Chiang Tao, "Economic Aid to Asiatic-African Countries by Communist China," *Studies on Chinese Communism*, February 28, 1967.
48. Larkin, *China and Africa, 1949–1970*, p. 94.
49. *People's Daily*, July 9, 1966.
50. *Ibid.*, March 15, 1968.
51. *The Standard* (Tanzania), July 6, 1968.
52. George T. Yu, *China and Tanzania: A Study in Cooperative Interaction* (Berkeley: University of California Press, 1970), p. 36.
53. *Ibid.*, p. 66.
54. *The Sunday Telegraph* (London), June 20, 1971; and *Hong Kong Standard* June 12, 1971.
55. *The Times* (London), April 30, 1972.
56. *Facts on File 1972.*
57. *Mainichi Daily News* (Tokyo), January 15, 1973.
58. Sreedhar and Ghosh, "China's Foreign Aid Programme"; and Yu, *China and Tanzania*, p. 65.
59. *The New York Times*, March 31, 1974.
60. Nielsen, *The Great Powers and Africa*, p. 230.
61. Larkin, *China and Africa, 1949–1970*, p. 186.
62. *The Annual Economic Survey, 1968* (Tanzania), p. 83.
63. Goldman, *Soviet Foreign Aid*, p. 46.
64. *People's Daily*, June 24, 1967.
65. *China Topics*, March 2, 1972.
66. *Far Eastern Economic Review*, November 7, 1970.
67. *Facts on File 1973.*
68. New China News Agency, February 26, 1974; and Carol H. Fogarty, "China's Economic Relations with the Third World," in *China: A Reassessment of the Economy* (Washington, D.C.: U.S. Government Printing Office, 1975).
69. For further details on the history of the project, see George T. Yu, "Working on the Railroad: China and the Tanzania-Zambia Railroad," *Asian Survey*, November 1971.
70. Larkin, *China and Africa, 1949–1970*, p. 99.
71. *The Standard* (Tanzania), November 7, 1969.
72. *Peking Review*, April 17, 1968.
73. *The China Quarterly*, Chronicle and Documentation, January-March 1971.
74. New China News Agency, November 16, 1971.
75. *The Washington Post*, November 10, 1972.
76. Nadine Gordimen, "Tanzania," *Atlantic*, May 1973.
77. *Facts on File 1973.*
78. *Ibid.*
79. "China and the Tazara Railroad Project," *Current Scene*, May-June 1975.

80. Larkin, *China and Africa, 1949–1970,* p. 102.
81. Yu, "Working on the Railroad."
82. *Ibid.; The New York Times,* February 12, 1971.
83. *The New York Times,* March 4, 1970.
84. *Weekly News* (Tanzania), January 30, 1972.
85. Yu, "Working on the Railroad."
86. *Asahi Shimbun* (Tokyo), June 23, 1970.
87. *The Washington Post,* November 10, 1970.
88. *People's Daily,* May 11, 1964.
89. Cooley, *East Wind Over Africa,* p. 65.
90. *Ibid.,* p. 57.
91. Colin Legum, "Peking's Strategic Priorities in Africa," in *Footnotes to the Congo Story,* Helen Kitchen (ed.) (New York: Walher and Co., 1967), p. 107.
92. "The Communist Economic Offensive through 1964," U.S. Department of State, Research Memorandum, August 4, 1965.
93. *The New York Times,* March 11, 1966; and Larkin, *China and Africa, 1949–1970,* p. 136.
94. *China Topics,* January 28, 1966.
95. *Kenya Weekly News,* July 14, 1967.
96. *The China Quarterly,* Chronicle and Documentation, October-December 1970.
97. *People's Daily,* May 4, 1974.
98. *People's Handbook 1965* (Peking), p. 230.
99. Larkin, *China and Africa, 1949–1970,* p. 94.
100. Gordon C. McDonald, *Area Handbook for the People's Republic of the Congo* (Washington, D.C.: U.S. Government Printing Office, 1971), p. 116.
101. *People's Daily,* February 6, 1965; June 13, 1965; and September 16, 1965.
102. M. Crawford Young, "The Congo Rebellion," *African Report,* April 1965.
103. McDonald, *Area Handbook for the People's Republic of the Congo,* p. 206.
104. Sreedhar and Ghosh, "China's Foreign Aid Programme."
105. Yuan Wei-lun, "Peiping's Economic and Technical Aid to Foreign Countries in 1969," *Issues and Studies,* March 1970.
106. *The China Quarterly,* Chronicle and Documentation, January-March 1971.
107. New China News Agency, October 20, 1972.
108. Radio Brazzaville, January 6, 1973.
109. See New China News Agency, July 30, 1973; and *China Quarterly,* Chronicle and Documentation, October-December 1973.
110. "The Communist Economic Offense through 1964," U.S. Department of State, Research Memorandum, August 4, 1965.
111. *People's Daily,* April 22, 1965.
112. Cooley, *East Wind Over Africa,* p. 57.
113. *Christian Science Monitor,* June 5, 1964.
114. New China News Agency, November 22, 1973.
115. "Communist Governments and Developing Nations: Aid and Trade in 1968," U.S. Department of State, Research Memorandum, September 5, 1969.

116. *Ibid.*

117. Yuan, "Peiping's Economic and Technical Aid to Foreign Countries in 1969."

118. *The China Quarterly,* Chronicle and Documentation, July-September 1971.

119. "Communist States and Developing Countries: Aid and Trade in 1972," U.S. Department of State, Research Study.

120. *The New York Times,* October 11, 1971.

121. *The China Quarterly,* Chronicle and Documentation, July-September 1972.

122. *China Topics,* March 1973.

Chapter 6
Summary and Conclusions

1. "Communist States and Developing Countries: Aid and Trade in 1970," U.S. Department of State, Research Study, September 22, 1971.

2. *Ibid.*

3. David A. Baldwin, *Foreign Aid and American Foreign Policy* (New York: Praeger Publishers, 1966), p. 23.

4. "The Communist Economic Offensive through 1964," Research Memorandum, U.S. Department of State, August 5, 1965.

5. Joseph J. Kaplan, *The Challenge of Foreign Aid: Policies, Problems and Possibilities* (New York: Praeger Publishers, 1970), pp. 347–348.

6. *Ibid.*

7. John Montgomery, *Foreign Aid in International Politics* (Englewood Cliffs, N.J.: Prentice-Hall, Inc., 1967), p. 29.

8. Lloyd D. Black, *The Strategy of Foreign Aid* (Princeton: Van Nostrand Publishers, 1968), p. 73.

9. "Communist States and Developing Countries: Aid and Trade in 1970," U.S. Department of State, Research Study, September 22, 1971.

10. *Ibid.*

11. Fogarty, "China's Economic Relations with the Third World."

12. Montgomery, *Foreign Aid in International Politics,* p. 71.

13. Kaplan, *The Challenge of Foreign Aid,* p. 310.

14. *Ibid.*

15. John Pincus, *International Aid and International Cost Sharing* (Baltimore: The Johns Hopkins Press, 1965), pp. 116–117.

16. According to the Organization for Economic Development and Cooperation, Western loans in 1973 had a 62 percent grant factor. See *Development Cooperation,* November 1974.

17. This is the second of China's "Eight Principles on Foreign Aid." See Appendix A.

18. "The Operational Aspects of United States Foreign Policy," Doc. No. 24, 87th Congress (Washington, D.C.: U.S. Government Printing Office, 1961), pp. 31–40.

19. "Communist States and Developing Countries: Aid and Trade in 1970," U.S. Department of State, Research Study, September 22, 1971.

Addendum

1. *The New York Times,* July 4, 1971.
2. *Ibid.,* November 23, 1971.
3. *Ibid.,* December 5, 1971.
4. *Financial Times* (London), September 26, 1972.
5. *U.S. News and World Reports,* June 19, 1972.
6. *The New York Times,* December 15, 1971; and *Prensa Latina* (Havana), October 25, 1972.
7. *World Report* (Tokyo), August 29, 1972.
8. Iraqi News Agency, June 25, 1971.
9. Ibid.
10. New China News Agency, September 8, 1971; and *The China Quarterly,* Chronicle and Documentation, April-June 1971.
11. New China News Agency, April 27, 1972.
12. *Malta News,* November 10, 1972.
13. *Daily Telegraph* (London) October 23, 1972.
14. Tunis Radio, September 7, 1972.
15. New China News Agency, July 2, 1973.
16. Bujumbura Radio, February 20, 1973.
17. Fogarty, "China's Economic Relations with the Third World."
18. *Ceylon Daily News* (Sri Lanka), May 11, 1972.
19. "China's Aid to Africa," in *Chinese and Soviet Aid to Africa,* Weinstein (ed.).
20. *Daily News* (Tanzania), November 13, 1972.
21. *China Topics,* March 1973.
22. *Current Scene,* September 1972.
23. *The New York Times,* April 15, 1973.
24. Lome Radio, September 26, 1972; and "Aid and Trade in 1972," U.S. Department of State, News Release, June 1973.
25. New China News Agency, February 13, 1973.
26. Logos Radio, November 5, 1973.
27. *China Topics,* March 1973.
28. *Current Scene,* December 1973.
29. *Ibid.*
30. *China Topics,* March 1973.
31. New China News Agency, December 12, 1972 and December 1, 1973.
32. New China News Agency, December 3, 1973.
33. *China Topics,* March 1973.
34. Fogarty, "China's Economic Relations with the Third World."
35. *Facts on File,* February 13–19, 1972.
36. *Miami Herald,* February 2, 1972.

37. *El Siglo* (Santiago), December 30, 1972.

38. *China Topics,* March 1973.

39. *Time,* August 7, 1972.

40. *The New York Times,* January 29, 1973; and *Current Scene,* February 1973.

41. "China's Aid to Africa," in *Chinese and Soviet Aid to Africa,* Weinstein (ed.).

42. *Facts on File 1974.*

43. Fogarty, "China's Economic Relations with the Third World."

44. New China News Agency, September 15, 1973.

45. Fogarty, "China's Economic Relations with the Third World."

46. New China News Agency, September 20, 1973.

47. Fogarty, "China's Economic Relations with the Third World."

48. *Facts on File 1975.*

49. *Ibid.*

50. *Ibid.*

51. New China News Agency, June 25, 1975.

52. *Le Monde* (Paris), September 13, 1975.

Bibliographic Note

No monograph has been written on China's foreign aid as an instrument of Peking's foreign policy. Nor has China's foreign aid been examined in any indepth foreign policy study. However, several books have been published that deal solely or partly with Chinese foreign aid. The most recent and only book-length study written on China's foreign aid per se is Wolfgang Bartke, *China's Foreign Aid* (New York: Holmes and Meier Publishers, 1975). This book contains a short (nineteen pages) essay on China's foreign aid, which includes some information on the mechanics of China's economic assistance, aid statistics, and a list of decision-makers responsible for negotiating foreign aid. The rest of the book is comprised of a list of Chinese aid agreements and projects. Little or no attention is given to military aid, aid to other Communist countries, or the reasons for giving aid. Other books that treat China's foreign aid program are Kurt Muller, *The Foreign Aid Programs of the Soviet Bloc and Communist China: An Analysis* (New York: Walker and Company, 1964); Sidney Klein, *The Foreign Trade and Aid Policies of China* (Hong Kong: International Studies Group, 1968); and Warren Weinstein (ed.), *Chinese and Soviet Aid to Africa* (New York: Praeger Publishers, 1975). The former two are now dated, but are well-written monographs. Muller's work deals primarily with the ideology and strategy behind the Communist nations' foreign aid programs and their other economic relations with non-Communist countries; but the emphasis is on the Soviet Union rather than China. Klein's book deals with China's trade policies more than its foreign aid. Weistein's book contains a number of new and well-written articles on Chinese aid to African countries, but the coverage is by no means complete.

Some other books that contain sections or information on Chinese aid include: Alexander Eckstein, *Communist China's Economic Growth and Foreign Trade: Implications for U.S. Policy* (New York: McGraw-Hill Book Company, 1966); Marshall I. Goldman, *Soviet Foreign Aid* (New York: Praeger Publishers, 1967); Nai-Ruenn Chen and Walter Galenson, *The Chinese Economy Under Communism* (Chicago: Aldine Publishing Company, 1969); *An Economic Profile of Mainland China* (Washington, D.C.: U.S. Government Printing Office, 1967); *China: A Reassessment of the Economy* (Washington, D.C.: U.S. Government Printing Office, 1975). Eckstein's book deals primarily with China's foreign trade, but in a number of cases the author relates aid-giving to increases in trade or notes why aid did not result in continuing trade relations. Goldman treats Chinese aid in the context of Sino-Soviet aid rivalry and presents an especially good analysis of their competitive aid-giving before the Afro-Asian Conference scheduled for

185

1965. Chen and Galenson relate aid to economic development. The two Congressional studies contain a number of highly analytical articles on China's economy, some of which relate to aid-giving, plus one short article in each that deals with China's aid program.

Some yearbooks or reference books also contain information on Chinese aid. For example, the yearbook published by the Far Eastern Economic Review Limited has regularly contained information on Chinese trade and economic activities, including foreign aid. The major focus is on Asian countries. A yearly reference book published by the Ministry of Defense in the Republic of China entitled *Yearbook on Chinese Communism* (in Chinese) has a section on Peking's foreign trade and usually information on its aid activities. The Area Handbooks written primarily by scholars at the American University and published by the U.S. Army contain a section on foreign policy and a chapter on economic development. These books were useful in checking the recipient countries' response to foreign aid, of course including China's, and helped ascertain whether Chinese aid was actually used and for what purposes.

In addition to these monographs and reference books a number of articles have been written partially or wholly on the subject of China's foreign aid. Following is a partial list: "The Communist Economic Offensive through 1964," Research Memorandum, U.S. Department of State; "Communist Governments and Developing Nations: Aid and Trade in 1968," Research Memorandum, U.S. Department of State; "Communist States and Developing Countries: Aid and Trade in 1970," Research Study, U.S. Department of State; "Communist States and Developing Countries: Aid and Trade in 1972," Research Study, U.S. Department of State; "Communist States and Developing Countries: Aid and Trade in 1974," Research Study, U.S. Department of State; Leo Tansky, "China's Foreign Aid: The Record," *Current Scene,* December 1972; W.F. Choa, "China's Aid to Developing Countries," *The China Mainland Review,* June 1965; Marshall I. Goldman, "Communist Aid: Successes and Shortcomings," *Current History,* August 1966; Peter A. Poole, "Communist China's Aid Diplomacy," *Asian Survey,* November 1966; "China's Aid Failures," *Asian Analyist,* March 1966; Sreedhar and S.K. Ghosh, "China's Foreign Aid Programme," *The Institute for Defense Studies and Analysis Journal* (New Delhi), July 1972; Sreedhar, "China's Economic Aid Programme in 1972," *China Report* (New Delhi), March-April 1973; Yuan Wei-lun, "Peiping's Economic and Technical Aid to Foreign Countries in 1969," *Issues and Studies* (Taipei), March 1970; Kang Hua, "An Analysis of Communist China's Economic Assistance to the Third World," (in Chinese) *Studies on Chinese Communism* (Taipei), October 1972; Hang Hua, "An Analysis of Communist China's Aid to African and Asian Nations in Railroad and Highway Construction," (in Chinese) *Chinese Communist Affairs Monthly* (Taipei), December 1972; Chiang Tao, "Economic Aid to Asiatic-African Countries by Communist China," (in Chinese), *Studies on Chinese Communism* (Taipei), February 1967.

Several newspapers and news magazines also supplied valuable information on China's aid diplomacy. *The New York Times* was the most useful because of its detailed index, which has a heading on foreign aid that lists donor countries. *The Christian Science Monitor* was also useful. *Time, Newsweek,* and the *Far Eastern Economic Review* regularly carry news on China's external activities. China Topics frequently devotes issues to China's external activities, including aid giving. In addition, *The China Quarterly* contains a section entitled chronicle and documentation and *Current Scene* a list of monthly activities that cites China's diplomatic events. *People's Daily* (in Chinese), the major newspaper published in China, *Peking Review,* China's major weekly news magazine, and reports of the New China News Agency provided original source material on aid negotiations, terms, etc., as well as China's aid policies and relations with foreign countries.

A number of books on China's foreign policy were useful in relating China's foreign aid donations to its external strategies and tactics. Among the most useful were: A. Doak Barnett, *Communist China and Asia: Challenge to American Policy* (New York: Harper and Row, 1960); Harold C. Hinton, *Communist China in World Politics* (Boston: Houghton Mifflin, 1966); Harold C. Hinton, *China's Turbulent Quest* (New York: Macmillan and Company, 1970); R.G. Boyd, *Communist China's Foreign Policy* (New York: Praeger Publishers, 1962); Vidya Prakash Dutt, *China's Foreign Policy, 1958–62* (Bombay: Asia Publishing House, 1964); Vidya Pakash Dutt, *China and the World: An Analysis of Communist China's Foreign Policy* (New York: Praeger Publishers, 1964); Peter VanNess, *Revolution and Chinese Foreign Policy* (Berkeley: University of California Press, 1971); Ishwer C. Ojha, *Chinese Foreign Policy in an Age of Transition* (Boston: Beacon Press, 1969); Arthur Huck, *The Security of China* (New York: Columbia University Press, 1970); Jerome Alan Cohen (ed.), *The Dynamics of China's Foreign Relations* (Cambridge: Harvard University Press, 1970); Herbert Passin, *China's Cultural Diplomacy* (New York: Praeger Publishers, 1962); J.D. Simmonds, *China's World: The Foreign Policy of a Developing State* (New York: Columbia University Press, 1970); Arthur Lall, *How Communist China Negotiates* (New York: Columbia University Press, 1968); A.M. Halpern (ed.), *Policies Toward China: Views from Six Continents* (New York: McGraw-Hill Book Company, 1965); Robert C. North, *China's Foreign Relations* (Belmont, Calif.: Dickenson Publishing Company, 1969); John Gittings, *The World and China, 1922–1972* (New York: Harper and Row, 1975).

Barnett's *Communist China and Asia* was especially useful in relating aid donations to foreign policy objectives during the 1950s. Hinton's *Communist China in World Politics* provided valuable insights into China's aims in negotiating border agreements and treaties of friendship, which I have linked to aid promises. Dutt's *China and the World* was helpful in connecting aid donations to a number of countries to China's dispute with India and fear of Indian expansionism, as well as China's desire to preserve a balance of power in South Asia. And VanNess' *Revolution and Chinese Foreign Policy* proved instrumental in showing a relationship between Chinese aid and its efforts to promote wars of national liberation.

On the subject of China's historical tribute system, which I relate to China's aid in chapter one, several sources were extremely useful. Among them were: John K. Fairbank (ed.), *The Chinese World Order: Traditional China's For-*

eign Relations (Cambridge: Harvard University Press, 1968); John K. Fair-
bank and S.Y. Teng, "On the Ch'ing Tributary System," *Harvard Journal of
Asiatic Studies,* June 1941; Immanuel C.Y. Hsu, *China's Entrance into the
Family of Nations: The Diplomatic Phase, 1858–1920* (Cambridge: Harvard
University Press, 1960); Immanuel C.Y. Hsu, *The Rise of Modern China*
(New York: Oxford University Press, 1970); Ten Ssu-yu and John K.
Fairbank (eds.), *China's Response to the West: A Documentary Survey
1839–1923* (New York: Atheneum Press, 1965); C.P. Fitzgerald, *The Chi-
nese View of Their Place in the World* (London: Oxford University Press,
1964). Relating the historical tribute system and traditional diplomacy to
contemporary China's foreign policy, some other sources were helpful, such
as: Mary C. Wright, *The Last Stand of Chinese Conservatism* (New York:
New York University Press, 1970); Ho Ping-ti and Tang Tsou, *China in Crisis,
Vol. I, II and III* (Chicago: University of Chicago Press, 1968); Chester C.
Tan, *Chinese Political Thought in the Twentieth Century* (Garden City:
Doubleday and Company, 1971); Jack Gray (ed.), *Modern China's Search
for Political Form* (London: Oxford University Press, 1967); Hu Shen, *Imperialism and Chinese Politics* (Peking: Foreign Languages Press, 1957).
On the subject of Peking's international perspectives and its foreign policy objectives, and on the tools of China's diplomacy, the books cited above on China's foreign policy were all useful. Especially instructive on Mao's view of
the world was Gittings', *The World and China, 1922–1972* and Hinton's
Communist China in World Politics. Passin's *China's Cultural Diplomacy*
and Simmond's *China's World* are particularily relevant to the tools of
China's foreign policy.
Concerning China's initial aid policies and relations with the Soviet Union in the
realm of aid, a number of monographs and articles provided beneficial in-
formation and insights. See Chu-yuan Cheng, *Economic Relations between
Peking and Moscow* (New York: Praeger Publishers, 1964); Alexander
Eckstein, "Sino-Soviet Economic Relations," in C.D. Cowan (ed.), *The
Economic Development of China and Japan* (New York: Praeger Publishers,
1964); Choh-ming Li, *Economic Development of Communist China*
(Berkeley: University of California Press, 1959); Yuan-li Wu, *The Economy
of Communist China* (New York: Praeger Publishers, 1965); Sidney Klein,
"Sino-Soviet Economic Relations, 1949–1962: A Sinologist's Sketch,"
Current Scene, June 1962; Oleg Hoeffding, "Sino-Soviet Economic Rela-
tions in Recent Years," The Rand Corporation, August 1960. These sources
were also instrumental in clarifying the relationship between China's economic development and its foreign aid-giving.
Bearing more directly on the Sino-Soviet dispute are: Donald S. Zagoria, *The
Sino-Soviet Dispute, 1956–1961* (Princeton: Princeton University Press,
1962); William E. Griffith, *The Sino-Soviet Rift* (Cambridge: M.I.T. Press,
1964); William E. Griffith, *Sino-Soviet Relations, 1964–65* (Cambridge:
M.I.T. Press, 1967); John Gittings, *Survey of the Sino-Soviet Dispute* (London: Oxford University Press, 1968); Zbigniew K. Brzezinski, *The Soviet
Bloc–Unity and Conflict* (Cambridge: Harvard University Press, 1960);
Alexander Dallin (ed.), *Diversity in International Communism* (New York:

Columbia University Press, 1963); Harold C. Hinton, *The Bear at the Gate* (Washington, D.C.: American Enterprise Institute, 1971); D. Beim, "The Communist Bloc and the Foreign Aid Game," *Western Political Quarterly,* December 1964; Clement J. Zablocki, *Sino-Soviet Rivalry: Implications for U.S. Policy* (New York: Praeger Publishers, 1966); C.F. Hudson et al., *The Sino-Soviet Dispute* (New York: Praeger Publishers, 1961); Jan S. Prybyla, "Soviet and Chinese Economic Competition within the Communist World," *Soviet Studies,* April 1964.

On China's aid to the four blocs and to individual countries in each bloc, a wide selection of sources was employed, too numerous to mention here. These are referred to in the footnotes of the chapters, and the reader is advised to check the chapters for sources.

Concerning conclusions made regarding China's foreign aid program, particularily the ways it is compared and contrasted to other foreign aid programs, a number of books on the subject of foreign aid were functional. Among them are: Lloyd D. Black, *The Strategy of Foreign Aid* (Princeton: Van Nostrand Publishers, 1968); John D. Montgomery, *Foreign Aid in International Politics* (Englewood Cliffs: Prentice-Hall, Inc., 1967); Joseph J. Kaplan, *The Challenge of Foreign Aid: Policies, Problems and Possibilities* (New York: Praeger Publishers, 1970); David A. Baldwin, *Foreign Aid and American Foreign Policy* (New York: Praeger Publishers, 1966); John D. Montgomery, *The Politics of Foreign Aid: American Experiences in Southeast Asia* (New York: Praeger Publishers, 1962); Robert A. Goodwin (ed.), *Why Foreign Aid?* (Chicago: Rand McNally and Company, 1962); H.J.P. Arnold, *Aid for Developing Countries: A Comparative Study* (Chester Springs, Pa.: Dufour Editions, 1962); Frederic Benham, *Economic Aid to Underdeveloped Countries* (London: Oxford University Press, 1961); Eugene R. Black, *The Diplomacy of Economic Development* (Cambridge: Harvard University Press, 1960); Herbert Feis, *Foreign Aid and Foreign Policy* (New York: St. Martin's Press, 1964); Amos A. Jordan, *Foreign Aid and the Defense of Southeast Asia* (New York: Praeger Publishers, 1962); George Liska, *The New Statecraft: Foreign Aid in American Foreign Policy* (Chicago: University of Chicago Press, 1960); John Pinicus, *Economic Aid and International Cost Sharing* (Baltimore: John Hopkins University Press, 1965); Gustav Ranis et al., *The U.S. and the Developing Economies* (New York: Norton and Company, 1964).

Index

Index

About the Author

John Franklin Copper is Lecturer in Government and Politics with the University of Maryland, Far East Division. He received the M.A. degree from the University of Hawaii in affiliation with the East-West Center, and the Ph.D. from the University of South Carolina. Dr. Copper has authored numerous articles on contemporary Chinese politics and international affairs, and writes for several Asian newspapers and magazines.